Mountain Biking Virginia

Help Us Keep This Guide Up to Date

Every effort has been made by the author and editors to make this guide as accurate and useful as possible. However, many things can change after a guide is published—trails are rerouted, regulations change, techniques evolve, facilities come under new management, etc.

We would love to hear from you concerning your experiences with this guide and how you feel it could be improved and kept up to date. While we may not be able to respond to all comments and suggestions, we'll take them to heart, and we'll also make certain to share them with the author. Please send your comments and suggestions to the following address:

The Globe Pequot Press
Reader Response/Editorial Department
P.O. Box 480
Guilford, CT 06437

Or you may e-mail us at:

editorial@GlobePequot.com

Thanks for your input, and happy travels!

Mountain Biking Virginia

Third Edition

An Atlas of Virginia's Greatest
Off-Road Bicycle Rides

Scott Adams

FALCON®

GUILFORD, CONNECTICUT
HELENA, MONTANA

AN IMPRINT OF THE GLOBE PEQUOT PRESS

Photo Credits: Scott Adams unless otherwise noted.

Library of Congress Cataloging-in-Publication Data is
available.

ISBN 0-7627-2656-3

Manufactured in the United States of America
Third Edition/First Printing

Contents

Coastal Virginia

Central Virginia

George Washington National Forest

Jefferson National Forest

Northern Virginia

Western Virginia

Southwest Virginia

Acknowledgments

A special thanks to all the folks who have ever supported my efforts and desires to get to this point. It goes without saying that I would be hard-pressed to manage my ideas and dreams without all of the regular and unending encouragement, extra helping hands, and borrowed elbow grease from those around me and from those who believe in me. Thanks.

Foreword

Andy Carruthers is one of the region's core mountain bike advocates, working diligently and successfully to keep local trails accessible to cyclists. Many thanks should go to him and all the volunteers who work to keep our trails open and healthy.

Trail Obstacles: Rocks, Roots, Trees and . . . Politics?

Mountain Biking Virginia will help you find new trails. Other books on bicycling (and a lot of trial and error) will help you to develop the skills to ride those new trails. Still other books will show you how to fix your bike when you get a flat tire on those trails. But what do you do when your favorite trails get closed to bikes? Well, there's no book to remedy that, really. It all depends on you.

Well, not quite. You see—it depended on you. When trails close and bikes are banned, chances are the "problem" had already existed for a while. Maybe a few cyclists had been rolling carelessly past hikers on the trail, frightening them. Or maybe a few cyclists had been riding muddy trails, damaging them. Or maybe the "problem" was that a vocal opponent of mountain bikes had been bending the park management's ear for the past year, worrying them. And finally, because management hadn't heard from bikers, management just gave in.

You see, if some people have their way, mountain bikes will be restricted to pavement, private property, rail-trails, and ski resorts in the off-season. Such people often get their understanding of our pastime from sensational television ads or magazine depictions of fearless teenagers engaged in death-defying feats. Sometimes, though, these people form their opinions based on a dangerous experience or a negative encounter on a trail. Fear motivates people. Scare someone today, even by accident, and your trail gets closed tomorrow.

Keeping Trails Open

Trail etiquette is a big part of the answer—the preventive solution. Just ask the International Mountain Bicycling Association (IMBA). Sure, the official IMBA "Rules of the Trail" are important. But simple courtesy, basic caution, and a little empathy for other trail users are the real requirements. In the long haul, they are more important than your bike gear, than your bike clothes—more important even than your bike. After all, a mountain bike isn't very useful if there isn't any place to ride it.

The second simple step to keeping trails open is to join together with other cyclists. Join your local mountain bike club or association so your head gets counted and your voice gets heard. Besides, it's often a great way to meet other riders and learn about trails before they're published in a book or a magazine. A year's membership rarely costs more than $20, the cost of a bike tire. You'll find it's well worth it.

Clubs

In Virginia, there are a few principal mountain bike groups that make a real difference. The major club in eastern Virginia is the Eastern Virginia Mountain Bike Association (EVMBA). In central Virginia it's a club called Mountain Bike Virginia. In northern Virginia, the Mid-Atlantic Off-Road Enthusiasts (MORE) handle things very well all the way into Maryland and D.C. In western Virginia, Mountain Bike Virginia and other trail groups keep things in order. All of these clubs are known for keeping trails open. For leading great rides. For building new trails and maintaining old ones. For raising money for parks. For educating riders. And, well, for giving mountain bikers a good name.

Better than Lincoln Logs

If you think breaking a sweat in the woods on your bike is fun, then working on trails might be more fun than you think. Who needs Erector Sets, Lincoln Logs, or LEGOs when you can build or maintain a real trail? Constructing a new tread way—or fixing an old one—will leave you with a sense of satisfaction that you can't buy in a bike shop. Skeptical? Call one of these local clubs and try it once. It's that simple. And it's fun.

IMBA

Speaking of simple, how much did your bike cost? And your helmet? And the bike rack for the car? Add it up and think about it. Then consider writing a check for the relatively paltry sum of $25 to the International Mountain Bicycling Association. The IMBA is the national voice for mountain bikers, and $25 gets you membership for a year—and helps support the group's effort to keep trails and land open to mountain bikers across the nation.

20-25-20

Twenty dollars to your local mountain bike group, twenty-five dollars to IMBA, and twenty hours a year as a trail volunteer. That's the recipe for access. That's the formula for keeping trails open and healthy. That's the ticket for preserving your fun. You've got the book and the bike. Time to do the rest.

This fine guide not only reveals some of the best shared-use trails around, it also makes clear one crucial fact: Cyclists' continued access to trails depends upon their courtesy toward hikers and equestrians and their willingness to help maintain those trails. The information in this book, and that message, is the key to some great riding!

Andy Carruthers

Introduction

From coastal beaches to mountain passes, cyclists will find endless possibilities for off-road riding in Virginia. This guidebook is designed to introduce you to some of the finest mountain biking this state has to offer. Each of the forty-eight featured rides includes a detailed map, instructions for how to get to the trailhead, where to ride once you arrive, and a description of the trails and the area. The rides range from easy jaunts accessible to first-time mountain bikers and families (many of the rides in this guide are also dog friendly) to hard-core rides that'll lead you up and over some of the most extreme terrain on the East Coast. Check the information at the beginning of each chapter to be sure that the ride you choose fits your ability level. Be honest with yourself about your ability. It's easy to get in over your head on a mountain bike ride, and the results can be serious. Moreover, since many of these rides venture into the backcountry, make sure you're prepared to be self-sufficient once you leave the trailhead.

I've divided this book into five sections, each representing a generally accepted region of the state. They are Coastal Virginia, Central Virginia, Northern Virginia, Western Virginia, and Southwest Virginia. While the majority of open riding can be found in the western parts of the state along the mountain ridges of the Alleghenies, cyclists will find plenty of opportunities for fine singletrack riding in the eastern half of Virginia.

While the first section of this book is titled Coastal Virginia, the region covered also includes much of the Tidewater, from Newport News north to Williamsburg. This region is essentially flat, offering little in the way of topography, but thanks to local mountain bike organizations and dedicated cyclists, mountain bikers have more than enough singletrack on which to spin their wheels. Places like Harwood's Mill, Waller Mill, York River State Park, and Carrollton-Nike Park are all under the watchful supervision of local clubs such as Eastern Virginia Mountain Bike Association and Mountain Bike Virginia. The trails at each of these locations are a testimony to the groups' will and desire for great places at which to ride.

Central Virginia includes much of the area between Richmond and Charlottesville, leading cyclists to Virginia's Piedmont, where flat terrain gives way to rolling hills, farmland, and distant views of the Blue Ridge Mountains. This is where both city parks and private property have become havens for the cycling community. Places such as Belle Isle in the heart of Richmond, Poor Farm Park near Ashland, and Panorama Trails outside of Charlottesville all attract thousands of mountain bikers each year. These riders pedal up and down the hilly, rocky terrain in tight switchbacks and limited space for solid training rides, evening workouts, and quick weekend adventures.

Northern Virginia is more of a geopolitical region of suburbs and sprawl spreading south and west from Washington, D.C. Like Richmonders, northern Virginians must search through the crowded region to find good riding. Unlike Richmonders, they must first do battle with hours of traffic and gridlock to get there. But locals need look no further than Wakefield Park and Lake Accotink, just a quarter mile off the Beltway, to get started. Here they'll find great off-road riding for a variety of skills, including everything from taxing singletrack to sluggish dirt paths. It's guaranteed to keep cyclists in the right mindset when they are just leaving work, tired of rush hour, and in need of a quick fix before heading home. But that isn't all. Northern Virginia is actually loaded with great places to pedal off road. Cyclists just need to be creative. Some of these rides are in fairly standard places, such as Burke Lake Park with its meandering pathway around the lake—great for novices and families. Other mountain bike trails had to be built. The trails in Fountainhead Regional Park, for example, were planned by the Northern Virginia Regional Park Authority in close collaboration with the Mid-Atlantic Off-Road Enthusiasts (MORE). The trail system at Fountainhead is a great circuit of tightly wound singletrack going up and down the hilly banks of the Occoquan Reservoir through a lush canopy of hardwood. Cyclists will find some of the best singletrack trails (huge steeps and rugged terrain) where they may least expect them—beneath the vast networks of power-line grids that provide the region with power. Some of the area's power-line right-of-ways offer up spectacular off-road terrain that even the most hard-core cyclists will love. Check out the Centreville Power Line ride as an example. I'm sure you'll come back smiling and exhausted.

Look west, however, and you'll see where mountain biking lives up to its name. Both western Virginia and southwestern Virginia are magnets for the serious cyclists thanks to nearly two million acres of public land stretching over two mountain ranges, the Blue Ridge and the Alleghenies, and covering nearly the entire western portion of Virginia from Front Royal to Abingdon.

The real treasure of the 1.7 million acres of national forest land in Virginia, however, is the fact that nearly every acre is open to the public (save for the wilderness areas scattered throughout). This means that cyclists don't need a landowner's permission to travel on any of the thousands of miles of trails and dirt roads.

In Virginia, there are two national forests that make up the state's huge parcel of public land: the George Washington National Forest and the Jefferson National Forest. The George Washington National Forest has over one million acres, 945,000 of which are in Virginia. It extends over 140 miles along the Allegheny Mountains in northwestern Virginia and attracts nearly four million visitors per year. Within this forest are more than 800 miles of trails open to mountain biking. Endless miles of dirt forest roads connect these trails, which wind up and down the mountain slopes and through the many valleys. In addition, camping is allowed at undeveloped sites almost anywhere within forest boundaries. The Jefferson National Forest has

690,000 acres of wooded mountains and valleys. It covers much of the state's southwestern portion, from the James River south to Mount Rogers. There are over 900 miles of trails and dirt forest roads open to mountain biking.

Located within the Jefferson National Forest is Mount Rogers National Recreation Area. More than 115,000 acres make up this mountainous wonderland, home to Virginia's two highest peaks—Mount Rogers (5,729 feet) and Whitetop Mountain (5,520 feet). There are over 400 miles of trails open to bike travel, all of which wind through the valleys and atop the highest peaks. Mountain biking is welcome throughout the Mount Rogers National Recreation Area, and because it is within national forest land, camping is allowed at undeveloped sites almost anywhere.

It's important to note that there are some restricted areas and trails within Virginia's national forests that allow only foot travel. Mountain bikers cannot ride on the Appalachian Trail under any circumstances and are also restricted from riding in any of the national forest's wilderness areas. None of the rides in this guide use either the Appalachian Trail or wilderness areas.

The rides included in this book are considered by many cyclists and forest rangers to be some of the more popular places and trails on which to ride in the national forests. While virtually all the trails and forest roads in both the George Washington and Jefferson National Forests are open to everyone, the rides in this guide attempt to avoid routes that might be sensitive to overuse or yield user conflicts.

At the end of each section I've listed a handful of honorable mention rides that certainly warrant attention and deserve to be ridden, but just didn't make it on my A-list this time around. Clearly, there are more rides in the Old Dominion than those that I have featured or listed in this book, but this guide should serve as a platform to help folks get started, find some great rides, and understand where to look for new rides on their own.

As always, happy riding and thanks for buying this book!

Getting Around Virginia

Area Codes

Virginia currently has five area codes: **540** serves Roanoke and western and northern Virginia excluding Arlington. **571** overlays with **703** to serve the Washington D.C. suburbs and Arlington area. **757** serves Hampton, Norfolk, and southeastern Virginia. And **804** covers Richmond, Lynchburg, and central Virginia.

Roads

For current information on statewide weather and road conditions and closures, contact the Virginia Department of Transportation (VDOT) twenty-four-hour HIGHWAY HELPLINE: (800) 367–ROAD (7623). (TTY users, call 800–432–1843); www.vdot.state.va.us.

Airports

Dulles International Airport (IAD) is 23 miles northwest of downtown Washington D.C. **Ronald Reagan Washington National Airport** (DCA) is in nearby Alexandria; www.metwashairports.com. **Richmond International Airport** (RIC) is located 7 miles east of downtown Richmond; www.flyrichmond.com. **Norfolk/ Virginia Beach International** (ORF) serves the Tidewater region; www. norfolkairport.com

Other major airports in Virginia include **Roanoke Regional Airport** (ROA); www.roanokeairport.com, **Shenandoah Valley Regional Airport** (SHD); www. flyshd.com, **Charlottesville Albemarle Airport** (CHO); www.cho-airport.state. va.us, and **Newport News-Williamsburg International** (NNW); www.phf-airport.org.

Most major airlines will carry your bicycle for $50 to $90. However, if you join the **League of American Bicyclists** (LAB), you can take advantage of their Bikes Fly Free program. For more information, contact LAB at (202) 822–1333; www.bikeleague.org.

To book reservations online, check out your favorite airline's Web site or search one of the following travel sites for the best price: www.cheaptickets.com, www. expedia.com, www.previewtravel.com, www.priceline.com, travel.yahoo.com, www.travelocity.com, or www.trip.com.

Train

Compared to other states, Virginia is well served by **Amtrak.** All trains stop at Union Station in Washington D.C. Amtrak carries boxed bikes for $12.00 (which includes a $7.00 fee for the box) to Alexandria, Richmond, Charlottesville, Petersburg, and Lynchburg.

The **Cardinal** offers by far the best Amtrak experience in Virginia. The train runs on Wednesday, Friday, and Sunday between Washington and Chicago. Special bike racks on board allow roll-on access to all stations for a $15 fee. The train stops at Manassas, Culpeper, Charlottesville, Staunton, and Clifton Forge. The train is rarely full along this segment of the journey, and the view from the lounge car is sublime.

Acela Regional Service serves Richmond, Williamsburg, and Newport News from New York and Boston several times a day. For more details, call (800) 872–7245 or visit www.amtrak.com.

VRE commuter rail service runs weekdays along two lines from Fredericksburg and Manassas to Union Station. Some of these trains have cafe cars with tie-downs for up to six bicycles. Call VRE at (800) RIDE–VRE to find out which trains carry bikes or visit www.vre.org/cafecar.htm.

Bus

Greyhound lines serve most larger towns and cities in Virginia, along with Dulles Airport, several times a day. Bicycles must be boxed, and a $15 fee applies. Bike boxes are for sale for $10 at major terminals; www.greyhound.com.

Local bikes-on-transit information for Virginia is located on the Internet at www.bikemap.com/transit/va.htm.

How to Use This Book

Mountain Biking Virginia features forty-eight mapped and cued rides and eighteen honorable mentions, as well as everything from advice on getting into shape to tips on mountain bike camping and getting the most out of cycling with your dog.

The book is divided into five sections, representing the five major geographic regions in Virginia. Within each section are the featured rides found in each of these regions. Each chapter is then divided into a variety of components. The ride specifications at the beginning of each ride are fairly self-explanatory. Here you'll find the quick, nitty-gritty details of the ride: where the trailhead is located, the nearest town, ride length, approximate riding time, difficulty rating, type of trail terrain, if dogs are permitted, and what other trail users you may encounter. There is also information on who to contact about trails, when trails are open, fees and permits required, and additional maps you may need. Our Getting There section gives you everything from dependable directions from a nearby city right down to where you'll want to park. The Ride description is the meat of the chapter. Detailed and honest, it's the author's carefully researched impression of the trail. While it's impossible to cover everything, rest assured that we won't miss what's important. In our Miles and Directions section, we provide mileage cues to identify all turns and trail name changes, as well as points of interest. Between this and our route map, you simply can't get lost. The Ride Information section contains more useful information including where to stay, what to eat, and what else to see while you're riding in the area.

The Honorable Mentions sections detail additional rides in each region that will inspire you to get out and explore.

How to Use the Maps

Getting There Map

This map helps you find your way to the start of each ride from the nearest sizable town or city. Coupled with the detailed directions at the beginning of each chapter, this map will visually lead you to where you need to be to hit the trails.

Regional Location Map

This map helps you find the general location of each ride discussed for a particular region.

Profile Map

This helpful profile gives you a cross-sectional look at the ride's ups and downs. Elevation is labeled on the left, mileage is indicated on the top. Road and trail names are shown along the route, with towns and points of interest labeled in bold.

Route Map

This is your primary guide to each ride. It shows all the accessible roads and trails, points of interest, water, towns, landmarks, and geographical features. It also distinguishes trails from roads and paved roads from unpaved roads. The selected route is highlighted, and directional arrows point the way. Shaded topographic relief in the background gives you an accurate representation of the terrain and landscape in the ride area.

The Maps

We don't want anyone, by any means, to feel restricted to just the roads and trails mapped here. We hope you will have an adventurous spirit and use this guide as a platform to dive into Virginia's backcountry and discover new routes for yourself. One of the simplest ways to begin is to just turn the map upside down and ride the course in reverse. The change in perspective is fantastic, and the ride should feel quite different. It will be like getting two distinctly different rides on each map. You may wish to copy the directions for the course onto a small sheet to help you while you're riding. Or you might take photocopies of the map and cue sheet. These pages can be folded into a bike bag or stuffed into a jersey pocket. Just remember to slow down or even stop when you read the map.

Interstate Highway		Airfield		Golf Course
U.S. Highway		Airport		Hiking Trail
State Road		Bike Trail		Lighthouse
County Road		No Bikes		Mine
Township Road		Boat Launch		Overlook
Forest Road		Bridge		Parking
Paved Road		Bus Stop		Picnic
Paved Bike Lane		Campground		Quarry
Maintained Dirt Road		Campsite		Radio Tower
Unmaintained Jeep Trail		Canoe Access		Rock Climbing
Singletrack Trail		Cattle Guard		School
Highlighted Route		Cemetery		Shelter
National Forest/County Boundaries		Church		Spring
State Boundaries		Covered Bridge		Swimming
Railroad Tracks		Direction Arrows		Train Station
Power Lines		Downhill Skiing		Wildlife Refuge
Special Trail		Equestrian Trail		Vineyard
Rivers or Streams		Fire Tower		Most Difficult
Water and Lakes		Forest Headquarters		Difficult
Marsh		Four-Wheel-Drive Trail		Moderate
		Gate		Easy

Coastal Virginia

George Washington National Forest

Jefferson National Forest

N

MARYLAND

66
Front
Royal

Washington, D.C.

Fredericksburg

WEST VIRGINIA

81
Harrisonburg

95
17

Staunton
Charlottesville
Onancock

Lexington
Tappahannock

64
13

Richmond

81
64

9 7
Lynchburg

8 6

77
Roanoke
460
5

Wytheville
Petersburg
Norfolk Atlantic
Ocean

81
VIRGINIA
4 2

95
A Virginia Beach

Abingdon
77
3 1

TENNESSEE

NORTH CAROLINA

1 Back Bay to False Cape

Start: From the Back Bay visitor center.
Length: 16.2 miles out and back; 27.7 miles of trails.
Approximate riding time: 1 to 4 hours.
Difficulty rating: Easy. Flat riding along the beach and dikes.
Trail surface: Flat packed gravel roads, sandy trails, and beach.
Land status: National wildlife refuge and state park.
Nearest town: Sandbridge.
Other trail users: Hikers and campers.
Canine compatibility: Don't bring 'em. Pets are allowed in False Cape but not in Back Bay except from October through March.
Fees and permits: $2.00—single-visit permit (foot/bike), $4.00—vehicles; tram is $6.00 for adults and $4.00 for children age twelve and younger; annual refuge pass—$15 per season.

Schedule: Back Bay dikes are closed from November 1 to April 1. The beach to False Cape is open year-round. The refuge is open daily from dawn to dusk. The visitor contact station is open 8:00 A.M. to 4:00 P.M. weekdays; 9:00 A.M. to 4:00 P.M. Saturday and Sunday. (Note: False Cape State Park and Back Bay National Wildlife Refuge are closed from the first Saturday through the second Saturday in October each year for the Game Management Program.)
Maps: USGS maps: Knotts Island (Virginia and North Carolina), North Bay; ADC map: Tidewater road map; Back Bay National Wildlife Refuge trail map; False Cape State Park trail map.
Trail contacts: Back Bay National Wildlife Refuge, (757) 721-2412, backbay.fws.gov; False Cape State Park, (757) 426-7128. The False Cape State Park Tram is managed by the Back Bay Restoration Foundation, (757) 498-2473.

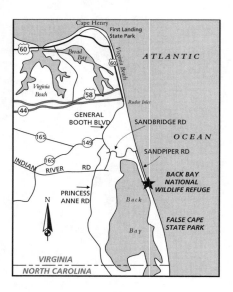

Getting There: From Virginia Beach Waterfront: Travel east on Shore Drive (U.S. Route 60) until it turns right, becoming Atlantic Avenue. At 40th Street, get in the right-hand lane. This is Pacific Avenue. Pacific Avenue becomes General Booth Boulevard after crossing the Rudee Inlet Bridge. Go 7 miles on General Booth Boulevard, then turn left on Princess Anne Road. Go 0.5 mile to the first light and turn left on Sandbridge Road. Take Sandbridge Road 5.6 miles, then turn right on Sandpiper Road. Follow Sandpiper Road 3.9 miles to Back Bay National Wildlife Refuge. The road ends at its parking lot. *DeLorme: Virginia Atlas & Gazetteer:* Page 35, C-7.

Seagulls will accompany you along the way.

The Ride

False Cape State Park, located on the southeastern tip of Virginia, is the least-visited park in the state, averaging fewer than 25,000 visitors annually. However, False Cape isn't for everyone.

To get there, you must be willing to travel off-road by bicycle, foot, or boat at least 10 miles round-trip through the nearly 8,000 acres of Back Bay National Wildlife Refuge. There is no vehicular access to the park, and hardy adventurers must lug in their own food, shelter, and hefty cans of bug spray (False Cape is renowned for its large insect population). The reward is one of the most isolated and unspoiled coastal environments on the East Coast.

Annually, hundreds of species of birds, including snow and Canada geese, tundra swans, and ducks, make this thin strip of Atlantic coastline their fall and winter home. River otters, white-tailed deer, mink, red and gray fox, muskrats, opossums, and raccoons also share this coastal habitat with a few nonnative species such as nutria wild horses and feral pigs. Yes, pigs!

Wild dunes and forests of loblolly pine, maple, and gnarled live oak grow right up to the persistent Atlantic surf, where sandpipers dodge the crashing waves and

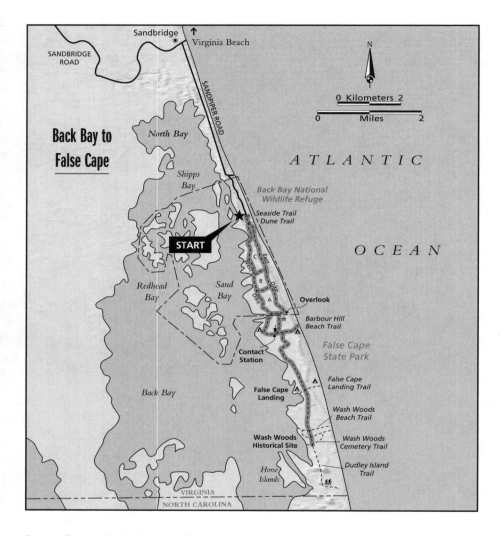

Back Bay to False Cape

forage for meals in the sand. Farther out in the ocean, brown pelicans and ospreys dive into the water in search of fish.

The adventure begins at Back Bay's visitor contact station, just south of the tiny coastal community of Sandbridge. Parking is plentiful, and the station is equipped with rest rooms, a telephone, maps, and information about the area. And since no motorized vehicles are allowed past this point, there is no other logical alternative but to leave the car and unpack your bike. Water is now available at the contact stations and first campsite, but cyclists should still carry plenty of liquid just in case.

The bike route starts on the east side of the visitor contact station and follows either the east or west dike south toward False Cape. Both dikes are topped with gravel and are well suited for cycling. Immediately before the Dune Trail, the two dikes split, but they reconnect at each of the three cross-dikes on your way south.

The arrangement of the different dikes and cross-dikes throughout the Back Bay Refuge forms large areas of marsh and wetland into an impoundment. Eight of these impoundments, or pools, exist in Back Bay. In fall and winter, the impoundments are filled, then planted with grass, plants, and other vegetation that serves as sustenance for the wintering birds and waterfowl this refuge protects. Both the east and west dikes lead directly into False Cape State Park, and one or the other will be clearly designated for the journey through Back Bay.

Cyclists may also choose to ride the 9-mile route along the beach from the refuge to the North Carolina border. Be aware, though, that the best time is from two hours before low tide until two hours after, when there's plenty of hard, wet sand on which to ride. If you want to come back along the beach, be sure to keep an eye on the incoming tide.

Once you reach False Cape State Park, you may find its coastal habitat very similar to Back Bay's—beautiful and unspoiled. There are numerous sights along the many miles of the park's bicycle routes, including the Wash Woods cemetery and church site and False Cape's wildlife lookout tower (within a quarter mile of Wash Woods)—a perfect place to view tundra swans and snow geese during the winter months.

At some point in the nineteenth century, a small community called Wash Woods developed on what is now the state park. Most of its residents were farmers and fishermen who carried their small parcels of crops and fish across Back Bay by boat to sell on the mainland. However, amid heavy storms and a battering ocean, and the fatal blow of a massive hurricane in the early 1930s, Wash Woods did not survive. All that remains are a church's foundation and steeple and a small cemetery. Most other traces of the community have been covered by the blowing sands. The Wash Woods historical site is the southernmost point that bicycles are allowed.

In December 1994, Back Bay National Wildlife Refuge implemented a seasonal dike closure from November 1 to April 1. This effectively closes the only roadways through the federal wildlife refuge to False Cape State Park. Officials at Back Bay felt hikers and bicyclists were disturbing the wintering waterfowl the refuge exists

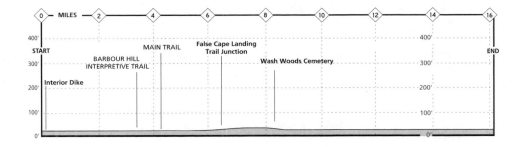

to protect. During these months visitors can take an electric tram from Little Island City Park, through the refuge, and on to False Cape. The tram makes a round-trip, picking up visitors at False Cape two hours after drop-off. However, the tram is not available to carry bicycles, so cyclists determined to arrive in False Cape State Park during the winter months must pedal the 10-mile round-trip along the beach.

Miles and Directions

0.0 START at the Back Bay National Wildlife Refuge visitor contact station. The bike trail starts on the east side of the visitor center. You will travel south along Back Bay's Interior Dike toward False Cape State Park.

0.2 The Interior Dike splits east and west. Take either the East Dike or West Dike to False Cape. Both dikes are clearly designated.

0.6 Begin passing Pool C, a large impoundment of marsh and wetland used for wintering birds and waterfowl. This and the other impoundments provide wildlife habitat year-round.

2.0 Reach the first cross-dike. Continue south on either the East or West Dike. Begin passing Pool B.

2.5 Reach the second cross-dike. Continue south on either the East or West Dike. Begin passing Pool A.

3.3 Reach the third cross-dike and False Cape State Park. Regardless of which dike you were riding on, you will enter False Cape on the Barbour Hill Interpretive Trail, which forms a 2.4-mile loop. This trail passes the observation tower (overlook). The observation tower is great for viewing the barrier spit's unique wildlife in its natural environment. This road will lead you to the state park contact station.

4.25 From the Barbour Hill Beach Trail and the visitor contact station, follow the Main Trail south toward False Cape Landing.

6.3 Reach False Cape Landing Trail. Continue straight on the Main Trail toward Wash Woods Historical Site.

7.5 Pass the Wash Woods Beach Trail (0.8 mile east to the Atlantic). Continue straight on the Main Trail.

7.8 Pass the Wash Woods Interpretive Trail (0.7 mile east to the Atlantic; 0.1 mile west to the Wash Woods Environmental Education Center). Continue straight on the Main Trail.

8.1 Turn left on the Wash Woods Cemetery Trail. Almost immediately you will come upon the old Wash Woods cemetery and church site. Bicycles are not permitted beyond this point. You may walk the last 2 miles of this trail (Dudley Island Trail) to the North Carolina border.

16.2 Return to Back Bay along these different trails, mixing them differently for a different ride. Or ride along the beach all the way to Back Bay for an unforgettable experience along a uniquely unspoiled coastline.

Helpful Mileage Information
5 miles—Back Bay to False Cape along the beach.
4 miles—False Cape to the North Carolina state line.
7.5 miles of ridable trails in Back Bay.
11.2 miles of ridable trails in False Cape.
27.7 miles—Total trails and beach open to bicycling.

Ride Information

Local Events and Attractions

Little Island City Park (swimming, surfing, fishing).
Virginia Marine Science Museum, located on General Booth Boulevard, is one of the top marine science museums in the nation. (757) 425-FISH; www.vmsm.com.

Accommodations

False Cape State Park Camping: Camping is permitted year-round, but reservations are required. The camping areas are Barbour Hill Bay, Barbour Hill Ocean, False Cape Landing Bay, and False Cape Landing Ocean. For camping information, contact the State Parks Reservation Center at (800) 933-7275; in Richmond dial (757) 225-3867.

2 First Landing State Park

Start: From the visitor center.
Length: 10.4 miles out and back.
Approximate riding time: 1.5 hours.
Difficulty rating: Easy. Relatively flat double-track.
Trail surface: Hard-packed dirt and sand.
Land status: State park.
Nearest town: Virginia Beach.
Other trail users: Hikers, joggers, campers, and dogs.
Canine compatibility: Good. Just be careful around the crowds of people who will be there in the warm months of the year. Pets must be leashed.

Fees and permits: Parking fees at First Landing State Park: $3.00 on weekdays, $4.00 on weekends, $2.00 during the off-season.
Schedule: 8:00 A.M. to dusk, year-round.
Maps: USGS map: Cape Henry; ADC map: Tidewater road map; First Landing State Park trail map.
Trail contacts: First Landing State Park, (757) 412-2300.

Getting There: From I-64 at Newport News: Approximately 100 miles from Richmond by way of I-64. Take I-64 east across the Hampton Roads Bridge-Tunnel into Norfolk to U.S. Route 13. Exit I-64 to U.S. Route 13 and follow this to U.S. Route 60. Turn right on U.S. Route 60 and go approximately 5 miles to the park entrance on the right. Turn right into First Landing State Park and follow the entrance road to the visitor center. (Following U.S. Route 60 from I-64 also works, but there are dozens of stoplights along the way. It is, however, an ocean-view way to go.) *DeLorme: Virginia Atlas & Gazetteer:* Page 35, A-7.

The Ride

This is a great ride for the family or the casual cyclist seeking an easy, relatively flat ride through a semitropical forest, complete with Spanish moss, bald cypress, lagoons, ospreys, and chicken turtles. Cyclists will pedal along the Cape Henry Trail, the park's only trail open to bikes. Be prepared for crowds, however, especially in the warm weather, as the park, named for the English settlers who first landed here in 1607 before reaching Jamestown, attracts over one million visitors a year.

You'll arrive at the state's most popular park along a narrow entrance road bordered by cypress swamps, high dunes, ospreys, and chicken turtles (an endangered species in Virginia, whose neck is nearly as long as its body). First Landing State Park attracts over one million visitors a year, but not merely because of its proximity to Virginia Beach or the famous boardwalk along the Atlantic Ocean. This national natural landmark has the distinction of being the northernmost location on the East

Pedaling along the Cape Henry Trail. Hey folks! Where are your helmets?

Coast where subtropical and temperate plants grow and thrive together. Warmed by Gulf Stream currents, the environment of this southeastern corner of Virginia is similar to that of more southern climates.

Garlands of Spanish moss hang from the thick branches of bald cypress, loblolly pine, osmanthus (wild olive trees), tall oaks, beeches, and almost everything else standing above ground. If you spent enough time here, you, too, would be cloaked in feathery garlands of moss.

"Early settlers called this area the great desert because they found its dense woods and swamps and huge sand dunes to be uninhabitable. Thousands of years ago the ocean lapped upon a shoreline about 50 miles west of here. As ocean and bay waters gradually receded, the wind and waves built a succession of sand dunes. As one row of dunes was being created, plant life was growing up on the one behind. Vegetation stabilized the shifting sand and the dunes became a permanent part of the landscape."—Department of Conservation and Recreation.

Today, some of those stabilized dunes reach 75 feet high and are among the highest natural points in southeastern Virginia.

The Cape Henry Trail is the only trail in the park open to bicycles, but it has something for everyone. All of the park's natural features, including the cypress

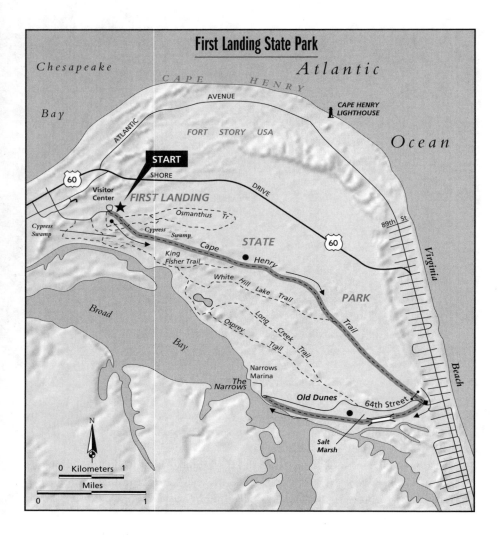

First Landing State Park

Chesapeake

Atlantic

CAPE HENRY

AVENUE

Bay

CAPE HENRY
LIGHTHOUSE

ATLANTIC

FORT STORY USA

Ocean

60

START

SHORE

Visitor
Center

FIRST LANDING

DRIVE

Cypress
Swamp

Osmanthus Tr

Cypress Swamp

Cape

STATE

60

King
Fisher Trail

Henry

White Hill Lake Trail

PARK

89th St

Broad

Long Creek Trail

Bay

Osprey Trail

Trail

Virginia

Narrows
Marina

The
Narrows

Old Dunes

64th Street

Beach

N

Salt
Marsh

0 Kilometers 1

Miles

0   1

swamp, salt marshes, old dunes, and The Narrows, can be reached along this hard-packed sand and dirt trail. The level terrain makes for very easy riding, so cyclists of all abilities will feel welcome here. There are dozens of bike rentals nearby.

You may want to start your ride just a few blocks west of the park at the Seashore Bike & Hobby Shop off U.S. Route 60 (where bike rentals are available). A paved section of the trail begins from the parking area next to this shop and leads you right into the park to the visitor center.

From the visitor center, follow the main trail left from the parking lot into the ocean breeze. Immediately, you will pass the bald cypress swamps, where thick-kneed cypress stretch out of the dark tannin-stained water through heavy Spanish moss.

Beyond the cypress swamps the trail resembles, more and more, old-growth forests of Virginia's past. Little has been done to change the landscape here since First Landing State Park, one of Virginia's first and oldest state parks, was established on June 15, 1936.

Once across 64th Street, the terrain changes a bit from the hard-packed sand and dirt that characterized the first section. Cape Henry Trail begins through some of the region's old dunes, developing into a looser surface of white sand. It then spans a long wooden bridge over the salt marsh. Be sure to watch and listen for the ospreys nesting in the trees high above the marsh.

The trail reaches its end at The Narrows, where a soda machine, bathrooms, and a cool place to rest await. Here you can watch shore fishermen cast their lines and boats navigate the channels to the ocean.

If you're interested in spending more time on the bike, take 64th Street east out of the park all the way to Virginia Beach. You can turn south and follow the board-walk nearly 10 miles along the Atlantic coastline to Rudee Inlet before the bike route ends.

Miles and Directions

0.0 START at the First Landing State Park visitor center. From the visitor center parking lot, follow the Cape Henry Trail east toward the Atlantic Ocean.

0.1 Pass through the bald cypress swamps. Cypress Trail is on the right. Osmanthus Trail is on the left. Bicycles are not allowed on any trail but the main trail.

1.3 Pass King Fisher Trail on the right.

2.2 Pass White Hill Lake Trail on the right.

3.5 Cross 64th Street. There is a portable toilet in the parking lot before 64th Street. Once across the road, a wooden bridge carries you over a small cypress swamp. This bridge is part of the Cape Henry Trail. Continue along the Cape Henry Trail toward Broad Bay.

3.8 Bear left, continuing on the Cape Henry Trail. Pass over a long wooden bridge spanning a salt marsh. Halfway across this bridge you can stop and sit on one of the viewing benches. This is a great spot to view the salt marsh and some of its inhabitants, such as local ospreys. Look for the osprey nests up in the trees growing from the salt marsh. Past this bridge, the trail becomes much sandier as it travels through some of the overgrown dunes along Broad Bay.

Bald cypress stretch out of the cypress swamp under a canopy of Spanish moss.

5.0 The Cape Henry Trail ends. Follow the paved drive a little farther to The Narrows.

5.2 Reach The Narrows. There are rest rooms and soda machines available here. Return to the visitor center along the same route.

10.4 Arrive back at your vehicle.

Ride Information

Local Information
Virginia Beach Information Center.
Chesapeake Bay Center.

Local Events and Attractions
Old Cape Henry Lighthouse, us-lighthouses.org/oldcape.htm.

Virginia Marine Science Museum, (757) 425–FISH; www.vmsm.com.

Accommodations
Eight campgrounds and twenty cabins for overnighters.

3 Great Dismal Swamp National Wildlife Refuge

Start: From Washington Ditch Road.
Length: 8.2 miles out and back; more than 140 miles available.
Approximate riding time: 1 hour along Washington Ditch Road.
Difficulty rating: Easy. Flat riding along a canal road.
Trail surface: Hard-packed dirt and gravel canal roads.
Land status: National wildlife refuge.
Nearest town: Suffolk.
Other trail users: Hikers and photographers.
Canine compatibility: Dog friendly.
Fees and permits: No fees or permits required.
Schedule: Open daily during daylight hours only. No overnight use is permitted. Closed all federal holidays.
Maps: USGS maps: Suffolk, Lake Drummond NW, Corapeake, Lake Drummond, Deep Creek.
Trail contacts: Great Dismal Swamp National Wildlife Refuge, (757) 986–3705; Dismal Swamp Visitor/Welcome Center, North Carolina, (252) 771–8333.

Getting There: From I–644 out of Hampton and Newport News: Cross the Monitor-Merrimac Bridge-Tunnel on I–664 toward Portsmouth. Exit on Route 58, traveling west to Suffolk. At Suffolk, turn left on East Washington Street (Route 337). Take Route 337 to White Marsh Road (Route 642). Turn left on White Marsh Road and follow the Great Dismal Swamp Refuge signs. After approximately 6 miles, turn left into the Washington Ditch entrance. Visitors may drive into a parking area at the boardwalk trail. *DeLorme: Virginia Atlas & Gazetteer:* Page 34, D-3.

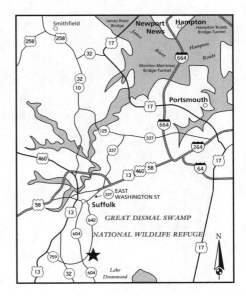

The Ride

With more than 140 miles of unpaved roads throughout this 109,000–acre wildlife refuge, the Great Dismal Swamp provides a variety of opportunities for off-road cyclists to explore one of the largest remaining wooded wetlands in the eastern United States. The Washington Ditch Road is just a small sampling, but certainly the most accessible route for cyclists interested in pedaling through the swamp's biological diversity to the mysterious and beautiful Lake Drummond.

When the full moon's pale light shines down upon the dark waters of the Great Dismal Swamp in just the right way, an ethereal lady in a white canoe is rumored to cruise soulfully across the still waters of Lake Drummond. Lake Drummond was

Washington Ditch Road is one of the many canal roads within the refuge.

said to have been created by what Native Americans described as a "firebird" falling to the ground. This account led people to believe that a meteorite burned through the atmosphere and landed in the thick marsh, burying itself deep in the swamp before the resulting 3,100-acre crater filled with water. More recent theories, however, suggest that the lake was more likely formed after a large wildfire ravaged the swamp and burned its trees to the ground. The swampy waters filled in and thus prohibited new growth, leaving what is now a beautiful lake in the heart of the swamp.

The Great Dismal Swamp is also filled with lots of history. It was discovered by the first colonial governor of North Carolina, William Drummond, in the late 1600s while on a hunting trip, and is one of only two natural lakes in Virginia (Mountain Lake near Blacksburg is the other). Our first president, George Washington, dug huge ditches here in the 1760s, attempting to drain the swamp. Runaway slaves often hid in the swamp's endless wilderness to evade capture. In 1929, the canal was purchased by the U.S. government for $500,000 from the Lake Drummond Canal and Water Company. Logging operations continued as late as 1976, deforesting the entire swamp at least once. Today the swamp is on the way to full recovery. Tall cypress trees, black bears, bobcats, and long-legged egrets make this national wildlife refuge their home. The 109,000 acres of the Great Dismal Swamp within the refuge represent only a remnant of a swamp that once covered more than one million acres. And even though this remnant has been altered numerous times by attempts to drain it, log it, and burn it, it is still one of the largest wooded wetlands in the eastern United States.

Its primeval forests, lush greenery, vast wildlife, and unexplained mysteries make the Great Dismal Swamp unique and enchanting to all who navigate its broad wilderness, from Native Americans and early European settlers to modern-day explorers.

The canals built by George Washington still exist, and more than 150 miles of unpaved roads open to bicycling currently crisscross through the refuge. The Dismal Swamp Canal, paralleling U.S. Route 17 on the refuge's east side, is the oldest man-made waterway still in use in the United States. Travelers can sail up this intracoastal waterway from Elizabeth City, North Carolina, to Portsmouth, Virginia.

Unfortunately, this world-renowned natural area is one of the most remote and inaccessible wildlife refuge's in the country. For centuries, the only means of accessing the swamp were either by foot or small boat—until recently. Many off-road cyclists have discovered the network of dirt roads in this 109,000-acre forested wetland to be excellent riding. However, there are few places to easily access any of the canal roads. Most of the refuge's dirt roads have no well-defined entrances, leaving cyclists to start on the refuge's western side, near Suffolk, and enter via the 5-mile Washington Ditch Road. This road is the shortest trek to Lake Drummond and branches to many of the other dirt canal roads within the refuge (it is also one of the first monuments named after George Washington). Additionally, the 1-mile, interpretive Boardwalk Trail from the parking area for the Washington Ditch Road into the thick-wooded refuge gives explorers a better perspective on the swamp, its inhabitants, and how the refuge is managed. The Jericho Lane entrance, also on the west side of the refuge closer to the town of Suffolk, offers additional access into the refuge.

The terrain is flat, and the difficulty level is virtually nil, but pedaling through the swamp allows cyclists to witness more of the swamp's lush greenery and wealth of wildlife than is possible on foot. This unusual and sometimes mystic national refuge is well worth all the time you can spend here.

Don't forget your bug spray when you come to visit the Great Dismal Swamp. Mosquitoes and other bugs can become fierce and annoying during the hot and humid summer months.

Miles and Directions

0.0 START from the parking lot at the Washington Ditch Road entrance.

1.1 Pass the ditch road on the left that heads due north. Take this road to other routes.

4.1 Reach Lake Drummond. Return back to the parking area the way you came.

Ride Information

Local Information
There are numerous Web sites with additional information about the **Great Dismal Swamp.** Simply type in "Great Dismal Swamp" on any search engine, and you're bound to come across something good.

The **Suffolk News-Herald** has an events listing and other great local information, available online at www.hamptonroadsmedia.com.

Local Events and Attractions
Planters Peanut Company is located in downtown Suffolk.

4 Carrollton-Nike Park

Start: From the Carrollton-Nike Mountain Bike Trail trailhead just past the last parking area. The trail starts at the edge of the woods at the mountain bike trail sign, next to the bike rack and red trash can.
Length: 2.5-mile loop.
Approximate riding time: 1 hour.
Difficulty rating: Easy to moderate. A good singletrack starter trail with a few log jumps and some rooty sections.
Trail surface: Winding, level singletrack covered in a soft layer of pine needles with the occasional dip and root obstacles.
Land status: County park.
Nearest town: Smithfield.
Other trail users: Hikers, dogs, and other park users.
Canine compatibility: Not bad. Plenty of water sources, but be careful of the paved trip

back to the park entrance if you make this trip into a loop, and be aware of the crowds. As at most local parks, leashes are required.
Fees and permits: No fees or permits required.
Schedule: 8:00 A.M. to dark, year-round.
Maps: USGS map: Benns Church.
Trail contacts: Isle of Wight Parks and Recreation, Public Recreational Facilities Authority, (804) 357-2291; Mountain Bike Virginia (mountain bike club), (804) 222-8006.

Getting There: From Newport News/ Hampton Roads: Cross the James River Bridge heading south on U.S. Route 17 toward the town of Smithfield. Less than 2 miles after crossing the bridge, turn right at the light onto Smith Neck Road (Route 669). Follow Smith Neck Road 1.7 miles to Titus Road (Route 668). Turn left on Titus Road and follow it back to Route 669. Turn left on Route 669 and drive 0.6 mile to the Carrollton-Nike Park entrance. Travel to the very end of the entrance road to the last parking area. Just past this parking area at the edge of the woods is the trailhead.
From Norfolk and Virginia Beach: Follow U.S. Route 17 north toward Newport News and the James River Bridge. Cross over the Nansemond River, continuing to the James River Bridge. Soon after U.S. Route 17 joins with Route 32 and U.S. Route 258, turn left at the light onto Smith Neck Road (Route 669). From here, follow the directions above.
DeLorme: Virginia Atlas & Gazetteer: Page 34, A-2.

Scenery like this, overlooking Jones Creek, will stop just about anyone for a while.

The Ride

Like a lot of regional parks, Carrollton-Nike is loaded with playing fields, baseball diamonds, jungle gyms, and lots of people (at least on nice weekends). Unique to this park, however, is its lengthy, wooded, singletrack mountain bike trail, built specifically for mountain bikers. Sure, anyone can use it, but its design suits off-road cyclists perfectly.

Admittedly, when I arrived here for the first time, I didn't have very high expectations. After all, the park is minutes from the James River Bridge, which crosses the mouth of the James just before it empties into Hampton Roads and then the Chesapeake Bay. Needless to say, the variety of terrain wasn't much to write home about. And when I saw all the soccer fields, the jungle gym, and the crowds of soccer league parents, I wondered if mountain biking would even be appropriate here. But my hesitation subsided the moment I discovered the trailhead, clearly labeled with a large Carrollton-Nike Mountain Bike Trail sign. As the trail led me into the woods at the far end of the playing fields, my entire outlook began to change.

Much like the Marle Ravine Trail at York River State Park, the Harwood's Mill Trail near Newport News, or even the Dogwood Trail at Waller Mill, the mountain bike trail here at Carrollton-Nike was designed and is well maintained by local

Carrollton-Nike Park

To (665)

668

669

TITUS ROAD

Titus Creek

NIKE

Jones Creek

PARK

ROAD

Old Nike missile site

Playing fields

P

START

Carrollton Branch

Cotton-peanut farm

((A))

669

N

0 Kilometers .25

0 Miles .25

cyclists. Mountain Bike Virginia has done a superb job of creating a real off-road treasure in a place that might otherwise be considered not worth traveling to. And for local cyclists easing their way westward to harder and harder trails, the route that winds and weaves its way within the woods along the perimeter of the park and the playing fields is a perfect introductory singletrack course.

The trail hops into the woods at the far end of the parking area near the rest rooms. Once you enter this stretch of woods between the marshes of Jones Creek and the playing fields, you'll probably forget about the soccer moms altogether, and for a couple of miles you'll be lost in a singletrack oasis of short ups and downs, creek crossings, tight, tree-hugging turns, and lots of great off-road riding. With the marshes of Jones Creek always present as a backdrop through the trees, your ride will be a delightful event through Virginia's scenic coastal environment.

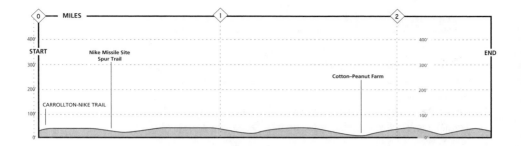

The trail winds up taking you along the perimeter of a local working farm before spitting you out of the woods and back in sight of the park's playing fields. Once you pop out of the woods at this point, you'll be next to a set of radio towers on a dirt road that bisects the cultivated field (this working field alternates between peanuts and cotton). Travel up this dirt road to the paved Nike Park Road (Route 669), turn left, and head back up to the park entrance.

While you're here, pedal west from the parking area past the rest rooms, and check out the old missile bunkers. The bunkers are completely sealed shut today, but this 150-acre park used to be home to a Nike missile base run by the U.S. Army.

You could easily spend an hour or two riding along the Carrollton–Nike Mountain Bike Trail, then tooling around the park's other foot trails watching wildlife and waterfowl in action on Jones Creek. So make sure to take the time to check out this marvelous singletrack mountain bike course and enjoy what other cyclists have created for our cycling pleasure.

Miles and Directions

0.0 START from the Carrollton-Nike Mountain Bike Trail trailhead at the far end of the playing fields near the parking area. The trail is well blazed and easy to follow. The trail is a fairly straightforward course through the woods in a confined area around playing fields, a working farm, and Jones Creek.

0.3 Continue on the main trail past the Nike missile site spur trail.

1.8 The working cotton and peanut farm is on the left.

2.1 Turn left onto Route 669.

2.3 Turn left on the park entrance road.

2.5 Arrive at your car.

Ride Information

Facilities

Very nice rest rooms are available during the park's operating hours. There are also drink machines near the rest rooms.

Local Events and Attractions

A number of mountain bike races are held here each year. Call one of the trail contacts to learn more about the current year's race schedule.

5 Harwood's Mill

Start: From the Harwood's Mill parking area.
Length: 5.2-mile loop.
Approximate riding time: 1 hour.
Difficulty rating: Novice to expert, with sections of flat, straight trails leading to twisting, obstacle-covered singletrack.
Trail surface: Twisting singletrack and dirt roads.
Land status: City park.
Nearest town: Newport News.

Other trail users: Equestrians and pedestrians may be encountered along the dirt roadways that connect each section of trail.
Canine compatibility: Dog friendly.
Fees and permits: No fees or permits required.
Schedule: Open daylight to dark, year-round.
Maps: USGS map: Poquoson West; ADC map: Virginia Peninsula road map.
Trail contacts: Newport News Park, (757) 888-3333; Eastern Virginia Mountain Bike Association, (757) 722-4609.

Getting There: From Newport News: Take I-64 to exit 258. Follow U.S. Route 17 (George Washington Memorial Highway) north for about 4 miles, then turn left on Oriana Road (Route 620). Cross over Harwood's Mill Reservoir and immediately turn left into the parking area for Harwood's Mill. The mountain bike trail starts across Route 620 from the parking area. *DeLorme: Virginia Atlas & Gazetteer:* Page 50, C-3.

The Ride

Cyclists on the Virginia Peninsula, from Williamsburg to Newport News, have been diligently developing excellent mountain biking routes in a region otherwise devoid of accessible off-road cycling terrain.

Far from the rugged landscape of the Appalachian Mountains or the peaks of Virginia's western highlands, mountain bikers in the Tidewater region have had to search far and wide for great places to ride. And if they couldn't find them, they created them.

The Harwood's Mill Mountain Bike Trail in Newport News Park and nearby Dogwood Trail at Waller Mill Park are evidence of the hard work and creative spirit of the many eastern Virginia cyclists who developed these trails. Both trail systems combine heavily forested, hilly terrain with winding, technical singletrack, guaranteed to challenge even the best off-roaders.

The narrow singletrack trails twist and turn throughout the trees so frequently that accidents would be inevitable without the control of a unidirectional traffic flow.

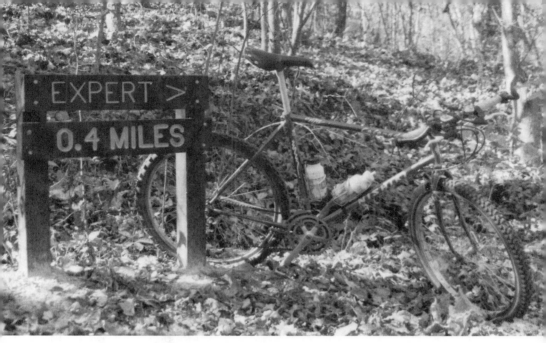

Professionally beveled park signs lead the way.

The Harwood's Mill trail system begins on Oriana Road across from Harwood's Mill. The most notable aspect of the Harwood's Mill Mountain Bike Trail is its categorized trail sections. Professionally beveled park signs head up each section of trail, marking them NOVICE, ADVANCED, or EXPERT. Wooden posts banded with corresponding levels of difficulty guide the way on the trails; one white band equals novice, two yellow bands equals advanced, and three orange bands equals expert.

An important facet of this ride's unique character is its unidirectional trail. *One way only, please!* The trails twist and turn so frequently, much of the singletrack being incredibly narrow, that accidents would be inevitable without some control. Backtrack on the dirt roads if you wish to return to a particular section of singletrack.

The novice section begins on relatively level terrain with a number of turns and twists through the trees—a good warm-up for things to come. The trail really doesn't begin to heat up, though, until you cross beneath the power lines to the trail's advanced section. Tight, narrow turns weave around trees and logs, darting up and down the hills alongside the reservoir. Beware of the many exposed roots along this section.

After finishing this section, you are rewarded with a leisurely ride along a forest road before heading toward the expert trail. Don't be fooled by this rating, though. At no time will you plummet down vertical drops to an unknown fate or climb deadly walls of slippery rock! The expert trail in Harwood's Mill was designed to challenge bike-handling skills on flat terrain, and for this purpose it is well suited. Tight corners, quick hills, obstacles, and pure singletrack make this section as fun and challenging as any bombardier mountain bike ride in the land.

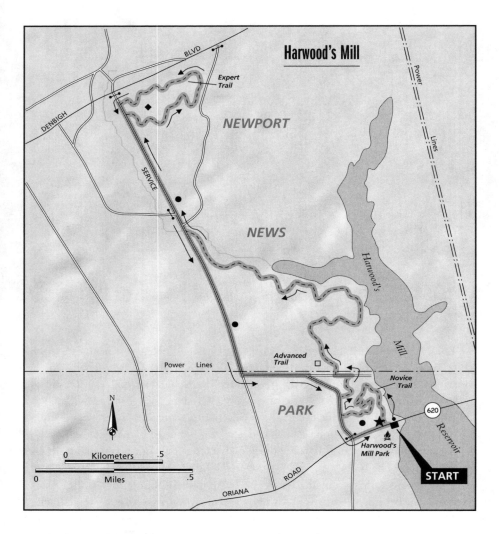

The rest of this roller-coaster-like ride is back to the start by way of dirt forest roads. (Note the clear-cutting in the forested area surrounding you. Let's hope they spare the land around these trails.) As you follow the dirt roads toward Harwood's Mill parking area, you'll pass many of the trailheads for this mountain bike park. Jump back on the trails if you wish, but remember, it's a one-way route only. And don't forget to thank the Eastern Virginia Mountain Bike Association and Newport News Department of Parks and Recreation for this fabulous off-road mountain bike playground.

Miles and Directions

0.0 START at Harwood's Mill on Oriana Road (Route 620). Cross Oriana Road to the Harwood's Mill Mountain Bike Trail. This is marked by a large sign at the start, detailing the rules of the trail. The first section of this trail is labeled NOVICE and is mostly easy terrain. It's marked with a white band on wooden trail posts.

0.55 Turn right on the dirt road, heading north.

0.6 Turn right, back into the woods, continuing to follow the novice singletrack trail.

0.7 Turn left on the gravel road that runs parallel with the power lines. Harwood's Mill Reservoir is down the road on the right.

0.8 Turn right at the ADVANCED trail sign, crossing beneath the power lines. This section is marked with two yellow bands and becomes quite a bit more difficult.

2.2 Leave the advanced trail and turn right on the dirt service road. There is a sign at this point directing you 0.4 mile down the road toward the expert trail.

2.6 Turn right into the woods on the expert trail (three orange bands). The expert trail is not hilly or steep, rather very technical, with obstacles across the trail at almost every turn.

3.4 Leave the expert trail and turn left on the dirt service road.

4.4 Turn left on the gravel road that runs parallel to the power lines.

4.6 Turn right on the dirt road, heading toward Oriana Road.

4.9 Turn left on Oriana Road. There is a dirt path on the other side of Oriana Road. Ride along this path back to Harwood's Mill Park.

5.2 Reach Harwood's Mill Park.

Ride Information

Local Information

For a Web site complete with local information, recreation, services, and more, go to the city of Newport News site at www.newport-news.va.us.

6 Newport News Park

Start: From the information and campsite office.
Length: 5.2-mile loop.
Approximate riding time: 30 to 45 minutes.
Difficulty rating: Flat, easy, wide, and scenic. A great place to come during lunch hour or on a lazy weekend.
Trail surface: Hard-packed dirt.
Land status: City park.
Nearest town: Newport News.

Other trail users: Walkers, joggers, and occasionally equestrians.
Canine compatibility: Dog friendly.
Fees and permits: Yorktown Colonial National Historical Park, $8.00 per car; bike/foot: $2.00 per adult, sixteen and under free.
Schedule: Open daylight to dark, year-round.
Maps: USGS map: Yorktown; ADC map: Virginia Peninsula road map; Newport News Park trail map.
Trail contacts: Newport News Park, (757) 888-3333; Yorktown Colonial National Historical Park, (757) 898-3400.

Getting There: From Newport News: Take I-64 to exit 250 on Fort Eustis Boulevard (Route 105) heading east. Immediately turn left on Jefferson Avenue (Route 143) and cross over the City Reservoir. Go approximately 1 mile to Newport News Park's second entrance. Parking, toilets, information, telephones, and bike rentals are available at the campsite office and information center. *DeLorme: Virginia Atlas & Gazetteer:* Page 50, C2.

The Ride

For cyclists interested in an incredible journey through American history, this easy off-road ride in Newport News Park is the perfect way to get started. Pedaling along a wide dirt path through one of the nation's largest municipal parks, off-road cyclists will enjoy a peaceful wooded setting in an area that saw battle in two of this country's greatest wars.

The Newport News Parks and Recreation Department has done much for the city's steadily growing number of mountain bikers, culminating in some great trails and tours for off-road cyclists all along the Virginia Peninsula. One such example is Newport News Park in Newport News. As one of the nation's largest municipal parks, Newport News Park has plenty of potential for supporting bicycling, both on- and off-road.

This leisurely ride through Newport News Park features an easy, off-road loop in the peaceful setting of a wooded environment. The previous chapter discusses the challenges of winding singletrack trails along the Harwood's Mill Mountain Bike

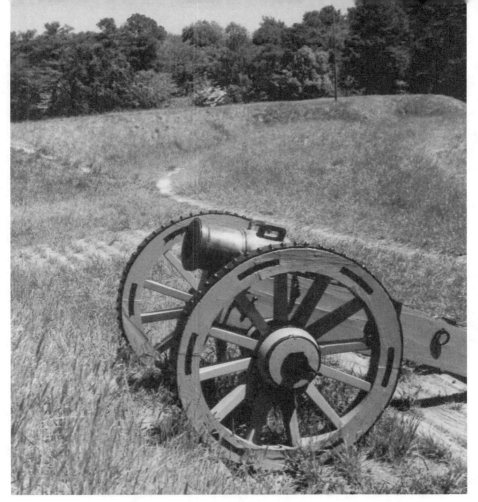

Artillery that helped buy our independence during the Revolutionary War.

Trail in the southern portion of Newport News Park. Both rides, however different, are perfect examples of what Newport News, one of America's oldest cities, has done for mountain biking, one of America's newest sports.

Founded in 1619, Newport News has since become a major American seaport. Early on, however, this point on the Virginia Peninsula at the head of Hampton Roads was no more than the setting for a small English colony trying to establish itself in the New World.

The city's name derives from the English sea captain Christopher Newport, who sailed from London in 1606 with an expedition of one hundred men determined to settle and explore the New World. Newport and the renowned Captain John Smith landed at what would be named Jamestown—the first English colony in America—on May 14, 1607. For those possibly confused, Plymouth, in Massachusetts, was the first English colony of families in the New World.

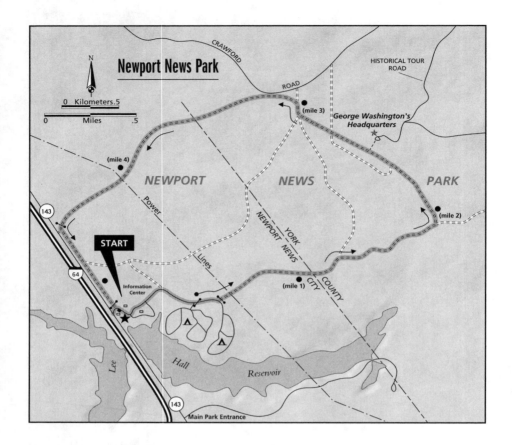

Captain Newport sailed back and forth from Jamestown to England throughout the following years for both supplies and news from the homeland. Legend holds that when word spread that Captain Newport was sailing back to the colonies, people would rush to the end of the peninsula to hear any news he brought back from their homes in England. In 1619, colonists on the peninsula officially adopted the name Newportes Newes for their small town in the New World.

Since Captain Newport's first landing at Jamestown, events on the Virginia Peninsula continued to shape America's destiny. In October 1781, rebel armies, under the command of General George Washington, battled with muskets and cannons to victory over the redcoats on the fields at Yorktown, and American independence was won from the British.

This independence, however, would not come without a price, and America would soon be at war once again—this time with itself. The land within the boundaries of today's Newport News Park once again soaked in the blood of American soldiers, only now it was brother against brother. On April 16, 1862, the violent thunder of Confederate and Union artillery echoed across the land in the first major

Civil War engagement on the peninsula. The Battle of Dam Number 1, as it was called, cost both sides a combined total of more than 3,000 men killed, wounded, or missing. After this battle, both sides continued up the peninsula toward Richmond, where they would clash again in the Seven Days Battle.

Today, original Civil War fortifications covering more than 10 miles still exist within the park, and most of these 140-year-old fortifications are in excellent condition. Some of the earthworks reach as high as 20 feet. The original Dam Number 1 is now beneath the surface of the Lee Hall Reservoir, but it can be seen from the footbridge, which crosses over the reservoir.

For cyclists interested in an incredible journey through American history, this easy, off-road ride in Newport News Park is the perfect way to get started. It begins from the second entrance to the park, at the campsite office entrance on the west side of the Lee Hall Reservoir. There is an information office with rest rooms, parking, free literature, and bike rentals. This loop is composed entirely of flat gravel and dirt roads that travel 5 miles through the park's northern section. Signs labeled BIKE WAY will direct you along the way.

Halfway around this hard-packed dirt loop, you can take a short trail through the woods directly to George Washington's Headquarters, where Washington planned his battle on the eve of victory over the British at Yorktown.

Consider taking the time to travel the nearly 14 miles of paved tour roads through Yorktown's Colonial National Historical Park. These quiet tour roads roll gently through the famous park, allowing for a close-up view of the battlefield on which American forces defeated the great British army in 1781 and ended British rule over the colonies. Interpretive signs and historical route markers guide the way. Return to George Washington's Headquarters to get back on the Newport News Park's mountain bike trail and head back to the ride's start.

Stop in at the Virginia Peninsula Visitor Information Center at the park's main entrance and find out more about the many different paved bike routes that the park service has to offer. Most of these routes were selected for their historic, scenic, and recreational interests and include loops from Yorktown to Jamestown to Williamsburg along gently rolling landscapes and lightly traveled roads.

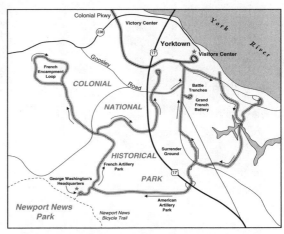

Bike through history at Yorktown's Colonial National Historical Park, accessible from Newport News Park's bicycle trail.

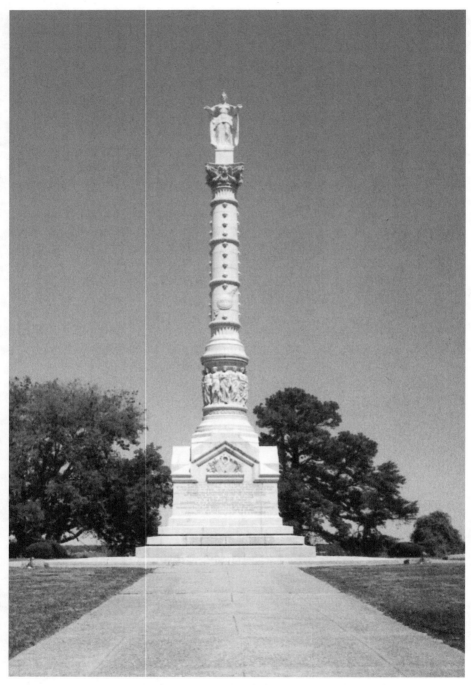

Yorktown Victory monument at the Colonial National Historical Park.

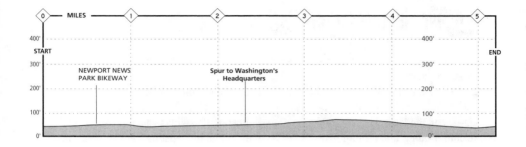

Miles and Directions

0.0 START at the campsite office and information center. If you forgot your bike, you can rent one from the information center. Turn right on the park access road, heading toward the camping areas.

0.5 Go through a gate. Continue on the park access road.

0.6 Turn left on the Newport News Park Bicycle Trail. Go around the gate if it is closed. This trail is a hard-packed dirt road and is almost completely flat.

2.4 Pass the dirt road on the right leading to George Washington's Headquarters.

4.6 Bear left at the gate, continuing on the bike trail. This last section runs alongside Route 143.

5.2 Reach the parking lot.

Ride Information

Local Information

For local information, recreation, services, and more, go to the Newport News Web site at www.newport-news.va.us.

Local Events and Attractions

Yorktown Colonial National Historical Park, (757) 898–3400.

7 Beaverdam Reservoir Park

Start: From the Route 606 entrance and the ranger station trailhead.

Length: 16-mile trail system with a long-term goal of about 25 miles of multiuse trails circumnavigating the lake.

Approximate riding time: 1 to 4 hours.

Difficulty rating: Easy to moderate, as most of the trail is flat singletrack. Lots of twists and turns with some exposed roots and a few sand traps will keep cyclists charged.

Trail surface: Twisty, wooded singletrack with tight turns tempered by an occasional straightaway through dense eastern hardwoods and a few moderate hills. Trails can get pretty soggy after wet weather thanks to the park's low elevation and proximity to the marshy reservoir.

Land status: County park.

Nearest town: Gloucester.

Other trail users: Hikers and equestrians.

Canine compatibility: Very good. There's plenty of water nearby for hydration. As in most local parks, though, dogs must be leashed.

Fees and permits: No fees or permits required. Trail log sign-in is required.

Schedule: Park hours vary throughout the year, but for the most part are 8:00 A.M. to sunset, year-round.

Maps: USGS map: Gloucester. Beaverdam Park has a trail map and other literature available at the main park entrance on Roaring Springs Road (Route 616).

Trail contacts: Beaverdam Park Manager Ranger Station, (804) 693-2107 or www.co.gloucester.va.us/pr/current/beaverdam.htm; Gloucester Parks and Recreation, (804) 693-2355.

Getting There: From Newport News/Hampton Roads area: Follow U.S. Route 17 north over the Coleman Memorial Bridge at Yorktown. Take U.S. Route 17 to Gloucester. Pass downtown Gloucester and continue on U.S. Route 17 north to the crossroads at Ark. Turn right here onto Fary's Mill Road (Route 606). Travel 2.6 miles on Fary's Mill Road to the secondary park entrance on the right. This isn't as clearly marked as the park's main entrance on Roaring Springs Road, so keep your eyes peeled. It shows up just after the bridge over the creek. Park in the gravel parking area (rest rooms, snacks, and drink machines are available here). The trailhead will be on the opposite side of the parking lot from the rest rooms, next to the trail sign-in book. *DeLorme: Virginia Atlas & Gazetteer:* Page 50, A-2.

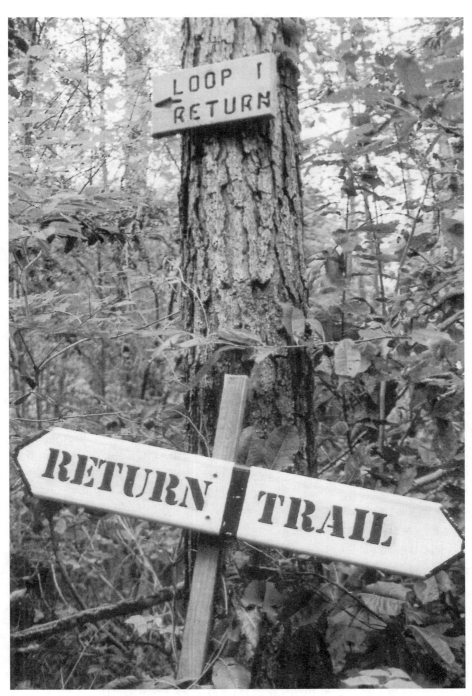

A well-marked trail makes riding here very easy.

It's always a bit odd to me when I stare across a beautiful lake surrounded by old hardwoods, teeming with wildlife, and home to such residents as the bald eagle, and think, incredulously, that this lake didn't even exist more than a dozen years ago! Before 1990, this area was mostly wetlands, open fields, woods, and a few creeks. In 1990 an earthen dam was built through Beaverdam Swamp, and the area was flooded, creating a 635-acre reservoir for the town of Gloucester's drinking water supply.

Today, rangers at Beaverdam Park claim this is one of the healthiest lakes in the state, and I'd have to agree. People come for miles to angle for the latest catch, including largemouth bass, sunfish, perch, channel catfish, eel, and crappie. The policies are mostly catch and release, with a scale at the main office for weigh-ins and ambitious record setters. And to the lake's credit, I watched an angler weigh in a largemouth bass at almost seven pounds before dropping it back in the water for another day. The main recreational uses at Beaverdam Park are unquestionably fishing and canoeing, although plenty of other activities are offered throughout the year (pick up a brochure from the park office for a list of all the activities available). But fishing was not the reason I came here, and I was eager to head up to the park's secondary entrance and check out its network of mountain bike trails.

The multiuse trail located at the northern end of the park at the secondary entrance on Fary's Mill Road is designed for hiking, horseback riding, and mountain biking. So far, the park, with the help of the Eastern Virginia Mountain Bike Association, has created six loops with trails extending all the way around to the ranger station and boat ramp. The trails all travel through a thick hardwood forest along the banks of the reservoir. Each of the loops is connected by the main Beaverdam Trail. The loops are a great way to break up the monotony of riding out and back and offer trail users more room to explore the park's northern and eastern edges. Each year more trails are added, so depending on when you arrive, there may be more to explore than expected. When all is said and done, the park plans to extend this trail system around the entire reservoir, creating a multiuse trail

HUNTING SEASON Be very careful when riding here during hunting season, which begins in the fall. Park boundaries are pretty narrow, and all the adjacent land is private property. For opening and closing dates for the current hunting season, call the Virginia Department of Game and Inland Fisheries, (540) 248-9360, or visit www.dgif.state.va.us.

nearly 25 miles long. The rangers readily admit, though, that this may not happen for some time, as the work will involve more than simply cutting a trail through the forest. Because of the swampy, low-lying terrain, a series of bridges and other trail connectors will need to be constructed. And the weather can also sometimes stand in the way of progress, as the park learned in 1999 when Hurricane Floyd blew through and caused extensive damage to the trails, closing Loop 4 for months.

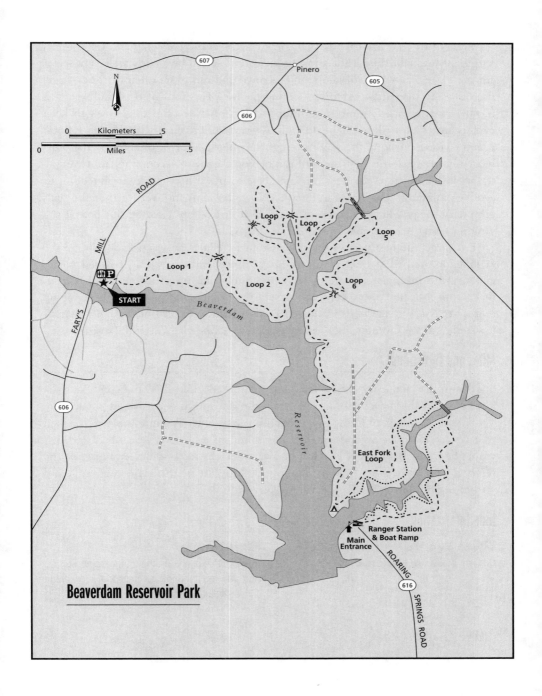

Beaverdam Reservoir Park

Beaverdam Trail is currently maintained by both the park staff and the Eastern Virginia Mountain Bike Association and is considered to be a fairly well-kept secret among trail users, who will rarely find a crowd and can more often than not enjoy time alone in the hardwood forests around the lake. This well-marked trail system is mostly level, with a few moderate hills and lots of twisty, fun singletrack to keep cyclists busy. Getting lost will be difficult, as wooden signs clearly label Loop 1, Loop 2, and so forth all along the way. Although it's not stated prior to entering the trailhead, my impression is that the trail is a bit too narrow to accommodate two-way traffic, so for caution's sake, it's probably best to travel in a clockwise direction to avoid running into oncoming trail traffic. Also, after rains and wet weather, the trails get pretty soggy and are known to flood. Call first before heading out here if the weather hasn't been cooperating prior to your visit.

For some, the best part of the trail system here at Beaverdam Park may be the facilities located right next to the trailhead. Excellent rest rooms, covered picnic tables, and drink machines are open to the public during park hours and help to make your visit here more comfortable and refreshing. Don't forget to bring along bug spray. Most of the trails in this far eastern section of Virginia are near marshy lowlands and are mosquito breeding grounds. You'll be glad you did. Trust me.

Miles and Directions

Start from the secondary entrance to Beaverdam Park just off Route 606. The trailhead is across the gravel parking area from the rest rooms and covered picnic area. Where you're going and how to get back is pretty obvious along this well-marked trail system (wooden signposts at the beginning of each loop lead the way), so it would be pretty hard to get lost. Just be aware that the park boundary alongside the reservoir is fairly narrow (it extends about 200 to 300 feet from the reservoir), and everything bordering the park is private property.

Ride Information

Local Events and Attractions
Historic downtown Gloucester.

Facilities
The facilities at the trailhead, including well-kept rest rooms, drink machines, and covered picnic tables, are excellent.

8 Waller Mill Park

Start: From the trailhead at the park entrance.
Length: 4.5-mile loop; 6 miles total.
Approximate riding time: 1 hour.
Difficulty rating: Difficult due to hilly, twisty singletrack through trees and over roots.
Trail surface: Hilly and wooded singletrack trails.
Land status: City park.
Nearest town: Williamsburg.
Other trail users: Hikers.
Canine compatibility: Dog friendly.
Fees and permits: No fees or permits required.
Schedule: Open 7:00 A.M. to 7:00 P.M. Closed for the winter (December–March).
Maps: USGS map: Williamsburg; ADC map: Virginia Peninsula road map; Waller Mill Park trail map.
Trail contacts: Williamsburg Parks Department, Waller Mill Park Office, (757) 220-6170; Eastern Virginia Mountain Bike Association, (757) 722-4609.

Getting There: From Williamsburg: Take Richmond Road (U.S. Route 60) east approximately 2 miles to Airport Road. Turn right on Airport Road (Route 645). Go approximately 1.5 miles on Airport Road to the Waller Mill Park entrance on the right. Dogwood Trail

begins opposite the entrance to the park. Seasonal bus: Take the Williamsburg Area Visitors Shuttle green route to stop 4 (U.S. Route 60 and Airport Road). Now on your bike, head east 1.5 miles on Airport Road to the Dogwood Trailhead on the left.
From Richmond or Newport News: Take I-64 to the Camp Peary exit. Make a hard right on Rochambeau Drive. Go approximately 1.5 miles past Bruton High School to Airport Road. Turn left on Airport Road (Route 645). The Waller Mill Park entrance is on the left. Dogwood Trail begins opposite the entrance to the park. *DeLorme: Virginia Atlas & Gazetteer:* Page 50, B-1.

The Ride

Sponsored by the Virginia Company of London, the colony of Jamestown was established in 1607. Hoping to make a profit on the land's untapped resources, the Virginia Company embarked on its mission from England in December 1606. Four months later, the first English colonists reached the shores of the New World.

They landed along the Virginia coast, selecting a safe site with deep water to moor their ships. On May 14, 1607, the colonists began creating what would become the first permanent English settlement in the New World, marking the beginnings of our nation.

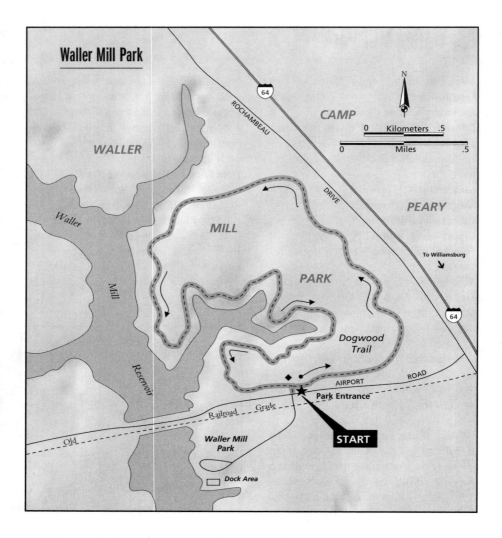

Waller Mill Park

Tobacco, the largest cash crop of its time, took root around 1613, stimulating the rapid growth of Jamestown along the James River and other English colonies settling down in eastern Virginia. By 1699, the seat of government in Virginia moved to Williamsburg. It remained there until 1780, when Virginians relocated it to Richmond to escape British troops. In 1694, a small college teaching arts, sciences, education, and law was granted its coat of arms. Today the College of William and Mary is one of the nation's oldest public colleges.

As towns and cities grew, Britain began imposing greater restrictions and higher taxes on colonists in this New World. This oppression ultimately led to the call for independence. More than six years after the war against Britain began, America won its independence on the fields of Yorktown, only a few miles from the site of the original settlement. A nation was born and a revolution won on this small piece of historic land along the Virginia Peninsula.

Today, U.S. history is revisited at Historic Jamestown, Colonial Williamsburg, and Yorktown Victory Center. Within minutes of each other along the Colonial Highway, these living museums bring to life the first chapters of America's history.

Moving forward through history to the present day, a new revolution is taking place on Virginia's historic peninsula—mountain biking, of course! In addition to Colonial Williamsburg, Historic Jamestown, Yorktown Victory Center, Busch Gardens Theme Park, and the College of William and Mary, the Virginia Peninsula offers some superior singletrack.

Only minutes from Colonial Williamsburg and a short bike ride from the College of William and Mary, the sensational Dogwood Trail awaits off-road riders eager to pedal supreme singletrack through hardwoods overlooking Waller Mill Reservoir. Loaded with hills, twisting trails, and inspiring scenery, this 4.5-mile loop contains the most exciting off-road riding in the Tidewater region.

Its home is Waller Mill Park, just off I–64 and within cycling distance from Williamsburg (actually, it's approximately 4 miles from downtown, so don't be fooled if you're not an avid cyclist). Dogwood Trail is maintained by the city of Williamsburg and is the park's only trail designated for bicycles, so it's particularly important to stay off the park's other trails.

The trail begins across from the park entrance on Airport Road. The first section of Dogwood Trail, traveled counterclockwise, is relatively new. Much of this portion of the trail was cut with the help of the Eastern Virginia Mountain Bike Association and is well marked. Negotiating many of the dips and turns of this wooded singletrack will get fairly tricky as you cut through the western half of Waller Mill Park. As the trail nears the reservoir, the terrain rolls more sharply, giving this already challenging trail an increased level of difficulty. At times, the trail crests some of the park's small ridges to reveal scenic views of the reservoir below. Following the loop brings you back to the start of the ride, where you can decide to call it quits or continue for another loop around the Dogwood Trail.

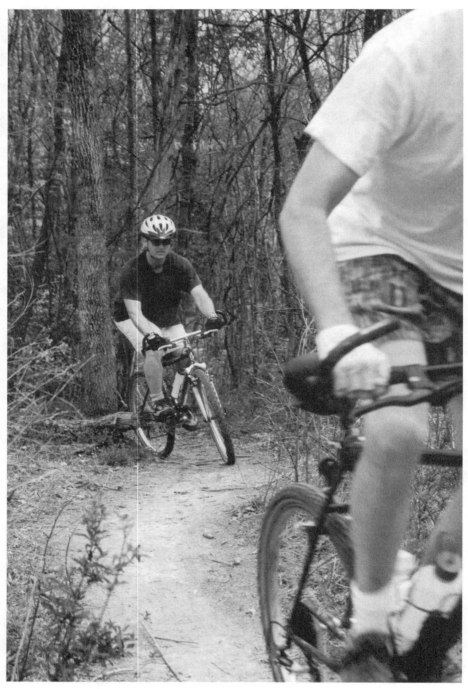

Tearing it up on the Dogwood Trail's exciting singletrack. This and York River's Marle Ravine Trail offer up some of the peninsula's finest riding.

Miles and Directions

0.0 START from the parking lot at Waller Mill Park. Follow the entrance road back to the park entrance. Dogwood Trail begins across Airport Road (be careful crossing this road). Immediately across the road and in the woods, Dogwood Trail splits either left or right. Turn right, following Dogwood Trail in a counterclockwise direction. **(Note:** Much like the Harwood's Mill Mountain Bike Trail in Newport News Park, Dogwood Trail must be traveled one way only—counterclockwise. While there are no signs dictating one direction over the other, counterclockwise appears to be understood as the preferred direction. The trails twist and turn frequently, the singletrack is very narrow, and passing anywhere on the trail would be difficult and dangerous. Ride with the flow to avoid any preventable accidents.)

2.3 Pass a wooden bench overlooking the reservoir. This is a perfect spot for a nice break.

3.0 Dogwood Trail contours the hill around the tip of the alcove.

3.5 Head away from the reservoir toward the start of the ride.

4.5 Reach the end of the loop at the trailhead for the Dogwood Trail. Care to make another loop before heading home?

Ride Information

Local Events and Attractions

Historic Jamestown.
Colonial Williamsburg.
College of William and Mary.

Yorktown Battlefield.
Historic Yorktown.
Colonial National Historic Park.
Busch Gardens Theme Park.

9 York River State Park

Start: From the visitor center.
Length: 14.5 miles of off-road bicycling trails.
Land status: State park.
Nearest town: Williamsburg.
Other trail users: Hikers and equestrians.
Canine compatibility: Dogs are welcome in the park and would love the trails, but as always they must be kept on leashes at all times.

Fees and permits: Parking: $1.00 per vehicle weekdays; $2.00 per vehicle weekends and holidays.
Schedule: Open 8:00 A.M. until dusk, year-round.
Maps: USGS map: Gressitt; ADC map: Virginia Peninsula road map; York River State Park trail map.
Trail contacts: York River State Park, (757) 566-3036 or www.state.va.us/~dcr/parks; Eastern Virginia Mountain Bike Association, (757) 722-4609.

Getting There: From Richmond or Newport News: Take I-64 south to exit 231B for Croaker on Route 607 North. At Croaker, turn right on Riverview Road (Route 606). Take this road for 1.5 miles to York River Park Road (Route 696) and turn left. Follow York River Park Road to the visitor center. Parking available for a fee. *DeLorme: Virginia Atlas & Gazetteer:* Page 50, A-1.

The Rides

There are six trails within York River State Park (nearly 15 miles worth) that are open to mountain biking. Some of them share use with equestrians and hikers. Of these six trails, however, two were developed exclusively for mountain bikes. They are maintained by local mountain bike volunteers through the Eastern Virginia Mountain Bike Association, which has successfully created a partnership between the state park and local cyclists looking for great places to ride.

Partnerships like this didn't used to exist, however, and cyclists had to warily creep onto public lands in hopes of riding some good trails without getting caught. Today, more and more parks are opening their arms and their land to cyclists, seeing mountain bikers as relevant and valuable trail users. York River State Park was one of the first and is certainly one of the best examples of parks that have embraced off-road cyclists. It has allowed local mountain bike volunteers to come in and, with park supervision, cut some of the best singletrack in eastern Virginia—to be used

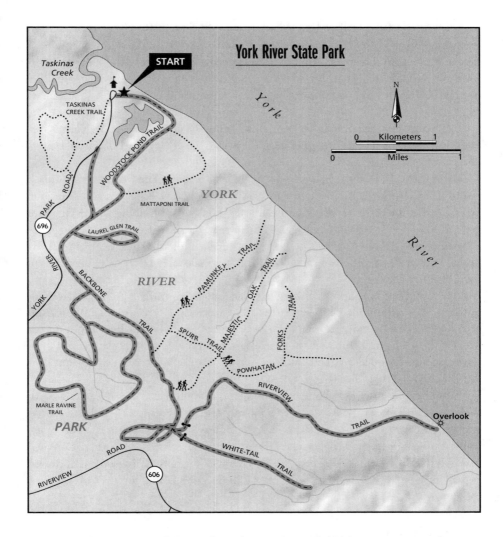

York River State Park

Taskinas Creek

START

TASKINAS CREEK TRAIL

WOODSTOCK POND TRAIL

MATTAPONI TRAIL

LAUREL GLEN TRAIL

PARK ROAD

696

YORK RIVER

BACKBONE TRAIL

YORK

RIVER

PAMUNKEY TRAIL

OAK TRAIL

MAJESTIC TRAIL

SPURR TRAIL

FORKS TRAIL

POWHATAN

RIVERVIEW

MARLE RAVINE TRAIL

PARK

RIVERVIEW ROAD

606

WHITE-TAIL TRAIL

TRAIL

Overlook

York River

N

Kilometers   1
0

0   Miles   1

exclusively by mountain bikers. The value to the park has been greater park atten-
dance, increased revenues, and a win-win situation for everyone.

   Currently, the trails open to mountain bikers fall into two categories: multiuse
trails, open for cyclists, hikers, and equestrians; and mountain bike trails, developed
exclusively for off-road cyclists. Woodstock, Backbone, Riverview, and White-Tail
are all multiuse trails within York River State Park and should be traveled with caution (bikes should always yield to everyone else on these trails). These trails are fairly
easy to pedal along and can be enjoyed by anyone interested in riding along unpaved
trails and bridle paths through the hardwood forests of eastern Virginia. The Laurel

Glen Mountain Bike Trail and the Marle Ravine Mountain Bike Trail are the park's two mountain-bike-specific trails, built and maintained by local volunteer mountain bikers. While Laurel Glen is meant to accommodate beginners to the sport along its relatively modest single- and doubletrack trails, the Marle Ravine Mountain Bike Trail packs lots of hills, switchbacks, bridges, and jumps into its 6 miles of advanced singletrack.

No matter what your skill level or riding interests are, it's clear that York River State Park is THE place to be in eastern Virginia for a great off-road riding experience.

Before mountain bikes and advanced singletrack dominated the minds of park visitors, however, York River State Park was (and still is) well known for its unique coastal environment. This is where freshwater from the Pamunkey and Mattaponi (mat-a-pone-EYE) Rivers converges to form the York River (this actually happens approximately 10 miles upriver), which then mixes with saltwater from the Chesapeake. The result of this convergence of fresh- and saltwater creates a habitat rich in marine and plant life.

At some point long ago in history, the ocean covered nearly all of Tidewater Virginia up to Richmond. The Eastern Shore, Chesapeake Bay, Virginia Beach, and most of eastern Virginia up to the city of Richmond were buried beneath hundreds of feet of ocean water. Today, fossil remains of prehistoric shellfish, sharks, and even whales can be found along the banks of the York River and its tributary streams near the park.

In the seventeenth and eighteenth centuries, when tobacco was the cash crop of the commonwealth, York River State Park was actually the site of a public tobacco warehouse called Taskinas Plantation. Local planters stored their crops in the warehouse before they were shipped across the Atlantic to England. The park was opened in its present form in 1980, to preserve a portion of this unique coastal environment and all its related marshes while also providing a unique area for day-use outdoor recreation.

Laurel Glen Mountain Bike Trail

Start: From the Laurel Glen trailhead off Backbone Trail near Woodstock Pond Trail.
Length: 2-mile loop.
Approximate riding time: 30 minutes.
Difficulty rating: Easy to moderate.
Trail surface: Hard-packed and sandy singletrack through woodlands, ridges, and swamps.
Other trail users: Hikers.

The Laurel Glen Mountain Bike Trail is made up of mostly gentle turns and hills with a few challenging climbs, drops, and log rolls. Cyclists new to the sport may want to consider pedaling along this trail first before trying to tackle the more challenging Marle Ravine singletrack.

Hammering along the Marle Ravine Mountain Bike Trail.

Marle Ravine Mountain Bike Trail

Start: From the Marle Ravine trailhead off Backbone Trail.
Length: 6-mile loop.
Approximate riding time: 1 hour.
Difficulty rating: Difficult due to twisting singletrack and short, steep ups and downs.
Trail surface: Hard-packed, narrow, twisty singletrack through woodlands and ravines.
Other trail users: Hikers and equestrians.

Considered by many to be one of the best rides in eastern Virginia, the Marle Ravine Mountain Bike Trail was designed by and built for mountain bikers. Another success story for the Eastern Virginia Mountain Bike Association, the Marle Ravine Trail shows what cooperation and initiative can do for an interest group. Though the terrain is less difficult than the terrain at nearby Waller Mill Park or Harwood's Mill Mountain Bike Trail in Newport News, the more than 6 miles of bicycling trails on this loop offer plenty of enjoyable off-road adventures for nearly all cyclists.

Riverview Trail takes you out to this overlook on the York River.

Woodstock, Backbone, Riverview, and White-Tail Trails

Start: From the visitor center.
Length: 8.3-mile trail combination.
Approximate riding time: 1 to 1.5 hours.
Difficulty rating: Easy due to fairly flat terrain along carriage roads.
Trail surface: Hard-packed old roadbeds and singletrack through upper woodlands and old-growth forest.
Other trail users: Hikers and equestrians.

This series of multiuse trails through the park offers mostly gentle turns and hills with a few challenging hills, dips, and log rolls through woodlands, ridges, and swamps.

The park's main trail, Backbone, begins at the visitor center, high on the banks of the York River. As the backbone to York River's trail system, Backbone Trail is a flat dirt pathway that carries cyclists into the park's hardwood forests and links riders to each of the other trails open to bikes. Not all trails in the park are open to bicyclists, so be careful to stay only on designated routes. The Woodstock Pond Trail, which is open to bicycles, follows a dirt road around the pond into the park before joining up with Backbone Trail. The other two multiuse trails open to bikes are the Riverview Trail and White-Tail Trail.

Riverview Trail is one of the park's more challenging multiuse trails. Narrow and sandy, this doubletrack winds its way through the park's forest toward the high banks of the river. Ivy and moss growing from the trees add to the thickness of the greenery, all the way to a spectacular view overlooking the river. Take a moment to climb down the steep cliffs, eroded and beaten by the river, and you may possibly find fossils of ancient fish and mammals.

White-Tail Trail leads you through the woods along the ridge on one of the park's many hillsides. This trail is more of a hard-packed, dirt forest road. It has a few quick descents, though it is mostly flat.

Ride Information

Concessions
Vending machines with snacks are available at the visitor center and Croaker Landing.

Local Events and Attractions
Annual Mountain Bike Duathlon (bike/run) in spring.

May and June—Kayak Below the Cliffs, groups of four or more, four-hour program, $50 per person for group of four, $40 per person for five or more, preregister (804) 214-9202.

June—National Trails Day, great day to hike. Call York River State Park for details.

Guided canoe trips on weekends.

Colonial Williamsburg.

Colonial Parkway.

Historic Jamestown.

Yorktown Battlefield.

Historic Yorktown.

Colonial National Historic Park.

Busch Gardens Theme Park.

Honorable Mention

Coastal Virginia

Listed here is one of the great rides in the coastal Virginia area that didn't make the list this time around but deserves recognition. Check it out and let us know what you think. You may decide that this ride deserves higher status in future editions, or, perhaps, you may have a ride of your own that merits some attention.

A Ipswitch: Chesapeake

Ipswitch has been around for years (once a Girl Scout park), and mountain bikers on the Chesapeake side of the bridge have made it their home for as long as mountain bikes have been around. There are trails everywhere, so making a loop may be difficult unless you're there with someone who knows the system. But honing your singletrack skills and gaining the "Ipswitch Advantage" is what most come here for. The trails are flat (you are near Virginia Beach, after all), but the singletrack is tight, twisty, and sandy. So if you're finding it too easy here, you're not trying hard enough. Watch out for BMXers who frequent Ipswitch seeking air on a series of jumps and doubles. Also, be aware that the trails at Ipswitch are being tainted with the occasional "bad element" that finds expensive bikes, cars, and roof racks to be perfect prey. Bad things have happened here, so keep your radar on, and go only in groups.

To get there from Hampton and Norfolk, follow I–64 east through Norfolk. Take the Indian River Road West exit. Once on Indian River Road heading west, make a left onto Level Green Boulevard (Level Green is a loop and has two entrances off Indian River. Take either). This turn is right by a gas station. Drive down Level Green for about 1 mile, then make a left onto Drew Drive. Take Drew about half a mile before coming to a three-way intersection and stop sign. Go through this stop sign and follow Drew Drive about a quarter mile, until the houses in this condo community disappear and there are trees on both side of the road. Park along the sides of the road. You should see a trailhead on your right just before the Ipswitch sign (this is the name of the condo community). Call HDK Cycles at (757) 424–6151 if you have any questions on how to get here or want someone to ride with. (*DeLorme: Virginia Atlas & Gazetteer:* Page 35, B-5.)

Central Virginia

10 Petersburg National Battlefield

Start: From the visitor center.
Length: 6 miles of trails.
Approximate riding time: 1 to 2 hours of riding. Those interested in more than bicycling at the park should set aside at least 2 to 4 hours to visit the main unit. To visit all the sites in the park, plan to spend at least a full day.
Difficulty rating: Easy, due to little elevation gain and smooth terrain.
Trail surface: Dirt trails and singletrack.

Land status: National park.
Nearest town: Petersburg.
Other trail users: Hikers, motorists, and Civil War buffs.
Canine compatibility: Dogs are welcome but must be kept on leashes.
Fees and permits: Costs vary from season to season. Be prepared to pay no less than $5.00 per person and $10.00 per vehicle during peak season (June through August) or as little as $3.00 per person and $5.00 per vehicle during off-season.
Schedule: Visitor center/museum open daily 8:00 A.M. to 5:00 P.M. with extended summer hours. The Park Tour Road closes at dusk. Park is closed December 25 and January 1.
Maps: USGS maps: Petersburg, Prince George; ADC map: Petersburg and Vicinity road map; National Park Service battlefield trail map.
Trail contacts: Petersburg National Battlefield, (804) 732–3531, www.nps.gov/pete.

Getting There: From I–95 at Petersburg: Take the Washington Street East (Route 36) exit into Petersburg. Go approximately 2.5 miles east on Route 36 to the Petersburg National Battlefield entrance on the right. Follow the entrance road through the tollgate to the parking lot at the visitor center. *DeLorme: Virginia Atlas & Gazetteer:* Page 48, C-3.

The Ride

Mountain biking at Petersburg National Battlefield used to conjure up thoughts of well-maintained gravel or paved trails along an interpretive route of signs and exhibits—nothing very exciting. Upon further inspection, however, this proved not to be the case.

The park is a wonderfully preserved site of American history, maintaining and protecting the very ground on which the largest battle and the longest siege of the

Civil War occurred. Nearly 70,000 Americans died in the Petersburg area during its nine-and-a-half-month siege. Reasons for such high casualties included attacks, counterattacks, artillery and mortar shells, sharpshooting, disease, and imprisonment by the enemy.

General Ulysses Grant firmly believed that the key to taking Richmond was first to take Petersburg. If Petersburg were captured, the Union army could cut off all of Richmond's railroad lines and roadways so vital to the Confederate capital's shipments of supplies and food. Many believed that if Richmond fell, the war would come to an end.

Cannons stand as monuments to the battles fought here in Petersburg.

Grant's Union forces began arriving in mid-June 1864 and would not fully smother the Confederate army for another nine and a half miserable months. After outnumbering Robert E. Lee's cold, hungry, and exhausted soldiers, Grant ordered an all-out assault on April 2. Lee's army collapsed. One week later, at Appomattox Courthouse, Lee surrendered; the war was over.

Today, Petersburg National Battlefield offers enough wooded trails open to bicycling that you would have to make plans *not* to ride to study its historical exhibits. Back roads and trails with such names as Attack Road and Encampment Trail take you cycling past massive Civil War earthworks and through dense forest that was once an open field of war. These trails are exciting and scenic and add a new dimension to off-road cycling. One day is not enough to hike all the trails in this park, though on a bike, you should have no worries about exploring each new off-road battlefield route.

Be sure, however, not to get too carried away on these great off-road trails; there is so much else worth seeing at this park. One such sight is a massive crater left by a federal attack (a 511-foot-long tunnel and four tons of gunpowder were used to blow up a Confederate battery). The resulting hole was nearly 170 feet long, 60 feet wide, and 30 feet deep. Unfortunately for the Union army, this attack, which took one month to prepare, turned out to be a horrible failure. After blasting the Confederate battery with the massive charge, Union troops dove right into the crater, rather than going around it, and were thereby trapped. Confederate troops then launched a counterattack and inflicted more than 4,000 casualties on the federal forces. There would be much more fighting before this siege ended.

The trails in this park are well maintained and don't present a very high level of difficulty. They are open to the public but are not meant for aggressive use. Ride gently on these historic paths and, by all means, stay on the designated trails. The Civil War earthworks are very fragile and can easily be scarred and damaged if ridden on. Take care of this national historic site and preserve it for future generations of cyclists and history buffs.

Miles and Directions

(**Note:** All of these trails connect, at some point or another, with the paved Park Tour Road. Leave your car at the visitor center and ride the bike lane along Park Tour Road to each of the different trails. Or, if you prefer, drive your car to the different parking areas along Park Tour Road and ride to the nearest off-road trail of your choice. Parking areas along Park Tour Road are shown on the map as small, black semicircles.

Because there are so many individual trails weaving through this park, it would be unreasonable to create a directional route. Instead, each of these trails is described individually, and it is left up to the reader to choose which trails to ride.)

Friend Trail

0.7 mile long. If you're riding into the park from the visitor center, this is the first trail you'll come across. Friend Trail starts on the right side of Park Tour Road, just across the bridge over Route 36. If you pass the traffic circle, you've gone too far. The trail dives down a set of steps into the battlefield wilderness and rambles along a picturesque, wooded path past Battery 8. Black U.S. troops captured this battery and renamed it Fort Friend for a large Friend House nearby. After it was captured, Fort Friend served as an artillery position during the siege of Petersburg. Shortly after crossing Harrison Creek, this trail ends on a one-lane paved road. Turn left on this road to get back to Park Tour Road.

Encampment Trail

1.5 miles long. This trail begins from the maintenance area just off Park Tour Road. The trail sign points into the woods. The trail is mostly a single-lane jeep trail that winds through the woods toward the site of the old Taylor Farm. The farm, located on a ridge overlooking the land west of the Taylor House, was quickly taken by troops at the start of the siege. During the Battle of the Crater, Union troops lined up nearly 200 pieces of artillery on this ridge and fired down upon Confederate troops.

Harrison Creek Trail

1.0 mile long. There is a small parking area on Park Tour Road where you can get on this trail. Harrison Creek Trail crosses the road at this point and takes you through the woods along a national historic route. The short section of trail north of Park Tour Road is a fun, winding singletrack along the creek that will challenge anyone's skills. South of Park Tour Road, the trail widens and allows for a more leisurely ramble through the forest.

During the siege, Confederate forces were driven back to Harrison Creek, where they dug in and held their line for two days. Later, in the last month of battle, Lee launched one last offensive. This offensive was called the Battle of Fort Stedman, and Lee's troops were stopped cold along this creek.

Attack Road

0.5 mile long. This old dirt road connects Route 109 to Park Tour Road within the park. Harrison Creek Trail and the unnamed service road south of Park Tour Road intersect with Attack Road and lead to the Union Camp and Battery 9. Attack Road is lined on either side with heavy earthworks, built large and high to guard against a Confederate attack on the Union encampment.

Jordon Point Road

0.3 mile long. This dirt road and two other roads, which together make a triangle, create what was an important supply route between Meade Station and the Union Camp. Meade Station provided a vital link along the rail line that brought Union supplies and medical equipment from City Point. This supply link ultimately secured the Union victory over Lee's troops. Lee's army, meanwhile, grew cold and hungry during the siege and fell to Grant's well-equipped troops.

Branch Trail

0.3 mile long. Branch Trail and Battery Trail are very similar. Both trails wind through the thick Petersburg Battlefield forest, weaving around massive trenches and earthworks set up by the Union army. Some of the earthworks are so high they cast shadows on the trail. Branch Trail takes you from Jordon Point Road to Park Tour Road, where you can follow the bike trail back to the visitor center.

Battery Trail

0.7 mile long. Battery Trail, like Branch Trail, weaves around the massive earthworks constructed by Union troops during the siege. This area is called Battery 9. Black U.S. troops captured this position on the first day of fighting and held it throughout the siege. From Jordon Point Road, Battery Trail takes you all the way back to the entrance road next to Route 36. The trailhead is opposite the trailhead for Friend Trail.

Ride Information

Local Events and Attractions

A seventeen-minute relief map presentation is shown on the hour and half hour at the visitor center.

Mid-June through mid-August, costumed interpreters demonstrate mortar and cannon firings and military life.

Accommodations

There are no places to stay in the park. However, a variety of hotels, motels, and RV camping sites are available in Petersburg and vicinity.

11 Pocahontas State Park

Start: From the park office and information center.
Length: There are more than 20 miles of off-road bicycle trails in the state park, including a great singletrack loop, an easygoing double-track loop, and miles of forest roads.

Land status: State park.
Nearest town: Chesterfield.
Other trail users: Hikers, equestrians, and dogs.
Canine compatibility: Dog friendly. However, dogs must be kept on leashes.
Fees and permits: There is a small parking, camping, and pool fee.
Schedule: Open 8:00 A.M. until dusk daily, year-round.
Maps: USGS maps: Chesterfield, Beach; ADC map: Richmond and vicinity road map: Page 23, E-8; Pocahontas State Park trail map.
Trail contacts: Pocahontas State Park, (804) 796-4255; Mountain Bike Virginia bike club, (804) 782-7903; Department of Conservation and Recreation, (804) 786-1712.

Getting There: From Richmond: Take I-95 south to exit 60. Follow Route 10 west approximately 7 miles to Beach Road (Route 655). Turn left on Route 655, go approximately 4 miles, and follow the signs. Turn right into the park. The park office is just up the road. *DeLorme: Virginia Atlas & Gazetteer:* Page 48, A-B1.

The Rides

Pocahontas is a familiar name associated with early colonial America. According to legend, this younger daughter of Powhatan (chief of a federation of Algonquian Indian tribes living in the Tidewater region) saved Captain John Smith's life. As the story goes, Powhatan's warriors captured Smith, the self-appointed leader of the first Jamestown settlers, and sentenced him to death. Pocahontas, whose real name was Matoaka, pleaded with her father to spare him. A relenting Chief Powhatan allowed Smith to go free.

Legend holds that as a young girl, Pocahontas often visited Jamestown. As she grew older, she would bring food to the settlers and warn the colonists of possible Indian attacks. Later, as a result of the settlers' kindness toward her, she chose to convert to Christianity and changed her name to Rebecca. While visiting Jamestown, she met John Rolfe, an early settler noted as the first commercial tobacco grower.

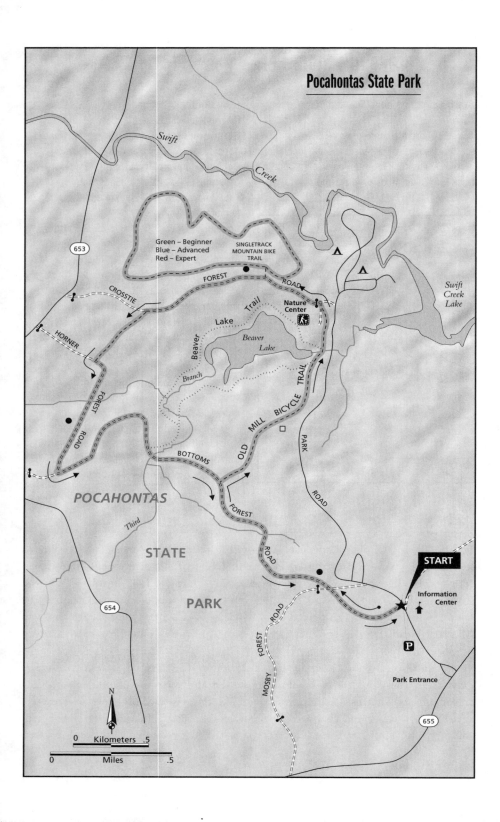

Pocahontas State Park

Green – Beginner
Blue – Advanced
Red – Expert

SINGLETRACK
MOUNTAIN BIKE
TRAIL

653

CROSSTIE

HORNER

FOREST   ROAD

Nature
Center

Beaver   Lake   Trail

Beaver
Lake

Branch

FOREST

ROAD

OLD MILL BICYCLE TRAIL

PARK

ROAD

BOTTOMS

FOREST

ROAD

POCAHONTAS

Third

STATE

654

PARK

Swift

Creek

Swift
Creek
Lake

START

Information
Center

P

Park Entrance

MOSBY   FOREST   ROAD

655

N

0   Kilometers   .5

0   Miles   .5

They married on April 5, 1614, had a child named Thomas, then sailed to England for a visit. She was one of the first Native Americans to visit London. During her stay, however, Pocahontas contracted smallpox and died in March of 1617.

The name Pocahontas means "playful one," which might explain why the Commonwealth of Virginia chose the name for this state park. Unlike many other parks in Virginia, the forestland surrounding Pocahontas is deeded to the park, not the state, which gives recreational activities priority over other land uses such as timber production. This arrangement serves this populated region in Virginia well, as Pocahontas State Park is within just twenty minutes of both Richmond and Petersburg.

Because of its proximity to these growing metropolitan communities, Pocahontas has been one of the state's busiest parks since the Civilian Conservation Corps built the first recreation area here in 1934. Today, hiking, swimming, horseback riding, and bicycling (both road and off-road) are all offered within the park's 7,604 acres. Along with the many trails that already exist for hiking and horseback riding, Pocahontas State Park has developed a number of outlets for eager cyclists. When you arrive, check them out separately or combine them into a single ride. Central Virginia cyclists have struck gold here at Pocahontas, and the recent popularity of mountain biking at the park will hopefully entice officials to consider opening up even more trails to bikes.

Singletrack Mountain Bike Trail

Start: From the Singletrack Mountain Bike Trail trailhead at the northern end of Old Mill Bicycle Trail.
Length: 10-plus miles of challenging singletrack.

Approximate riding time: 1 hour.
Difficulty rating: There are three marked trails, classified beginner, intermediate, and difficult.
Trail surface: Hilly and technical singletrack.

Pocahontas State Park opened the Old Mill Bicycle Trail to bikes back in the early 1990s, before most other parks had even caught on to mountain biking. But the Old Mill Trail, as nice as it is, wasn't quite enough for the growing masses of central Virginia mountain bikers who were looking for more of a challenge and a place to test their skills. Dan Soper, the park's chief ranger, stepped in and, in cooperation with the Mountain Bike Virginia bike club, developed the park's latest all-singletrack addition, geared solely to the needs of singletrack-hungry cyclists. Mountain bikers love it.

Within the Singletrack Mountain Bike Trail loop, located at the northern end of the Old Mill Bicycle Trail, there are three trails to follow: Green, Blue, and Red. Green is easiest, Blue is intermediate, and Red is for expert cyclists. The trailhead is clearly marked with a sign labeled SINGLETRACK MOUNTAIN BIKE TRAIL, and all trails within the loop start from this point.

The Old Mill Bicycle Trail crosses this bridge at the Beaver Lake dam.

If you're new to the sport, stick to the Green Trail, which is classified as easy. This 2-mile trail offers a good introduction to singletrack, but doesn't force the inexperienced cyclist to overdo it. If you want a challenge, head straight for the Blue or Red Trail. While the Red Trail is labeled expert, many consider the intermediate Blue Trail, which is also the longest trail at about 4 miles, to be the most fun. Cyclists on the Blue Trail will love the technical challenges combined with a few taxing uphill efforts for a good hearty workout. But if difficult is what you came for, then difficult is what you'll get on the expert Red Trail. While this nearly 4-mile stretch of expert riding may not require the same amount of stamina as the Blue Trail, it'll tax your concentration, challenge your confidence, and build bike-handling skills you didn't even know existed. The Red Trail is full of chest-high log jumps, huge steeps, and what downhill racers describe as monster g-outs (the *g* stands for "gravity"). A g-out is an abrupt dip with a sharp transition.

Cyclists are asked to register at the trailhead so the park staff can keep track of how much use the trails receive. Who knows? If there's enough use here (and the trail's popularity suggests there is), perhaps the park will consider opening even more new trails. Keep on biking!

Pocahontas State Park Forest Roads

Start: From the visitor center.
Length: 10 miles of forest roads open to bikes.
Approximate riding time: Varies.
Difficulty rating: Easy due to fairly flat terrain along carriage roads.

Trail surface: Hard-packed old forest roads and grassy doubletrack through what used to be classified as state forest land.
Other trail users: Hikers, equestrians, and dogs.

In addition to Pocahontas's singletrack loops and the bike trail around Beaver Lake, there are more than 10 miles of old, grassy forest roads open to bikes. All of the forest roads are clearly marked and roll gently up and down through what was once designated state forest land. It's been awhile since Pocahontas State Park has functioned also as a state forest, and it has been trying to shed the old state forest moniker for some time. Today, all the land surrounding the park is considered state parkland and is open to the public for recreational use. Pick up a brochure at the park office for trail maps of all the forest roads, and head out into the woods to create a variety of loops and out-and-back rides.

Old Mill Bicycle Trail

Start: From the park office and information center.
Length: 6.1-mile loop around Old Mill Bicycle Trail.
Approximate riding time: 1 to 1.5 hours.
Difficulty rating: Easy.

Trail surface: Hard-packed dirt trails around Old Mill Bicycle Trail. Technical singletrack around the mountain bike loop.
Other trail users: Hikers, equestrians, and dogs.

The Old Mill Bicycle Trail begins from the information center near the park entrance and follows Bottoms Forest Road into Pocahontas State Forest. The terrain is rolling, and many of the trails are wide and inviting, allowing cyclists of all abilities to enjoy the wooded environment of this state park. Upon reaching the first split in the trail, turn right, following the white arrows painted on the ground. This will lead you counterclockwise around Beaver Lake, ensuring traffic travels in one direction. From here, the trail narrows and winds beneath a leafy canopy of tall hardwood and pine forest. In less than 1 mile you will cross a small footbridge past the dam and climb a short, steep hill to the nature center. Bear left around the nature center on Crosstie Forest Road and continue along the rolling forest roads. Signs along the route point the way.

Miles and Directions—Old Mill Bicycle Trail

0.0 START at the park office and information center. Bottoms Forest Road starts just across from the parking lot on the left side of the Park Road.

0.5 Bear right, continuing on Bottoms Forest Road. Signs along the trail will direct you.

1.2 Reach the main loop. Turn right on Old Mill Bicycle Trail. Follow the white arrows painted on the ground. These arrows point you in a counterclockwise direction around the loop.

2.1 Cross a little bridge over the creek on the other side of the Beaver Lake dam. This section is very scenic.

2.3 Reach the nature center. You must go in front of the nature center to stay on the trail. Turn left on Crosstie Forest Road.

3.1 Bear left, continuing on Crosstie Forest Road.

3.3 Follow this forest road through a tunnel of tall loblolly pines.

3.4 Turn left on Horner Forest Road.

4.1 Turn left on Bottoms Forest Road.

4.7 Pass Beaver Lake Trail on the left. (Bikes are not allowed on this trail.)

5.0 Reach the beginning of the bicycle loop. Bear right, following Bottoms Forest Road through the woods, back to the start of the ride.

6.1 Arrive back at the parking lot.

Ride Information

Accommodations

Camping and group cabins are available. Call for reservations at (800) 933-PARK or (804) 225-3867.

Snack bar near the pool is open during the summer season.

Local Events and Attractions

Swimming pool at the park—open Memorial Day to Labor Day.

Edgar Allan Poe Museum, Richmond, VA, (804) 648-5523.

Museum and White House of the Confederacy, Richmond, VA, (804) 649-1861.

Hollywood Cemetery, Albemarle and Cherry Streets Richmond, VA. Buried here among the many graves are two U.S. presidents (James Monroe and John Tyler), Jefferson Davis (president of the Confederacy), Confederate general J. E. B. Stuart, and 1,800 Confederate soldiers.

12 Belle Isle

Start: From the Belle Isle parking lot.
Length: Many miles of trails.
Approximate riding time: Varies with distance.
Difficulty rating: Easy around the island's perimeter trail. Difficult on the inner island's hilly singletrack.
Trail surface: Gravel path around the island's perimeter and rugged, hilly singletrack on the island's higher ground.
Land status: City park.

Nearest city: Richmond.
Other trail users: Hikers and dogs.
Canine compatibility: Bring 'em if you've got 'em. Dogs love it here. Just be careful with the crowds.
Fees and permits: No fees or permits required.
Schedule: Open daylight to dusk, year-round.
Maps: USGS map: Richmond; ADC map: Richmond and vicinity road map; Belle Isle Interpretive Guide and Trail Map.
Trail contacts: Park Naturalist, James River Park, City of Richmond Parks and Recreation, (804) 780–8130; James River Park Visitor Center, (804) 780–5311.

Getting There: From I–95 through Downtown Richmond: Take exit 74B to Franklin Street. Turn right on Franklin Street. At the first light, turn left on Fourteenth Street. Go 1 block and turn right on Main Street (one way) at the light. Follow signs to Belle Isle and the Tredegar Iron Works. Turn left on Fifth Street. Go 2 blocks, cross over the Downtown Expressway, and turn left on Byrd Street. Turn right at the Federal Reserve Building on Seventh Street. At the fountain, bear right on Tredegar Street to the Belle Isle parking lot. *DeLorme: Virginia Atlas & Gazetteer:* Page 58, D-1.

The Ride

Belle Isle, part of the James River Park System and one of Richmond's most popular city parks, is located in the heart of Virginia's state capital, just across the river from the Richmond Riverfront. This fifty-four-acre island in the middle of the James River attracts thousands of visitors annually. Its high cliff walls, rushing rapids, stone ruins, and fascinating history together make this island one of the most unique mountain biking spots in the Richmond area.

But before I digress, let me warn you that we're talking about Richmond here, where a good cluster of trails often means a local park crowded with more bikes, walkers, and dogs than you can count on a calculator. But to the island's credit,

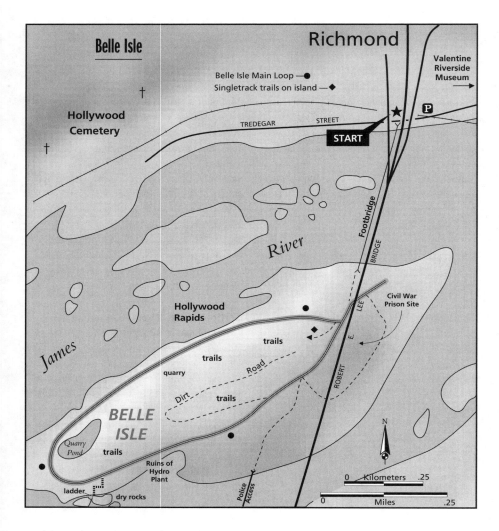

Belle Isle

Richmond

Belle Isle Main Loop —●
Singletrack trails on island —◆

Valentine
Riverside
Museum

Hollywood
Cemetery

TREDEGAR   STREET

START

Footbridge

River

BRIDGE

Hollywood
Rapids

Civil War
Prison Site

LEE

trails

E.

trails

quarry

Road

ROBERT

James

Dirt   trails

BELLE
ISLE

Quarry
Pond   trails

N

Ruins of
Hydro
Plant

0   Kilometers   .25

ladder   dry rocks

Police
Access

0   Miles   .25

cyclists interested in an afternoon ride can pedal across the river over the footbridge beneath the Robert E. Lee Bridge directly from downtown Richmond. On the island, cyclists will find huge drops, rocky and rooty singletrack, quick turns, and some great scenery. Views of Hollywood Cemetery, the Richmond skyline, sunsets over the James River, and the rushing Hollywood Rapids are always a good reason to pedal over to the island, whether or not you're looking for a workout.

Formerly a Native American fishing village, Belle Isle once provided great harvests. Its shores yielded American freshwater mussels, which still exist along the banks of the James. During America's colonial period, the island was called Broad Rock Island because of its large granite walls. It had a general store, crops growing on the east side, and a ferry that transported folks to and from the island.

The Civil War brought to the island a gruesome role. The northeastern section was used as a prisoner-of-war camp for captured Union soldiers. More than 20,000 prisoners were sent here, and at one time as many as 8,000 Union prisoners of war were detained in the island's notorious tent city. Thousands of these prisoners subsequently died of dysentery and other diseases.

During the Industrial Revolution, ironworks came to Belle Isle. Ruins of the old Iron Rolling, Milling, and Slitting Manufactory still exist on the east side along the main trail. This plant ran on water power and slave labor in the early nineteenth century and produced such products as horseshoes, nails, spikes, copper pots, and bowls.

Also during this time, a man named James Bell built a racetrack on the flat land of then Broad Rock Island's east side. Hundreds arrived nightly to "Bell's Island" to gamble and watch the races. It is reported that when James Bell left the island, ladies of Richmond attempted to restore the island's image by renaming it with the "more refined" French title of *Belle Isle,* which means "the good island."

Today Belle Isle is used exclusively as an outdoor recreation area for Richmonders weary of the city's skyscrapers and pavement. The Belle Isle footbridge transports visitors from Tredegar Street over the James River to Belle Isle's eastern flatland. The main trail around the island starts to the right of the bridge. This main trail makes a 1-mile loop around the island, passing many of the historical artifacts left to ruin. For cyclists, this path is short and can be crowded on nice days, weekends, and holidays. Don't even try to ride here on Memorial Day or July 4. However, if you spin up the high hills of the inner island, you'll find a network of singletrack trails crisscrossing the island's high ground. While the trails up here may not be worth writing your friends in Colorado about, they do have a lot of great drops and climbs (about twenty in all), ranging in difficulty from not so steep to nearly vertical. Because of the island's size (very small), you could be doing these same drops and climbs all afternoon—for a quick sense of singletrack bliss in a city better known for its history than its hills.

These trails, though not technically closed to bikes, aren't recommended to cyclists by the park service because of their difficulty level and danger. Trails on the inner island are not maintained and should be approached with great caution and responsibility. In short, cyclists have to behave and stop crashing down cliff walls, breaking collarbones, and causing the park service unnecessary grief, which might result in its banning bikes on the island altogether. Ride only on the inner trails and avoid the cliffs on the island's north side near the Hollywood Rapids. Remember to be careful, and you're guaranteed a great, although brief, ride on Belle Isle.

Miles and Directions

0.0 START at the Belle Isle parking lot next to the Valentine Riverside Museum. Turn right, heading west, on Tredegar Street to the footbridge ramp. Cycle up the ramp and cross over the James River. Please be cautious and considerate of other footbridge traffic (people and dogs). It's a narrow bridge so you may want to walk the bike across.

0.25 Reach Belle Isle. From here, pedal to the right along the dirt path. The main bike path around the island is easy to find from here.

0.3 Reach the main bike route around the island. You may circle the island in either direction.

1.2 Reach the end of the loop. To return to the car, take the footbridge back over the James River to the parking lot.

1.5 Reach the parking lot.

Option: If you want to explore the hilly singletrack trails within the island, go straight at mile 0.3 and climb the dirt hill toward the center of the island. This hill is a short, steep climb. Once you're up this hill, there are riding trails everywhere. Many of these trails are quite difficult, and some are downright hard. There are enough trails within this island to spend an afternoon exploring. The park service warns that many of the trails on Belle Isle are steep and rocky and should be treated with great caution.

As you pedal around the main loop of Belle Isle, you may notice a number of places to access the singletrack trails within the island. There are also a number of areas posted with signs that say NO BIKES. Please don't ride in these areas.

When the weather is dry and the water is low, some cyclists like to explore the dry rocks on the south side of the island. Walk across the metal walkway from the main trail, then climb down a ladder to the rocks. Don't expect to ride with much speed, however. With lots of technical bike-handling skills, some cyclists can maneuver from one rock to the next without falling into the river.

Keep in mind, on weekends and holidays Belle Isle gets very crowded. Be extremely cautious when riding around here, and by all means keep the speeds down.

Ride Information

Restaurants

Third Street Diner at the corner of Third and Cary. Great diner food serving breakfast 24/7. Perfect for breakfast after a late afternoon bike ride.

Local Events and Attractions

Richmond's Riverfront, bordering Richmond's downtown along the James River, creates a 1-mile corridor from the historic Tredegar Iron Works through Kanawha Canal and Haxall Canal. There are events here all year long. For more information, go to www.richmond riverfront.com.

13 Powhite Park

Start: The trailhead starts into the woods at the far end of the circular drive.

Length: There are approximately 8 miles of singletrack on which you can ride.

Approximate riding time: Varies depending on how long you want to have fun.

Difficulty rating: Moderate to difficult; the hilly, twisty nature of the singletrack here requires both stamina and skill. There are a few flat sections and only a couple of resting spots.

Trail surface: Wooded, narrow, twisty singletrack with some muddy sections.

Land status: Regional park.

Nearest town: Richmond.

Other trail users: Hikers and dogs.

Canine compatibility: Dog friendly.

Fees and permits: No fees or permits required.

Schedule: Open daylight to dusk, year-round.

Maps: USGS maps: Richmond, Bon Air, Drewrys Bluff, Chesterfield.

Trail contacts: Mountain Bike Virginia bike club, (804) 782-7903.

Getting There: From Downtown Richmond: Take the Powhite Parkway (Route 76) south toward Chesterfield. Take the Jahnke Road East exit just after crossing over the Chippenham Parkway. As you head east on Jahnke Road, you will cross back under the Chippenham Parkway and will see almost immediately the Powhite Park entrance across the median on your left. Drive another 50 yards to the light at the Chippenham Medical Center and make a U turn to get back to the park entrance. Make a right into the park and proceed to the end of the entrance road to the circular drive (cul-de-sac). Park here. The trailhead starts into the woods at the far end of the circular drive. If the gate to the park entrance is closed, park at the post office across the street.

From the West End or the South Side of Richmond: Take the Chippenham Parkway to the Jahnke Road East exit and follow the directions above. *DeLorme: Virginia Atlas & Gazetteer:* Page 58, D-1.

The Ride

For a long while, years ago, Powhite Park (pronounced po-white) was a big question mark to local cyclists. Could we ride there or couldn't we? Well, of course, we all did for many years regardless, but we always wondered whether—or rather when—we'd get kicked out for good. Well, that time never came, and today mountain bikers have

Hard-core cyclists love Powhite's maze of switchbacks, off-camber descents, log crossings, and challenges like the great Doublerock Jump and the Buzz.

pretty much adopted the park as their own, even helping the park service maintain the trails.

Times sure have changed, and thankfully so in the case of Powhite Park, located right on the border of Richmond and Chesterfield County near the Chippenham Medical Center. So good are the trails here that once you've ridden the fast, rocky descents, the scenic side trails, and the must-ride half pipe, you'll be coming back again and again. Certainly one of the most attractive aspects of this park, aside from its singletrack trail network, is its proximity to the greater Richmond area. Its convenient location allows die-hard cyclists and all of us working saps around the state capital a convenient place to zip on over to after a hard day's work. Powhite Park is located just off Chippenham Parkway across the street from the Chippenham Medical Center, making it a convenient drive from just about any direction. Of course, trying to get there right after work may pose a challenge as the parkway can back up pretty quickly with traffic. While sitting in traffic, you might hardly notice the wooded hillsides between the Powhite and Jahnke Road exits or even know that this area is a regional park and one of the city's finest off-road playgrounds.

GET CONNECTED If you are so inclined, it is possible to travel from Powhite Park to the James River Park by pedaling east on Jahnke Road to Westover Hills Boulevard (turn right on Forest Hill Avenue to get to Westover Hills Boulevard). Head down the hill next to the Nickel Bridge, and you'll end up at the James River Park, which is full of trails. Crossing over the Nickel Bridge will take you into Maymont Park and Dogwood Dell, where more mountain bike trails await. And if you follow the trails within the James River Park heading east, you will eventually reach a small pedestrian footbridge that crosses over the James River onto Belle Isle, where even more singletrack awaits (see Ride 12). Who says you need a car around here?

You'll find the trailhead buried behind the trees right at the end of the park entrance road (at the head of the circular drive). Jump into the woods here and be ready to drop hard, down a quick descent into the park. At the bottom of the descent, you'll come to a swampy area that you must wade through to get to the main trail system. Future plans may someday include constructing a wooden bridge over this typically muddy mess, both to ease the slog factor for cyclists and to relieve the swampy ground from so much traffic. Once you're past this area and into the main trail network, you've got lots of options from which to choose. The trails are fairly well marked, and getting lost will be tough—major roads and neighborhoods surround the park on all sides.

Be sure not to miss some of Powhite's finest features while you're here. While this maze of switchbacks, loops, log crossings, and off-camber descents will keep you entertained, challenges like the great Doublerock Jump (a tricky descent) and the

The trails at Powhite Park are perfect for any singletrack lover in the Richmond area.

Buzz (a half pipe with a series of quick dips through a dirt ravine) will keep you coming back again and again.

Miles and Directions

Due to the nature of this trail network, there's really no point in trying to create specific trail directions for cyclists to follow. Instead, enter the park at the main trailhead at the far end of the circular drive, head downhill and across the swampy area, then simply go where your bike takes you. The trails will dictate where you should and shouldn't go, and various signage throughout the park denotes private property. Please—no trespassing. You can spend the better part of an afternoon at Powhite Park, so hit the trails and have fun!

Ride Information

Local Events and Attractions

Edgar Allan Poe Museum, Richmond, VA, (804) 648-5523.

Museum and White House of the Confederacy, Richmond, VA, (804) 649-1861.

Hollywood Cemetery, Albemarle and Cherry Streets, Richmond, VA. Buried here among the many graves are two U.S. presidents (James Monroe and John Tyler), Jefferson Davis (president of the Confederacy), Confederate general J. E. B. Stuart, and 1,800 Confederate soldiers.

14 Poor Farm Park

Start: From the Archery Range trailhead.
Length: More than 13 miles of trails.
Approximate riding time: 2 to 3 hours.
Difficulty rating: Hilly, rugged singletrack makes this a moderate to difficult ride filled with roots, rocks, tight squeezes, big drops, and, at times, high traffic.

Trail surface: Roots, rocks, climbs, and twisty singletrack.
Land status: County park.
Nearest town: Ashland.
Other trail users: Hikers, dogs, nature tours, and the occasional archer.
Canine compatibility: Good. Dogs love this place as much as mountain bikers do.
Fees and permits: No fees or permits required.
Schedule: Open daylight to dark, year-round. Trails are sometimes closed after heavy rains.
Maps: USGS map: Hanover Academy.
Trail contacts: Hanover County Parks and Recreation, (804) 798–8062; Hanover Visitor Information Center, (804) 752–6766; Mountain Bike Virginia bike club, (804) 782–7903.

Getting There: From Richmond: Take I-95 north to Ashland. Take Route 54 West at Ashland. Follow Route 54 West approximately 5 miles to Liberty Middle School. Turn left on Route 810, pass Liberty Middle School, and follow the signs for Poor Farm Park. Route 810 ends at the gravel parking lot for the park. *DeLorme: Virginia Atlas & Gazetteer:* Page 58, B-1.

The Ride

Richmond's mountain bikers know that finding good singletrack in the area is somewhat difficult. Like many of Virginia's urban areas, Richmond is far removed from the rugged hills of the Allegheny Mountains and the vast public land of the state's national forests. Richmond's terrain, in fact, is typically flat to rolling (at best), and much of the surrounding land is privately owned. But as in many other urban areas hard-pressed for singletrack, there are exceptions. While the Richmond area might, at first, appear to be a dry well for off-road riding, upon closer inspection, cyclists will find a spring of singletrack delight in a regional park called Poor Farm Park, just west of nearby Ashland.

The park is located next to a middle school, and within its boundaries are playing fields, volleyball sandpits, soccer fields, picnic tables, and an amphitheater. But don't let these leisurely amenities fool you. Behind this regional-park facade, through the woods and down the hill from the playing fields, lies a vast network of off-road cycling adventure, growing year by year into some of the best off-road riding in central Virginia. Hills, steep trails, big drops, tough climbs, and fast descents abound in this woodland region and will keep cyclists of all interests and abilities content.

This is a small regional park, so don't expect days of endless exploration. But you can easily spend a few hours pedaling Poor Farm's wooded trails, honing that singletrack savvy and humbling face-plant steeps. And, if you manage to cross Stagg Creek (there's now a footbridge that takes you there), miles of singletrack await your tread beneath both the power lines and farther over in a whole series of newly cut trails.

One of the best ways to get onto the trail system at Poor Farm is to enter at the Archery Range trailhead. From the gravel parking lot at the end of the park entrance road, ride through the open gate, pedaling past the volleyball sandpits toward the soccer fields. Just beyond the sandpits, on the right side of the field, there is a large wooden sign hanging in front of a trail opening. This is the trailhead for the orange-blazed Archery Range Trail.

This trail will lead you downhill toward Stagg Creek, where you can go one of two ways. Turning right at the end of the descent allows you to continue following the loop around the archery course. A left turn will take you on a narrow trail marked with blue and white blazes along the creek. Both of these trails are challenging, with plenty of obstacles and steep hills guaranteed to keep you on your toes.

Besides these two main trails, you can branch off on a side trail to explore a little deeper into the park. Some of these trails are longer than others and have different degrees of difficulty.

The best way to approach cycling in this park, though, is to not worry about following specific routes. Rather, pedal your way into the woods on one of these many trails and just start riding, making up loops of your own.

Please be aware, of course, that this is a regional park, open to all types of trail users. On most days there are certain to be other people enjoying the trails, particularly hikers and dog walkers. Richmond is lucky to have this place. Remember to be courteous to the other trail users. They have a right to be here, too.

Miles and Directions

As far as the trails go, each year a very enthusiastic Poor Farm Park–loving mountain bike group adds more. It would be silly to try and create a loop that people should follow, so instead my best recommendation is to just go out and get lost for a few hours. When you are very lost, keep in mind these few major landmarks: the playing fields where you parked your car, the hills, Stagg Creek, and the power lines—in that order. So if you start wondering where you are and run out of playing fields, hills, creek, or power lines, then you're heading away from your car, and you may want to start thinking of which way is back. If you're on the east side of Stagg Creek (where most of the trails are), simply head uphill, and in one place or another, you'll end up back at your car.

Start from the Archery Range trailhead just off the soccer fields. If you're into really hilly, sketchy, rocky singletrack trails, travel down toward the creek and head left. If you like flatter but very rooty trails through dense woods, cross Stagg Creek (there's a wooden footbridge along the trail near the amphitheater). Over here, you'll find a whole new set of trails winding and zigzagging through the woods (my personal favorite area—just be careful to stay off private property). If you like tight, smooth singletrack, stay on either side of the parking lot on the east side of the creek. There's an adrenaline-pumping downhill near the amphitheater and a couple more beneath the power lines.

Cyclists travel from as far away as Fredericksburg to ride at Poor Farm, and so far as I know, no one has gone home disappointed. Whether you're looking for a good after-work ride or some technical skill training that will knock your shorts off, Poor Farm Park will deliver.

Ride Information

Local Events and Attractions

Poor Farm Park is home to a number of great mountain bike races each year, including the Virginia Point Series. Get in touch with your local bike shop for scheduled races or contact the Mountain Bike Virginia bike club at (804) 782-7903.

Restaurants

The town of Ashland has lots of restaurants and hosts various festivals throughout the year.

15 Cumberland State Forest

Start: From Bear Creek Lake State Park.
Length: 40 to 50 miles of forest roads and trails.
Approximate riding time: Varies with distance.
Difficulty rating: The trails and forest roads are rated easy to moderate.
Trail surface: Flat to rolling dirt roads, singletrack around Bear Lake, and doubletrack trail segments.
Land status: State forest.

Nearest town: Farmville.
Other trail users: Hikers and motorists (light).
Canine compatibility: Dog friendly.
Fees and permits: There is a fee to enter Bear Creek Lake State Park. Expect to pay up to $2.00 per person and $5.00 per car.
Schedule: Open dawn till dusk, year-round.
Maps: USGS maps: Gold Hill, Hillcrest, Whiteville.
Trail contacts: Cumberland State Forest, (804) 492–4121; Bear Creek Lake State Park, (804) 492–4410.

Getting There: From Richmond: Take U.S. Route 60 west from Richmond approximately 40 miles to Cumberland State Forest. U.S. Route 60 travels through the forest. Turn right off U.S. Route 60 just east of Cumberland Courthouse onto Route 622. Take Route 622 north 4.5 miles, then turn left onto Route 629. Route 629 leads you into Bear Creek Lake State Park where you can park. *DeLorme: Virginia Atlas & Gazetteer:* Page 56, D-2.

The Ride

Between the Appalachian and Blue Ridge Mountains to the west and the flat coastal plains to the east lies Virginia's Piedmont region, characterized by its gently rolling hills and quiet valleys. This is an area of few extremes, where the terrain is neither hilly nor flat, and pines, cedars, and hardwoods grow side by side. Land from Manassas to Danville makes up Virginia's Piedmont, and just like Virginia's mountains and coast, off-road bicycling has found its way into this central region.

The majority of accessible mountain biking terrain in the Piedmont region is primarily within Virginia's state forests. The Virginia Division of Forestry administers four state forests in the Piedmont region: Cumberland, Appomattox-Buckingham, Prince Edward–Gallion, and Pocahontas State Forests, all of which comprise nearly 50,000 acres. This area constitutes the largest publicly owned land open to mountain biking east of the Blue Ridge Mountains.

While mountain biking is popular in the state forests, Virginia's forests are primarily managed for such things as watershed protection, timber production, and

The forest has many uses. Timber is one of its greatest resources.

research. For example, several natural areas in the different state forests are intended for use as outdoor laboratories for students of ecology, botany, and other natural sciences. In these areas, timber cutting and recreation (such as mountain biking) are strictly prohibited.

While the natural areas are safeguarded from overuse, there are many areas in Virginia's state forests that are specifically designed for public use. Within each forest is a state park that provides a variety of outdoor activities, from camping and picnicking to swimming, boating, hiking, and cycling.

HUNTING SEASON For opening and closing dates for the current hunting season, call the Virginia Department of Game and Inland Fisheries at (540) 248-9360; www.dgif.state.va.us.

Cumberland State Forest is singled out in this guide as the representative state forest. It is also the headquarters for Virginia's Piedmont state forests. The other three state forests mentioned are similar in size and terrain, and all have many miles of unpaved forest roads and trails ideal for off-road bicycling.

Cumberland State Forest is situated in the heart of Virginia, just 35 miles west of Richmond and only a half hour's drive from Farmville. Its nearly 17,000 acres of flat-to-rolling terrain are filled with forest roads, dead-end trails, and dirt paths.

Many of the dirt roads lead you through scenic hardwood and pine forests and past the natural habitats of deer, turkeys, quail, squirrels, rabbits, and raccoons. The areas that are absent of trees, which I'm sure you'll notice if you come for a visit, have been harvested by the state. The bare spots have been replanted, however, and will be closely monitored in the years to come. Cyclists are welcome on all the dirt forest roads.

One note of caution to anyone venturing into the forests: Please be aware that the state forests make up a significant portion of land open to public hunting in central Virginia. Be aware of hunting seasons, and be careful not to get caught in the woods during a deer hunt.

Miles and Directions

Start at Bear Creek Lake State Park. Bear Creek Lake State Park is a small state park with a forty-acre lake as its main attraction. Camping, picnicking, hiking, fishing, and swimming are some of the activities popular here. There is also a modern bathhouse and a full-service concession area. Leave your car at the lake and hit the forest roads and trails for a good day's bike ride, then return for a cool swim and hot shower.

Most of the roads are maintained forest service roads used by loggers for harvesting timber. There are countless dead-end trails and dry-weather roads that are gated. All of them branch off the main forest roads. Most of these trails are seeded to reduce erosion and improve game habitat. They travel into the woods sometimes up to half a mile before ending. At that point, just turn around and head back to the main road. These trails provide a wonderful diversion from the main forest roads and bring cyclists much closer to the forest's natural setting.

Folks interested in singletrack should head out on the Willis River Trail, which starts near Bear Creek Lake and travels north through Cumberland State Forest for nearly 16 miles. The trail is fairly secluded but never too far from a forest road. It rolls up and down over a variety of short climbs and descents. The trail is fairly well marked, so pick up a map and go for as long as you desire.

Note on the map the shaded area above Route 622. Cumberland State Forest continues well north of this road. In fact, only about half of the state forest is mapped in this guide. Be sure to get the Virginia Department of Forestry's *Guide to Virginia's Piedmont State Forests* if you wish to travel farther into the forest. In addition to Cumberland State Forest, the Virginia Department of Forestry's guide also provides detailed maps of Appomattox-Buckingham State Forest, Prince Edward-Gallion State Forest, and Pocahontas State Forest. Each of these four state forests has many miles of great forest roads and trails suitable for mountain biking.

(**Note:** Because Cumberland State Forest has so many individual forest roads and trails suitable for cycling, it would be unreasonable to create a single loop. Instead, cyclists are encouraged to use the forest map provided and select their own routes. For this reason, there is no profile map available.)

Ride Information

Local Events and Attractions

Lee's Retreat Driving Tour, Farmville. For information, go to www.leesretreat.com.

Accommodations

Bear Creek Lake State Park has a number of campgrounds available to the public, as well as parking, information, toilets, and showers. Call ahead for current information on prices and for reservations; (800) 933-PARK.

In Addition

Mountain Biking With Your Dog

Many people love to bring their canine companions along on mountain bike trails. Our furry friends make great trail partners because they're always good company and they never complain. If you take your dog mountain biking with you, or you're considering it, remember that there are a number of important items to keep in mind before hitting the trails.

Getting in Shape

It would be no better for your dog than it would for you to tackle running a marathon without first getting into good physical condition. And if your pet has been a foot warmer much of his life, you will need to train him into reasonable shape before taking him along on those long weekend bike rides.

You can start your dog's training regimen by running or walking him around the neighborhood or, better yet, a local park. Frisbees and balls are also great tools to help get your dog physically fit for those upcoming mountain bike rides. Always remember that on a trail your dog probably runs twice as far as you ride. Build your dog's exercise regimen based on the mileage you plan to ride each time you head out. If you're going on a 5-mile trail, assume your dog needs to be in shape for a 10-mile trail. Gradually build up your dog's stamina over a two- to three-month period before committing him to arduous afternoons of trying to keep up with you as you pedal along on your bike.

Training

Teaching your dog simple commands of obedience may help keep both you and your dog out of a heap of trouble out there on public trails. The most important lesson is to train your dog to come when called. This will ensure he doesn't stray too far from the trail and possibly get lost. It may also protect him from troublesome situations, such as with other trail users or perhaps coming in contact with local wildlife. Also teach your dog the "get behind" command. This comes in especially handy when you're on a singletrack trail and you run into other bikers. Teaching your dog to stay behind you and your bike and to follow your lead until the trail is clear is a valuable and important lesson. Remember also to always carry a long leash with you in case, despite all your prior training, you still have to tie your dog up to a tree at a campsite or obey local leash laws on crowded trails.

There are a number of good dog training books on the market that should help you and your dog stay out of trouble with other trail users. Also, look to your local

Society for the Prevention of Cruelty to Animals or kennel club for qualified dog trainers in the area.

Nutrition

Nutrition is important for all dogs. Never exercise a dog right after a meal. Feed your pet a high-quality diet such as Hills Science Diet or Iams. These products have higher-quality ingredients and are more nutritionally balanced than generic grocery store dog foods. They may be more expensive than some generic brands, but your dog doesn't need to eat as much to get the same nutrition and calories. If you insist on feeding your dog a grocery store diet, stick with the Purina brand, as it is better for your dog than most others in this class.

Trail Tips

- Try to pick your riding trails near lakes or streams. The biggest threat to your dog when biking is the heat, and water is essential to keep him cool. If the trail doesn't have water nearby then you need to bring as much liquid for him as you would drink yourself. A small lightweight plastic bowl can be used to give your dog water, or you can purchase a collapsible water bowl made from waterproof nylon. You can also use a water bottle to squirt water into your dog's mouth.

- Do not take your dog riding with you on a really hot day—hotter than eighty degrees. To avoid these temperatures, take your dog riding in the early morning or evening, when the air is cooler and safer for your pet.

- Watch for signs of heat stroke. Dogs with heat stroke will pant excessively, lie down and refuse to get up, or become lethargic and disoriented. If your dog shows any of these signs, immediately hose him down with cool water and let him rest. If you're on the trail and nowhere near a hose, find a cool stream and lay your dog in the water to help bring his body temperature back to normal.

- Avoid the common foot pad injuries. Don't run your dog on hot pavement or along long stretches of gravel road. Always bring a first-aid kit that includes disinfectant, cotton wrap, and stretchy foot bandage tape so you can treat and wrap your dog's paw if it becomes injured. You might also want to look into purchasing dog booties, useful for protecting your dog's pads and feet during long runs outdoors.

- Be sure to keep your dog's nails trimmed. If your dog's nails are too long, they might catch on an object along the trail and lead to soft tissue or joint injuries.

- Don't take your dog on crowded trails, and always carry a leash with you. Remember, just because you love your dog doesn't mean other people will.

16 Charlottesville Dirt Ride

Start: From the Stony Point Elementary School.
Length: 20.3-mile loop.
Approximate riding time: 2 to 2.5 hours.
Difficulty rating: Moderate. Technically, there are few challenges, as this ride follows well-maintained gravel roads and pavement; physically, the ride is a bit longer than most and has a fairly steady climb near the start and middle of the route.
Trail surface: Hilly dirt roads and paved roads.

Land status: Public roads.
Nearest town: Charlottesville.
Other trail users: Motorists.
Canine compatibility: Not good. Too many roads.
Fees and permits: No fees or permits required.
Schedule: All roads open to the public year-round.
Maps: USGS maps: Barboursville, Keswick, Charlottesville East.
Trail contacts: Virginia Department of Transportation HIGHWAY HELPLINE, (800) 367-ROAD or www.vdot.state.va.us; UVA Mountain Bike Club, scs.student.virginia.edu/~ bikeclub; Charlottesville Albemarle Bicycling Association (CHABA), www.chaba.home stead.com.

Getting There: From Charlottesville: Take Route 20 north for approximately 8 miles to the Stony Point Elementary School. Park here. You can access Route 20 from I-64 and from U.S. Route 250 as well. *DeLorme: Virginia Atlas & Gazetteer:* Page 68, D-2.

The Ride

When I wrote the first edition of this book a number of years ago, I must have traveled thousands of miles throughout Virginia in search of good places to mountain bike. My bike, car, and I passed through countless towns, big and small, on our way to one trailhead, then another, and another. I got to see a lot of the state and learn a lot more about how rich, dynamic, and diverse Virginia really is. One town I passed through time and time again was Charlottesville, located right in the center of the state amid the foothills of the Blue Ridge Mountains.

It didn't take long to grow fond of this beautiful little city of slightly more than 40,000 people and home to such well-known Americans as Thomas Jefferson, James Monroe, and even James Madison (if you consider Montpelier in the Charlottesville area). Don't let this population figure fool you though. The surrounding area has well over 100,000 residents and is growing strong. Thomas Jefferson's Monticello

Thoroughbreds grace Charlottesville's horse country.

rests upon Carter Mountain overlooking the town, commanding a breathtaking view of the rolling countryside and his prestigious University of Virginia, founded in 1819. The university is now home to more than 11,000 students.

The surrounding countryside is a great place to spend the day pedaling a bike past wineries, old plantations, fields of dogwood, and, of course, horses, horses, horses. Not every off-road ride, as you will see along these quiet back roads, need be a mountainous adventure with white-knuckled descents and bone-jarring trails. A change every now and then can be very enjoyable.

Change of pace is precisely why this scenic loop is included in the book. I designed this ride to showcase some of the treasures central Virginia has to offer, while for the most part keeping you off the pavement. The ride doesn't take you to every place I'd like to show you, but it's great for the leisurely mountain biker with an appetite for the scenery and solitude of some peaceful back roads through the rolling foothills of central Virginia.

The ride begins at the Stony Point Elementary School just off Route 20. Park your car in the school parking lot. You will travel up a quiet mountain road to the top of Charlottesville's Southwest Mountains before descending quickly toward the small town of Cismont. The Southwest Mountains have the highest peaks east of the Blue Ridge. Snacks and refreshments are available at the corner store along Route 231. Be careful along the next section of this ride on Route 22, as it is a bit more heavily traveled by cars.

Cruise through the equally small towns of Cobham and Cash Corner (food and drinks available) before heading back over the Southwest Mountains through Turkeysag Gap. Horse farms and colorful gardens provide the scenery all the way back to the mountain. The rest of the ride is along more of the numerous back roads in this region, all of which are scenic, quiet, and peaceful—perfect for a leisurely ride through the countryside.

This may be the most off-road riding many could wish for. If you live in the central Virginia region, especially near Charlottesville, you'll be pleased to know there are miles and miles of back roads like the roads presented on this ride. Many of these paths pass through old farmland, past exquisite horse stables, and near central Virginia's famous wineries. Rides like this help bring folks much closer to the area's rural landscape than paved roads can deliver. So take some time to explore this off-road experience, and I'm sure you'll be pleased with your discoveries.

(Note: Check out the Sugarloaf Mountain and The Waltons ride in the central Virginia Honorable Mentions section for another great ride along some of the peaceful back roads in the Charlottesville area.)

Miles and Directions

0.0   START at Stony Point Elementary School. Parking available. Turn right on Route 20 (paved).

0.3   Turn right on Stony Point Pass (Route 600) (hard-packed dirt and gravel). This road takes you through Charlottesville's Southwest Mountains.

3.4   Reach the summit. There's a small clearing here, but no real view except in the winter when the foliage is thin.

4.2   Route 600 changes to pavement.

4.4   Route 600 changes back to dirt.

4.7 End of the descent. Pass a very large horse stable on the left.

5.7 Cross Gordonsville Road (Route 231). Continue straight along the paved road through the small town of Cismont. You'll find snacks, a soda machine, and refreshments at the Chevron station on this corner.

6.0 Turn left on Louisa Road (Route 22).

8.5 Arrive in the tiny town of Cobham. Turn left on Route 640 (paved). Heading back toward the mountain, this flat, paved road showcases the magnificent horse farms and stables that make this area famous.

10.5 Cross Gordonsville Road (Route 231). Get some snacks or drinks at the Cash Corner store. Stay on Route 640 (paved).

12.0 Route 640 changes to dirt and gravel and begins climbing back over the Southwest Mountains.

13.3 Reach the summit and cross through Turkeysag Gap.

15.4 Turn right on Stony Point Road (Route 20) (paved). Bobbi's grocery store is at this intersection.

15.6 Turn left on Gilbert Station Road (Route 640).

15.7 Start climbing (dirt).

16.8 Reach the summit of this climb.

17.5 Bear left. Do *not* turn right on Brocks Mill Road (dirt).

17.7 Turn left at this intersection onto Route 784 (dirt).

18.2 Paved descent.

18.4 Cross a small bridge at the bottom of this descent (dirt).

19.7 Turn left at the stop sign on Route 600 (paved).

20.2 Go straight through the intersection of Route 20 and Route 600.

20.3 Reach the Stony Point Elementary School. This ride would be fun on one of those horses!

Ride Information

Local Information

Charlottesville/Albemarle Convention and Visitor's Bureau, www.charlottesvilletourism.org.
C-Ville Weekly, Charlottesville's news and arts weekly, www.c-ville.com.

17 Observatory Hill

Start: McCormick Road near the University of Virginia's McCormick Observatory.
Length: 7-mile combination of singletrack loops and trail segments.
Approximate riding time: Varies depending on rider's discretion.
Difficulty rating: Moderate to difficult due to roots, rocks, hill climbs, and other trail obstructions.
Trail surface: Narrow, technical singletrack in a very hilly, wooded environment.
Land status: University of Virginia property.
Nearest town: Charlottesville.
Other trail users: Hikers, trail runners, and dogs.
Canine compatibility: Dog friendly.
Fees and permits: No fees or permits required.
Schedule: Dawn to dusk, year-round.
Maps: USGS map: Charlottesville West; ADC map: Albemarle County: Page 35, G-10.
Trail contacts: Mountain Bike Club at the University of Virginia, (804) 293–9092 or www.studentvirginia.edu/~bikeclub; Charlottesville Albemarle Bicycling Association (CHABA), www.chaba.homestead.com.

Getting There: From Downtown Charlottesville: Travel west on West Main Street, which then becomes University Avenue. Cross Emmett Street where University Avenue becomes Ivy Road. Continue for 0.5 mile and turn left on Alderman Avenue. Proceed on Alderman Road and turn right on McCormick Road at the Observatory Hill Dining Hall. Follow McCormick Road uphill. At the very top of the climb, bear a hard right at the water tanks. McCormick Road continues climbing sharply. Just up the road a bit more, you can park your vehicle on the side of the road, where you'll find the first of a number of marked trailheads. *DeLorme: Virginia Atlas & Gazetteer:* Page 67, D-7.

From UVA: Follow McCormick Road west through the grounds toward Slaughterhouse Recreation Center. Cross Alderman Road. Continue following McCormick Road uphill and follow the directions above.

Public Transportation: From the bus transfer point at Second and Water Streets, take Charlottesville Transit Service bus route 4 (Fry's Spring) to the intersection of Jefferson Park and Fontaine Avenues. Now on your bike, pedal west on Fontaine Avenue for 0.5 mile to the southeast corner of the trail network on the right, just past the University of Virginia's Piedmont Apartments.

The McCormick Observatory, resting atop Mount Jefferson (O-Hill), is nearly 130 years old and still works like a charm.

The Ride

What a bunch of lucky folks those UVA students are. They enjoy a beautiful campus with all the luxuries a fine university can offer: great instructors, a wonderful library, state-of-the-art facilities, and a dynamic downtown scene with all that a young crowd could want. But if that's not enough, students interested in burning off some post-class stress have an amazing network of mountain bike trails literally across the street from the main university grounds. And this is no ordinary terrain. O-Hill throws the "mountain" into mountain biking and keeps it coming for a whole afternoon of power riding and technical skill work. Sharp climbs; long, fast descents; rocky minefields; and some smooth runs all come together at O-Hill to create an atmosphere of real mountain bike adrenaline—and it's all right next to campus. Granted, after a few days spent here, cyclists will start to see the limitations this small plot of land presents. But nothing so close can beat the workout and the technical skills training O-Hill offers.

For those of us not lucky enough to have such backyard training grounds, it may be difficult to appreciate its proximity. But there's no denying the challenges and great off-road riding this hill provides, whether you live five minutes away or have

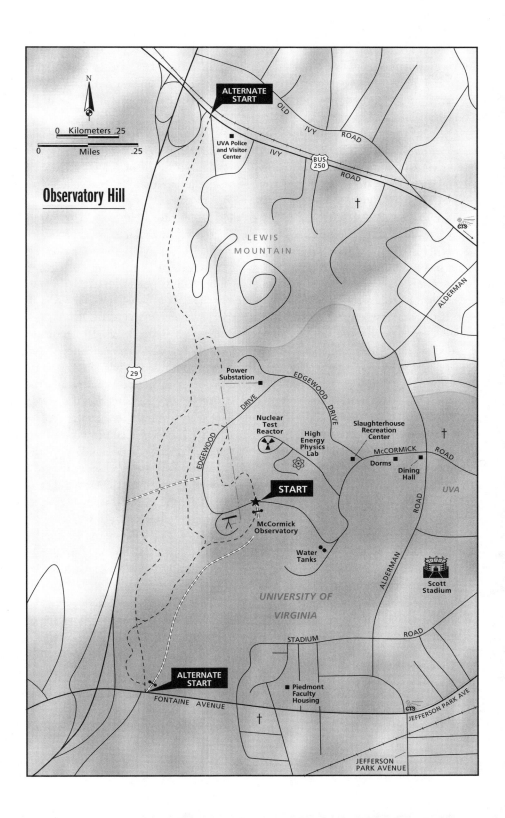

to travel an hour to get here. The fact is, it's a great ride no matter where you're from. And with the university next door, countless restaurants and bars within walking distance, and more things to do in this small Blue Ridge city than you can shake a stick at, there's little reason not to come here in the first place. So while you're here, bring along your bike and go for a huge workout on O-Hill.

Okay, so I'm a bit excited about this place. I've lived in Virginia all my life and never before have I had the opportunity or the luxury to go somewhere that didn't require time spent first in a car (growing up in northern Virginia left me a bit jaded). To find such a gem in the middle of town that isn't just another city park filled with baby buggies, little kids, and soccer fields is a real treasure.

To know a little more about this place called Observatory Hill may help visitors appreciate these trails even more. The name of the hill on which the observatory rests is actually Mount Jefferson, named, of course, for this town's most famous resident. It was Jefferson's intent, when designing the University of Virginia, to include an observatory and a center for astronomical study. Unfortunately, he didn't live to see his plan to completion (he died in 1826), but the idea to build an observatory as part of the university didn't die with him. In 1877, Leander McCormick, a Rockbridge County native and founder of McCormick Harvesting Machine Company, donated a 26.25-inch telescope to the university. An observatory, which bears McCormick's name, was built atop Mount Jefferson to house the telescope and various other astrometric instruments. Construction on both the observatory and the director's house (the large house next to the observatory now named the Alden House after the observatory's third director) began in 1882 and was completed in 1884. It's interesting to note that, in the early 1800s, Leander McCormick's father, Robert, invented the mechanical reaper. Thanks to many improvements to the reaper by Leander, a successful patent application, and brisk sales to farmers across the Midwest, the McCormick family became one of the nation's richest families.

Today the observatory offers regular tours to interested visitors, so check out its schedule and take the opportunity to see how an actual observatory tower works.

Returning to more important matters, Observatory Hill offers a maze of technical and steep singletrack trails, rocky dirt roads, and some of the best mountain biking a downtown could offer. O-Hill is bounded on all sides by paved roads, apartments, and private homes; therefore specific trail directions are not needed for this ride because it would be difficult to get lost. Be alert for other trail users, especially on weekends and late afternoons. Don't hesitate to call the Mountain Bike Club at the University of Virginia to get involved in trail maintenance and improvement.

Miles and Directions

There are a handful of starting points for the trails at O-Hill, so take your pick. A lot of folks drive up McCormick Road to the observatory, park their car, and start at the gated trailhead on the left. Others find it easier to pedal over to Fontaine Avenue and start riding at the gated forest road just before U.S. Route 29 (starting here helps to avoid finishing on top of the hill, which may help some riders avoid climbing to the top altogether). If you choose the Fontaine Avenue trailhead, you can still cruise the hilly and fun singletrack that contours the base of Mount Jefferson pretty much all afternoon without having to crank your way up to the top of the hill. But hey, where's the downhill fun in that? A third starting point is just off Ivy Road (U.S. Route 250 Business) past the UVA Police and Visitor Center and an Amoco gas station. There's a place to park under the trees, where the trailhead begins.

Ride Information

Local Information

University of Virginia, www.virginia.edu.
Charlottesville Transit Service, (804) 296–RIDE, www.transit.ci.charlottesville.us.
University of Virginia's Department of Astronomy, www.astro.virginia.edu.
Charlottesville/Albemarle Convention and Visitor's Bureau, www.charlottesvilletourism.org.

Hyperville (Charlottesville Web site), www.hyperville.com.
C-Ville Weekly, Charlottesville's news and arts weekly, www.c-ville.com.

Local Events and Attractions

The O-Hill Meltdown Mountain Bike Race, held annually toward the end of April. Contact the Mountain Bike Club at the University of Virginia for details.

18 Walnut Creek Park

Start: From the bicycle parking lot.
Length: Approximately 15 miles of singletrack.
Approximate riding time: 2 to 3 hours.
Difficulty rating: Moderate to difficult. Technically, the rocks, roots, and off-camber singletrack presents a challenge to most any rider, while the length and hilly terrain will keep the heart working and the sweat pouring. Less ambitious riders may want to spend their time along the less strenuous lakeside trails.
Trail surface: Rocky, rooty singletrack with occasional creek crossings through dense hardwood.
Land status: County park.

Nearest town: Charlottesville.
Other trail users: Hikers, trail runners, and anglers.
Fees and permits: $2.00 for Albemarle County residents; $3.00 for all nonresidents (city of Charlottesville residents should bring $3.00).
Schedule: Open year-round.
Maps: USGS map: Alberene.
Trail contacts: Albemarle County Parks and Recreation Department, (804) 296-5844; Mountain Bike Club at the University of Virginia, (804) 293-9092 or www.studentvirginia.edu/~bikeclub.

Getting There: From Charlottesville: From I-64 take U.S. Route 29 south for approximately 10 miles. Turn left onto Route 708 and follow it for approximately 5 miles. Turn right onto Route 631 (Old Lynchburg Road). The park is half a mile past the intersection of Route 708 and Route 631. Once in the park, follow signs for bicycle parking into the first lot. A large trail map is posted on the bulletin board in the parking lot. Don't forget to pick up your trail map from the entrance gate. *DeLorme: Virginia Atlas & Gazetteer:* Page 55, A-7.

The Ride

If it isn't obvious right from the outset, this trail system was designed and is maintained by Charlottesville area mountain bikers. Trail names such as the Blue Wheel, Extreme Sports, Blazing Saddles Trail, and Bike Factory Trail all get their monikers from local "C-ville" bike shops. Wahoo Way throws in a sprinkle from the Mountain Bike Club at UVA. And Outward Bound Trail finds its roots in Orange County's Outward Bound. Let's not forget Wilkins Way, named after Doug Wilkins of the Mountain Bike Virginia bike club, who, along with so many others, has worked very hard in cooperation with the Albemarle County Parks Department to develop this amazing system of multiuse trails at Walnut Creek Park, just 10 miles south of Charlottesville.

This old farmhouse is one of the relics you'll see along the way.

Since its inception a few years back, central Virginia mountain bikers, trail runners, and hikers have all volunteered thousands of hours to design, build, and maintain these fantastic multiuse trails for our enjoyment. And their efforts have paid off big. Today there are more than 13 miles of clearly marked singletrack trails on which to ride. These trails lead cyclists and other trail users over tight, twisting routes through a dense hardwood forest surrounding a twenty-five-acre lake. There are countless log jumps, hairpin turns, quick descents, hills, ravines, and just about everything a well-planned trail system can throw at you.

The first thing to do when you arrive, aside from paying your park fee at the gate, is to pick up a trail map from the gate attendant. Clearly labeled and in color, the map will detail every trail in the park and what color blazes you'll need to follow to stay on track. Once you get into the woods, colored diamond blazes corresponding to the map help guide the way. It'll be just plain difficult to get lost in this park.

Following the map, park in the trailhead parking lot next to the lake and follow the yellow blazes (Chimney Trail) across Walnut Branch and into the woods. After crossing the creek, you'll have a few options. The recommended loop to follow is the red trail (Wilkins Way). Follow this color all the way back to this point. The red loop (4 miles around) is the park's original singletrack trail. You'll see from both the map and the additional trails within the park that things have come a long way. The red trail leads you around the eastern portion of the park and packs a real punch to anyone who takes on this moderate to difficult singletrack. Just about every obstacle these folks could build into this trail they did, including hairpin turns, steep hills,

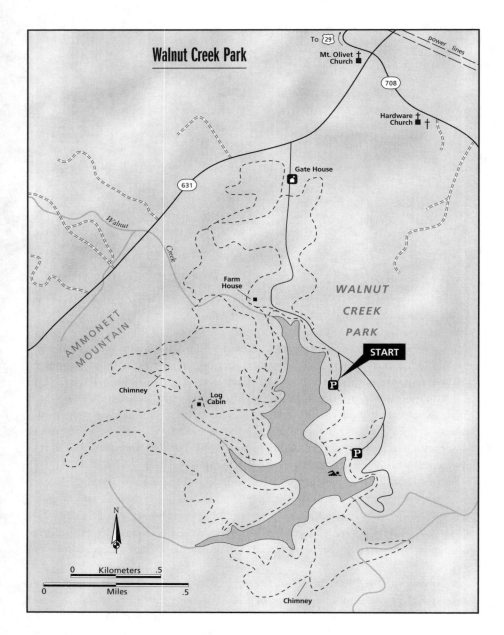

strategically placed logs, streams, and gullies—you name it. This loop will give anyone a good workout. Along the way, you'll notice a number of other, newer connector trails. Trail combinations are endless, so just go out there and have fun. Just keep in mind, it's recommended when on the red trail that you travel *clockwise* to avoid trail collisions.

Once you're done pedaling and it's time to cool off, swing on over to the beach house and go for a dip in the lake. Between Memorial Day and Labor Day, swimming and drinking water are available. There are plenty of other things to do at Walnut Creek Park, including canoeing, kayaking, hiking, and fishing. So come prepared to spend some time here and bring a good set of legs for the red trail.

Miles and Directions

The trails are well blazed with colored plastic diamonds that correspond to the trail map handed out at the entrance gate. You won't have much trouble figuring out where you are and will find that it's difficult to get yourself lost. For a great starter loop, begin at the trailhead parking area and hook up with the red trail (Wilkins Way). This 4-mile trail, the park's first, leads you through hairpin turns, steep hills, strategically placed logs, streams, gullies, and more, to give you a taste of what's in store for anyone heading off into the woods at Walnut Creek.

Ride Information

Local Information

University of Virginia, www.studentvirginia.edu.
Charlottesville/Albemarle Convention and Visitor's Bureau, www.charlottesvilletourism.org.

Local Events and Attractions

A swimming beach and swim area is available at the second parking area.

19 Panorama Trails

Start: All rides must begin from the trailhead parking area and trail signboard.

Length: More than 30 miles of singletrack.

Approximate riding time: Varies depending on rider's discretion.

Difficulty rating: Trails range from easy to difficult, depending on route taken and length of ride.

Trail surface: Primarily narrow, twisting singletrack with hills, rocks, roots, and off-camber sections; approximately 3 miles of interior farm roads; rolling terrain with open pasture meadows, hay fields, mature hardwood forests, stream crossings, and tricky log crossings.

Land status: Private property.

Nearest town: Charlottesville.

Other trail users: This is a mountain bike venue only, so you'll have the trails completely to yourself.

Canine compatibility: Leave the pooch at home. Dogs aren't allowed.

Fees and permits: A permit is required to access Panorama Trails. Day passes cost $8.00 and can be purchased from local bike shops or directly from Panorama Trails, LLC prior to arriving. Annual permits are also available through Panorama Trails, LLC. Check their Web site at www.panoramatrails.com for more information.

Schedule: Open dawn to dusk for daytime riding from January 15 through October 1. Open 10:30 A.M. to sundown on Sunday and Tuesday through Thursday from October 1 through January 14. Night riding is available year-round on Wednesday and Thursday, but you must have three or more riders present. Trails are generally closed during and immediately following wet weather. In addition, hours may change during hunting season. Call ahead or check the Web site.

Maps: A black-and-white trail map is provided with purchase of a day pass. Detailed, full-color trail map and guide is available for purchase at local retail outlets. Detailed color trail-map boards located at trailhead and interspersed throughout property.

Trail contacts: Panorama Trails, LLC, message line for current trail conditions at (434) 974–7849, trailboss@panoramatrails.com, www.panoramatrails.com.

Getting There: From U.S. Route 29 North:
Turn right (toward the airport) onto Route 649 (Airport Road) north of Charlottesville. Bear left onto Route 606 at the airport. At the T intersection, take a left onto Route 743 (Earlysville Road). Proceed south on Earlysville Road for approximately 1.5 miles before making a right onto Route 844 (Panorama Road). If you cross the bridge over the reservoir, you've gone too far.

From U.S. Route 29 South: Turn left on Route 631 (Rio Road) just north of Fashion Square Mall in Charlottesville. After 1 mile, make a right at the stoplight onto Route 743 (Earlysville Road). Proceed approximately 2 miles, crossing over the reservoir, before making a left onto Route 844 (Panorama Road).

Panorama Road is a residential road in a residential area with a lot of foot and horse traffic. Please follow speed limit signs (10

Cruising along the Big Easy.

mph) and be very courteous. Panorama Road dead-ends into Panorama Farms. Follow the farm driveway downhill, across the bridge, then uphill to the first road on the right. Look for the large trail signboard and the parking area through the gate on the right. *DeLorme: Virginia Atlas & Gazetteer:* Page 68, D1.

The Ride

A local secret since 1996, Panorama Trails is now open to the public as one of central Virginia's premier mountain biking destinations, and perhaps one of the best in the entire state.

Located minutes from Charlottesville on just under 900 acres of prime Blue Ridge real estate, Panorama Trails takes advantage of every contour of its sprawling farmland. More than 30 miles of sweet singletrack weave up and down Panorama's rolling, pastoral terrain, through hay fields, open meadows, and mature hardwood forests; over creeks and streams; and alongside scenic lakes and the Rivanna River Reservoir. The scenery is nothing short of extraordinary as, with each turn in the trail, cyclists are treated to magnificent views of the Blue Ridge Mountains, which rise up against the western sky as a stunning backdrop to these groomed trails.

Many of the trails at Panorama are ideal for beginners and intermediates. But the carefully designed, meticulously constructed, and well-maintained trail system serves up some serious challenges to even the most adventurous mountain bikers. Steep climbs, fast and rocky descents, roots, off-camber turns, and lots of long, uninterrupted loops will keep cyclists focused as they pedal along the myriad of trails that twist over hilly farmland.

The key to Panorama's success comes from its focus. From the very beginning, proprietor Drew Murray knew he had something special to offer—and it wasn't dairy cows and soybeans. Outdoor recreation was burgeoning, trail access was limited, and agricultural use wasn't paying the rent. So rather than sell chunks of land to local developers for a windfall, the family pursued other sustainable uses and developed several successful ventures, including Panorama Trails. Having explored the property since childhood, Murray knew every hill, valley, and ridge on this vast expanse of land. With pocket saw, hand clippers, and lawnmower, Murray cut and blazed miles of mountain bike trails over the contours of their property. Many years and untold hours of sweat equity later, Panorama Trails became one of the hottest "secret" destinations for local cyclists. But only friends and acquaintances—and those lucky enough to overhear the hushed excitement—knew about it. That is, until 2001, when Murray opened the trails to the public and invited all to come and ride what can only be described as an innovation for modern-day land use and sustainability.

Since the gates were opened to the public, Panorama Trails has been host to dozens of events, including the Rollin' River Rambler, a point-to-point mountain bike race ranging from 6 miles for kids to 22-plus miles for pro and expert classes.

The Blue Ridge Mountains serve as a constant backdrop to the trails at Panorama Farm.

Other events include cyclocross races as part of the Virginia State Series in late November and December, the Holiday Duathlon (run-bike-run), and weekly night rides. Future events will include midsummer races, a mountain bike festival, and some night racing. The best part is that all the races are set up with point-to-point courses, something very few venues anywhere can achieve.

Even though the proprietors of Panorama Trails know how to put on an event for cyclists, it's the day-to-day riding that makes this a special place. Because the trails were designed and cut specifically for cyclists and because the terrain is so diverse, mountain bikers who come here for an evening workout or a weekend adventure will not leave disappointed. Color blazes abound and large, color trail-map boards are strategically placed throughout the property. Plenty of parking is available with portable rest rooms nearby.

Because this is private property and a lot of money is spent to develop and maintain the trails, run events, provide maps, and keep things humming, cyclists interested in riding here must first obtain a valid trail permit. These permits are available at a number of local Charlottesville bike and outdoor stores. A trail map, an accident waiver, and passes to stick to your bike and car window are included with the price of a day permit. Annual permits are also available through Panorama Trails, LLC. Check their Web site at www.panoramatrails.com for a listing of local stores that carry day passes and for current prices of annual passes. Panorama Trails does close the trails during and immediately following periods of wet weather and will occasionally hold hunts during hunting season. So check their message line, the Web site, or the trailhead notice board for current conditions and information on closures.

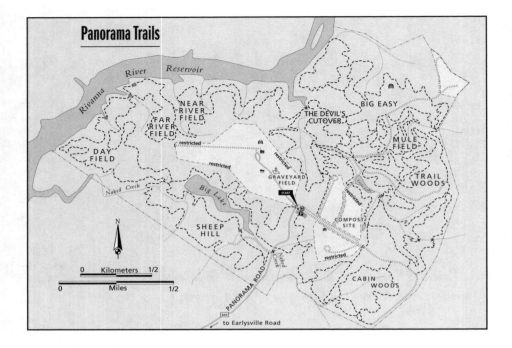

Miles and Directions

All rides begin from the trailhead parking area as described in the directions. Take a moment to study the large color map board to get your bearings and to figure out your riding agenda for the day. New trails are being added all the time, and the map board is updated at least once a year to reflect these changes.

If you're up for a long and challenging ride around the perimeter of the farm, start with the blue trail and head east toward Cabin Woods. The blue trail winds its way through hardwood forest over rolling terrain along the northern end of the property and carries you west toward the Big Easy and the orange trail. The orange trail through the Big Easy is probably one of the most unique trail segments in the state. It snakes its way through wide open fields with spectacular views of the mountains to the west. This is a great destination near dusk for watching the sun slip behind the mountains and cast an orange glow over the evening sky. To continue along the perimeter of the farm in a straightforward approach, follow the white/yellow blazes from the orange trail until you reach the intersection with the white trail. Be sure to bear right on the white trail and head south along the reservoir (bearing left will take you back toward the parking area). The white trail traverses through thick woods, along the marshy riverbank, up and down old cattle-grazing fields, and back north toward the parking area through mature hardwoods. This perimeter route, depending upon some of the options you take in between can total more than

15 miles in length and take a couple hours. So bring plenty of water and expect to be out on the bike for some time.

For killer trails and technical riding, head due west following the white blazes from the parking area over to The Devil's Cutover and rip it up on twisting, rocky, hilly singletrack. The Big Easy is nearby if you need a break, but with trail combinations and plenty of exploration, you could spend a couple of hours just trying to maneuver over this terrain.

For long stretches of open, rolling terrain, head south across Panorama Road and hitch up with the yellow trail. The yellow trail takes cyclists around Big Lake, then farther south toward the reservoir. The route is hilly but not as technical, allowing you to really open it up on some of the descents. You can loop back on the white trail in either direction and expect a lengthy ride. However, you'll have covered less than half of the entire property, so save some energy for more riding.

With so many trails and endless combinations, the best bet at Panorama is to pick a direction and just start exploring. You'll run out of energy and time before running out of trails, and getting lost is part of the fun. But with detailed trail maps positioned throughout the farm, and one to carry with you when you purchase a day pass, it's hard to stay lost for too long.

Ride Information

Local Information

University of Virginia, www.virginia.edu. Check the **Panorama Trails online calendar** for scheduled race and festival events, www.panoramatrails.com. **Albemarle County,** www.albemarle.org. **City of Charlottesville,** www.charlottesville.org.

Local Events and Attractions

Monticello (Thomas Jefferson's house), www.monticello.org. **Charlottesville's downtown pedestrian mall,** with countless shops and restaurants, Main Street in downtown Charlottesville.

Honorable Mentions

Central Virginia

Compiled here is an index of great rides in the central Virginia region that didn't make the list this time around but deserve recognition. Check them out and let us know what you think. You may decide that one or more of these rides deserves higher status in future editions, or, perhaps, you may have a ride of your own that merits some attention.

B Dogwood Dell

In a most unlikely place, cyclists have discovered a series of singletrack trails just behind downtown Richmond's open-air amphitheater, Dogwood Dell. The amphitheater holds as many as 3,000 people, who sit on grassy benches during warm months to watch everything from local musicians to Shakespeare plays. The trail network, thought to have as many as 6 miles worth of singletrack, could never hold as many folks as the amphitheater, but it still affords intermediate to advanced cyclists plenty of playtime in the woods. The singletrack is tight but smooth, traveling up and down through dense hardwood and over creeks and gullies. Mountain bikers love this little place in the city and follow the orange arrows through the woods with enthusiasm. Its proximity to the Fan and Virginia Commonwealth University (VCU) makes this a prime spot for singletrack-seeking cyclists stuck downtown.

To get there, head toward the James River down Boulevard to Maymont Park. The trail system at Dogwood Dell lies behind the Carillon (the large bell tower), accessible from a number of places just off the dirt access road left of the bell tower. Jump into the woods and have fun. (*DeLorme: Virginia Atlas & Gazetteer:* Page 58, D1-2.)

C Hollywood Farm

Hollywood Farm is considered by just about everyone who's ever been here to be some of the best riding south of D.C., east of Richmond, north of Hampton Roads, and just about every place in between. It is chock full of twisty, rooty, extremely tight singletrack (narrow your handlebars for this ride) that weaves in and out, creating a network of nearly 9 miles of interlacing trails. The only problem is, it's on private property. So far the property owners have been more than accommodating by allowing cyclists on their land, but they insist that visitors play by the rules (wear a helmet) and stay away during hunting season. To best understand your boundaries, keep the railroad tracks on one side and the open fields on the other. Everything in between is ridable.

The ride is just east of Fredericksburg near the Stafford/King George County line. From Fredericksburg, follow Route 3 east approximately 5 miles to Hollywood Farm Road (Route 601), just before the county line (if you've crossed into King George County, you've gone too far). Turn left on Hollywood Farm Road and go approximately 2 miles to a dirt road on the right just after the railroad tracks. Turn in here, park, and ride. For more information, call Bike Works at (540) 373–8900 or the Fredericksburg Cyclists (bike club) at (540) 373–1451 or visit www.bikefred. com. (*DeLorme: Virginia Atlas & Gazetteer:* Page 70, B–C 3.)

D Sugarloaf Mountain and The Waltons

This is a wonderful back-roads ride through the foothills of the Blue Ridge Mountains, located approximately 20 miles south of Charlottesville just off U.S. Route 29. From Rockfish (Route 617), turn right on Route 623, then left on Route 640 (Wheeler Cove Road). Route 640, a scenic dirt road, winds through Thoroughfare Gap. Turn right on Dutch Creek Road (Route 641) toward Sugarloaf Mountain. A jeep road leads you from Route 641 to the top of Sugarloaf Mountain. This 3-mile ascent is incredibly steep, but a breathtaking view of the Blue Ridge foothills awaits at the top. And since you're in the area, make a quick drive over to Schuyler, just off Route 6 and Rockfish Road, where you can visit the Waltons Museum and the Hamner House. This is the town and the house from which the popular television show *The Waltons* was based. The house in which Earl Hamner grew up can be visited year-round. Check out the official Waltons Web site at www.thewaltons.com for more information. (*DeLorme: Virginia Atlas & Gazetteer:* Page 55, B-5.)

E James River State Park

James River State Park is the state's newest park. It officially opened June 20, 1999, and intends to meet the needs of a wide range of users, including mountain bikers. The park, which is still under development, currently offers cyclists access to 20 miles of multiuse trails, most of which are gravel forest roads and grassy doubletrack. And if things go well, park management hopes to build, with the help of local cyclists, some technical singletrack to challenge the more hard-core central Virginia mountain bikers. This scenic park along the James River offers a lot more than pleasant mountain bike trails. When you come, bring along a fishing pole, canoe, or tent and plan to spend a weekend. There are currently fifteen primitive campsites, six picnic shelters, and three rest rooms.

The park is fairly remote, so people will be coming from many directions. A good starting point is from a small crossroads called Bent Creek at the intersection of U.S. Route 60, Route 26, and Route 605. From here, head north on Route 605 at the James River Bridge. Travel 7 miles to Route 606. Turn left on Route 606 and follow the signs into the park. (*DeLorme: Virginia Atlas & Gazetteer:* Page 55, C-D5.)

F Appomattox-Buckingham State Forest and Holliday Lake State Park

Appomattox-Buckingham State Forest is located 30 miles east of Lynchburg off Route 24. Part of Virginia's Piedmont Forest System, there are over 19,700 acres of rolling terrain here, making this Virginia's largest state forest. Miles of unpaved forest roads, trails, and dead-end paths, most of which are ideal for off-road bikes, wind through this pine and hardwood forest. Holliday Lake State Park is situated within the forest, with information, a bathhouse, rest rooms, camping, and showers. Park officials dedicated a multiuse trail named Carter Taylor Trail back in 1996. It is geared toward mountain bikers interested in pedaling from Holliday Lake. This generally easy 12-mile loop from the lake was designed to ease the traffic on Lakeshore Trail around Holliday Lake and give cyclists a little more room to have fun. For more information about Holliday Lake State Park, call (804) 786–1712 or visit www.state.va.us/~dcr/parks/holliday.htm.

Of course, don't overlook the nearby Appomattox Courthouse, where Confederate general Robert E. Lee surrendered to Union general Ulysses S. Grant to end the Civil War. The Appomattox Courthouse National Historic Park is just down the road from Holliday Lake State Park on Route 24, north of Appomattox. For more information about Appomattox Courthouse and the history that made it famous, visit www.nps.gov/apco/index.htm. (*DeLorme: Virginia Atlas & Gazetteer:* Page 45, A-6.)

G Prince Edward-Gallion State Forest

Located off U.S. Route 360, 16 miles east of Farmville and 48 miles west of Petersburg, Prince Edward-Gallion State Forest is very similar to Appomattox-Buckingham State Forest, only smaller. As part of Virginia's Piedmont Forest System, there are nearly 7,000 acres of forested terrain, with miles of unpaved forest roads on which to ride. Twin Lakes State Park, located within the state forest just off U.S. Route 360, is host to 6 miles of multiuse trails built for hiking, horseback riding, and biking, taking visitors through the hardwood forest surrounding the lakes. The Prince Edward-Gallion Multiuse Trail is a 14-mile loop adjacent to the state forest and is open to hikers, bikers, and equestrians.

Twin Lakes State Park has a multitude of accommodations, ranging from campsites with electric hookups to full-service cabins. All reservations must be made through the reservation center at (800) 933–PARK. Bike rentals are also available, so call ahead and make plans to spend a weekend here. For more information call (804) 786–1712 or visit www.state.va.us/~dcr/parks/twinlake.htm. (*DeLorme: Virginia Atlas & Gazetteer:* Page 46, C-2.)

Northern Virginia

George Washington National Forest

Jefferson National Forest

N

MARYLAND

66 25 24 J
Front 23 22 Washington, D.C.
Royal 21
20
Fredericksburg
H

WEST VIRGINIA

81 Harrisonburg
Staunton Charlottesville
Lexington 64
64 17
95 Tappahannock Onancock
Richmond
13
64 Atlantic
Ocean
77 Lynchburg 460
Roanoke Petersburg Norfolk
Wytheville VIRGINIA 95 Virginia Beach
81
Abingdon 77

TENNESSEE

NORTH CAROLINA

20 Prince William Forest Park

Start: From the Prince William Forest Park Visitor Center.

Length: Varies depending on route chosen. (There are 8.2 miles of unpaved roads open to cyclists.)

Approximate riding time: Varies depending on route chosen.

Difficulty rating: Moderate.

Trail surface: Paved and unpaved park roads.

Land status: Administered by the National Park Service.

Nearest town: Dumfries.

Other trail users: Hikers, motorists, naturelovers, and pyrite collectors.

Canine compatibility: Dog friendly.

Fees and permits: A three-day family pass is $4.00 per vehicle within the park; $2.00 for cyclists and walk-ins.

Schedule: Open daily from dawn to dusk. Registered campers and cabin campers have twenty-four-hour access. The visitor center is open between 8:30 A.M. and 5:00 P.M.

Maps: USGS map: Joplin; ADC map: Prince William County road map.

Trail contacts: Prince William Forest Park Visitor Center, (703) 221–7181; National Park Service, (703) 759–2915.

Getting There: From the Capital Beltway (I–495): Take I–95 south toward Richmond for 20 miles to exit 150, Joplin Road (Route 619 West). In one-tenth of a mile, turn right from Joplin Road to the park entrance road. The visitor center is about 1 mile down this road. *DeLorme: Virginia Atlas & Gazetteer:* Page 76, D-3.

The Ride

Down here in Prince William County lies a relatively large park, preserved as one of the few remaining piedmont forest ecosystems in the National Park Service system. Within its 18,000 acres are 35 miles of hiking trails, hundreds of acres open to primitive camping, a scenic paved road looping through the park (creatively named Scenic Drive Road), and a plethora of wildlife and plant life for city folks to enjoy. Four miles of the Scenic Drive Road have a dedicated bike lane, providing a paved, relatively flat surface ideal for beginning bicyclists. More experienced cyclists with mountain bikes have the option of off-road biking on any of the ten fire roads in the park.

At one time, Prince William Forest Park's thousands of acres of forestland were extensively farmed for tobacco. Then, when the hills eroded and the earth could no longer support their crops, farmers turned to dairy farming, already well established throughout the county. But for those living in the Quantico Creek area, this enterprise, too, failed. The Civil War was equally taxing for those already struggling here. The Confederates blockaded the Potomac, requiring large numbers of troops for support. Those living in the vicinity of the blockade were required to provide the troops with timber and food, and found that what little they had before the war was no longer enough.

FALL LINE Prince William Forest Park lies along the border between two physiographic zones: the Piedmont and the Coastal Plain. Many of the faulted rocks represent the fall line, a unique geological feature where streams form falls or rapids as they leave the harder rocks of the Piedmont and enter the softer rocks of the Coastal Plain.

In 1889, a mining operation near the confluence of the north and south branches of Conduce Creek provided a much-needed boost to the area's economy. But a strike over wages closed the high-grade pyrite ore mine in 1920, bringing down with it any hope for the area's recovery. It was soon thereafter that the United States government bought the land, resettling nearly 150 families, and with the Civilian Conservation Corps began the effort to "return the depleted land to an ecological balance."

Originally established as the Chopawamsic Recreational Demonstration Area by an act of Congress in August 1933, Prince William Forest Park, a unit of the National Park Service, is mandated to "conserve the scenery and the natural and historic objects and the wildlife therein and to provide for the enjoyment of the same in such manner and by such means as will leave them unimpaired for the enjoyment of future generations." The park contains the largest example of an eastern piedmont forest ecosystem in the national park system and is a sanctuary for native plants and animals in the midst of this rapidly developing metropolitan area.

All kinds of outdoor activities are available within the park for haggard Washingtonians to enjoy. One of them is bicycling. Riding on park trails, unfortunately, is prohibited. However, there are many unpaved roads throughout the park that can be used by cyclists. Many of these roads are separate out-and-back fire roads; you may need to ride along the paved Scenic Drive Road to create loops. Scenic Drive Road is very well maintained and road cyclists from all around often come to Prince William Forest Park just to ride this paved loop, getting quite a workout from its hilly terrain.

To witness the progress this 18,000-acre forest has made in reclaiming what was once depleted and eroding farmland is a wonderful experience. And riding your mountain bike along the forest roads through the park gives you an up-close look at this process in action.

Folks looking to do more than just bike can explore as many as 35 miles of hiking trails along ridges, into valleys, and beside the two main creeks in the park. Scenic Drive Road provides access to all the trails and features within the park. Bicycles are not allowed on any of the park's hiking trails.

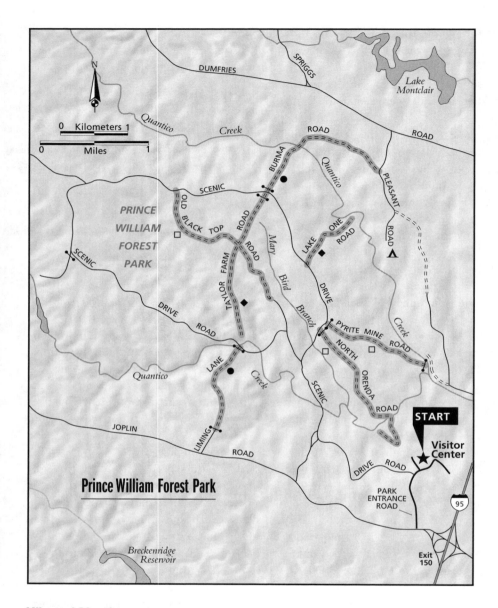

Miles and Directions

Liming Lane Fire Road

0.8 mile long. This forest road is, for the most part, moderately easy. It begins from the parking lot on Scenic Drive Road and takes you out of the park's boundaries to Joplin Road.

Taylor Farm Road

1.5 miles long. From the northern part of Scenic Drive Road, Taylor Farm Road is mostly level until it drops sharply to the South Branch Quantico Creek. The first nine-tenths of this road are part of the 9.7-mile South Valley Trail, which travels the circumference of this part of Prince William Forest Park.

Burma Road

1.5 miles long. Burma Road starts out as an easy forest road, then crosses over a series of hills, making this section moderately difficult. This forest road crosses Quantico Creek and takes you to Pleasant Road. From here, you can create a loop back to Scenic Drive Road. Following Pleasant Road past Cabin Camp, you can gather "fool's gold" at the site of the old pyrite mine. Cross Quantico Creek again and take Pyrite Mine Road back to Scenic Drive Road.

Pyrite Mine Road

1.0 mile long. This forest road takes you from Scenic Drive Road to Quantico Creek, the North Valley Trail, and the old pyrite mine. The trail is moderate in the beginning, then becomes steep at the end.

North Orenda Road

1.2 miles long. This is a moderate forest road that takes you down to the South Branch. Across the creek is South Orenda Fire Road, which leads you back to the visitor center.

Lake One Road

0.6 mile long. Lake One Road starts from the parking lot along Scenic Drive Road and takes you down a moderately steep hill to Quantico Creek.

Old Black Top Road

1.6 miles long. Old Black Top Road starts from the Turkey Run parking area and travels north, crossing Taylor Farm Road, then connects with Scenic Drive Road. The terrain is moderate and offers a good challenge through the middle of the park.

Ride Information

Local Information

Prince William County Convention and Visitors Bureau, (800) 432-1792, www.nps.gov/prwi.

Local Events and Attractions

Lazy Susan Dinner Theater, (703) 550-7384.
Waterworks Water Park, www.pwcces.com/waterworks.
Historic town of Occoquan, www.occoquan.com.
Harbor River Cruises in Occoquan, (703) 385-9433.

Historic Occoquan Spring Arts and Crafts Show, (703) 491-2168.

Accommodations

Oakridge Campground, $10 a night.
Turkey Ridge Run Campground, $30 a night.
Cabin Rental, (703) 221-5843.

Organizations

Friends of Prince William Forest Park, www.bmsi.com/fpwfp.

POTOMAC MILLS SHOPPING CENTER

Around here it's hard to really get away from it all no matter how hard you try. This point is never more evident than when you drive a bit farther south of Prince William Forest Park on I-95 to one of Virginia's greatest tourist attractions—Potomac Mills Shopping Center, a destination shopping attraction that brings in more than 13,000 bus tours each year. Potomac Mills was named in the *Washington Post* on September 8, 1991, as the top-rated tourist attraction in the state of Virginia, ahead of both Colonial Williamsburg and Busch Gardens—and it claims to hold that rating even now!

With its more than fifty-two acres of parking and 1.7 million square feet of fully enclosed shopping space, it's easy to understand how this super-regional specialty mall brings in the foot traffic. The mixture of outlet stores and off-price retailers draws cost-conscious shoppers from around the globe. It's really somewhat bewildering to wander Potomac Mills's crowded walkways, past its hundreds of shops and thousands of people. The thought of getting back on the bike and pedaling to Prince William Forest Park becomes all the more enticing. But, hey, if you're down in the area anyway, why not head to the largest, most crowded single-floor shopping mall on the planet? Buy some Power Bars and Lycra shorts, then head back north and hit the trails.

21 Fountainhead Regional Park

Start: Fountainhead Park.
Length: 4.5 miles.
Approximate riding time: 1 hour.
Difficulty rating: Moderate to difficult.
Trail surface: Technical singletrack and doubletrack.
Land status: Northern Virginia regional park.
Nearest town: Springfield.
Other trail users: Hikers, boaters, swimmers, equestrians, campers, and anglers.
Canine compatibility: Dog friendly.
Fees and permits: $3.50 per car at Burke Lake Regional Park for nonresidents of Fairfax County.
Schedule: Open daily from dawn to dusk, March to November.
Maps: USGS map: Occoquan; ADC map: Northern Virginia road map.
Trail contacts: Northern Virginia Regional Park Authority, (703) 352-5900, www.nvrpa.org; Fountainhead Regional Park, (703) 250-9124; MORE (Mid-Atlantic Off-Road Enthusiasts), (703) 502-0359, www.more-mtb.org.

Getting There: From the Capital Beltway (I-495): Take exit 5 west onto Braddock Road. Head south on Route 123. Continue past Burke Lake Park to the Fountainhead Regional Park sign on the right side of the road. Turn right at this sign on Hampton Road. Follow Hampton Road to the park entrance on the left. Park in the first parking lot on the right. The trailhead is to your left. *DeLorme: Virginia Atlas & Gazetteer:* Page 76, C-3.

The Ride

Here's your chance to ride a trail designed by mountain bikers for mountain bikers. As soon as your ride begins, you'll notice the thought that went into these trails. Curves and twists in the landscape will require your total concentration. Thanks to the efforts of the local mountain bike advocacy group, MORE (the Mid-Atlantic Off-Road Enthusiasts), riders in the Washington area can enjoy this great network of singletrack trails along the Occoquan Reservoir in southern Fairfax County.

The Doag Indians were the first to inhabit this area because of its abundance of natural resources. They called it Occoquan—"at the end of the water"—because of its proximity to the river. As with most eastern American Indians, the Doags soon succumbed to English settlers, leaving the name Occoquan as one of the few legacies of their existence. During the Civil War, this area served as a strategic line of defense between the North and South. Such famous Civil War battlegrounds as Bull Run are just a few miles upstream.

Cruising along Fountainhead's mountain bike trail.

Today, the area is part of the larger Bull Run Recreation Area and is managed by the Northern Virginia Regional Park Authority (NVRPA). This off-road bicycling trail is the first of its kind for mountain bikers in northern Virginia. The NVRPA envisions it as an example for the region—a pilot program of sorts. If no user conflicts arise from this experiment, the NVRPA will consider opening more trails for off-road cyclists in the region. Let's set a good example here and help ensure the growth and acceptance of off-road bicycling trails throughout this area.

Your ride starts in the main parking lot as you head toward the marina. From the lot, pedal toward the trail entrance (staging area). This trail is one-way traffic only, so don't plan to travel it in any direction but clockwise. After a brief, fast, and technical downhill, you will bear left at the first trail intersection. Be sure to avoid the right fork in this trail—it is for equestrians and hikers only. A small technical stream crossing leads you to the first turn and the beginning of the loop. The trail takes you

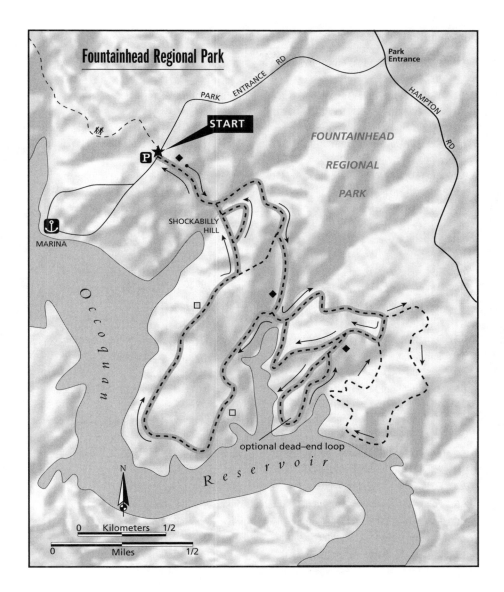

Fountainhead Regional Park

Park Entrance

PARK ENTRANCE RD

START

FOUNTAINHEAD REGIONAL PARK

HAMPTON RD

P

SHOCKABILLY HILL

MARINA

O c c o q u a n

optional dead-end loop

R e s e r v o i r

N

| 0 | Kilometers | 1/2 |
| 0 | Miles | 1/2 |

around and back on a series of small loops, offering up to 5 miles of technical, challenging singletrack. If, after your first or second loop, you're up for it, head out to the marina and rent a boat or even play a game of miniature golf.

While you're here, don't miss the quaint, historic downtown of Occoquan, rich with history, antiques shops, arts and crafts, and great restaurants. You'll also find the nation's first automated gristmill. And don't forget to check out a host of historic homes and businesses, some of which have been in operation for more than 200 years.

Miles and Directions

0.0 START at the Red Trail trailhead, which is approximately 10 yards to the left of the Nature Trail.

0.2 Turn left at this intersection and continue downhill toward the creek crossing. The trail, clearly marked as a "bike trail," briefly joins a hiking trail.

0.26 Take a left before a major creek crossing. Remember this is a one-directional trail. This is the only way to go. On your way back, you will have to negotiate Shockabilly Hill with its steep drop-offs. This is visible on the other side of the creek.

0.35 Cross the small creek and continue following the red blazes. Get ready to climb.

0.5 After a series of twists and one challenging ascent, turn left at the trail intersection, continuing down a gradual descent. Pay close attention to the exposed roots and stumps—unless you want to sample the soil! Turning right will take you to Shockabilly Hill.

0.84 There is a sharp, sudden left switchback toward the bottom of the hill. Continue following the red blazes away from the reservoir. Do not go across the creek.

0.86 Turn right at this point and cross the small creek. Continue back toward the reservoir.

0.9 After a short steep hill, you will be directly across from the previous switchback. Continue left, following the red blazes. The direction is clearly marked.

1.16 Continue following the trail signs and red blazes.

1.37 Turn right at this trail intersection. (Continuing straight takes you along the new loop.)

1.53 Turn left, following the trail toward the "optional dead-end loop." Prepare for a fun descent. This is a two-way section, so be careful.

1.61 Bear right onto the singletrack. After a twisty descent, the trail curves to the left, offering a great view of the reservoir.

2.1 You have completed the optional dead-end loop. Turn right and continue up the two-way-traffic section of trail.

2.2 Turn left at this intersection and continue down a fast descent. Keep alert, because you will have to turn left abruptly.

2.3 Follow the trail to the left.

2.5 Follow the switchback to the right. The trail continues to be blazed red.

2.66 Follow the trail to the left at another sign pointing to the parking lot. Go over the small wooden bridge and continue following the red blazes.

2.7 Turn left to follow the red blazes.

With trails designed to take advantage of the area's elevation and terrain, riding here isn't always the easiest option.

4.16 Reach Shockabilly Hill. Continue straight down this hill only if you are an expert. These directions lead you to the right, following the "easier" alternate route.

4.3 Turn right over the wooden bridge. If you choose, turn right immediately after the bridge and do the loop again. Otherwise, continue straight toward the red/yellow blazes.

4.35 Turn right over the small wooden bridge.

4.5 Arrive back at the trailhead.

Ride Information

Local Information

Occoquan information, www.occoquan.com.

Fairfax County Convention and Visitors Bureau, (800) 7FAIRFAX; www.visitfairfax.org.

Local Events and Attractions

Historic town of Occoquan, www.occoquan.com.

Harbor River Cruises in Occoquan, (703) 385-9433.

Historic Occoquan Spring Arts and Crafts Show, (703) 491-2168.

Accommodations

Bennett House Bed and Breakfast, Manassas, VA; (703) 368-6121.

Sunrise Hill Farm B&B, Manassas, VA; (703) 754-8309.

In Addition

The Fountainhead Trail Project: A Groundbreaking Event

The Fountainhead Regional Park Mountain Bike Trail opened in the spring of 1997. Until then, bicycles were not permitted on any of the trails within the park. The trail is a single-direction trail (clockwise), clearly marked with trail signs and red blazes. If at any point the red blazes are on the back of the trees rather than on the front, then you are going in the wrong direction and should turn around.

As mentioned earlier, the Fountainhead Regional Park Mountain Bike Trail represents an important opportunity and major breakthrough for cyclists in the Washington metropolitan area. It was planned by the Northern Virginia Regional Park Authority (NVRPA) in close collaboration with the Mid-Atlantic Off-Road Enthusiasts (MORE) and was initially funded, in large part, by REI (Recreational Equipment, Incorporated). This flagship mountain bike trail project was designed specifically by mountain bikers for mountain bikers and will serve as a real litmus test. Other park officials who may be interested in constructing and maintaining mountain-bike-specific trailways at their parks are watching it closely.

A paved trailhead and two-way access trail is lined with split-rail fence to resist erosion and discourage "trail braiding." The trail was designed to take advantage of the area's elevation and terrain, and water bars are widely employed on its steeper grades, including new rubber-belt-style devices popular in California. Overall trail usage is expected to be very high, quite possibly exceeding 500 users per month. Please take extreme measures when riding here to ensure this trail's success and durability. The trail is built. Now it's our turn to make sure it stays open.

The number (703) 250–2473 is a dedicated trail line with daily updated messages about trail conditions, closings, and openings. Cyclists should always call this number before heading out to the trail. The Fountainhead Regional Park number is (703) 250–9124.

22 Wakefield Park/Accotink Trail

Start: From the Wakefield Park Recreation Center.
Length: 6.1 miles.
Approximate riding time: 1 hour.
Difficulty rating: Main loop is rated easy. Off-shoot trails are more difficult.
Trail surface: Singletrack and dirt trails.
Land status: County parks.
Nearest town: Annandale.
Other trail users: Hikers.
Canine compatibility: This is a pretty crowded place, so unless your dog is well trained, it may be best to leave him behind.
Fees and permits: No fees or permits required.
Schedule: Open daylight to dark year-round.
Maps: USGS map: Annandale; ADC map: Northern Virginia road map; Fairfax County Park Authority trail map.
Trail contacts: Fairfax County Park Authority, (703) 246–5700; Lake Accotink Park, (703) 569–3464.

Getting There: From the Capital Beltway (I–495): Exit west at exit 5 onto Braddock Road. In less than 0.2 mile, turn right on Wakefield Park's entrance road. Go 0.6 mile to the parking and recreation center on the left. Phones, water, rest rooms, and food are available at Wakefield Recreation Center. *DeLorme: Virginia Atlas & Gazetteer:* Page 76, B-4.

The Ride

Host to countless mountain bike races and cross–country races throughout the season, Wakefield Park has become somewhat of a local stronghold for mountain bike excitement in northern Virginia. With the nearby power lines behind Wakefield Park and trails that are perfect for a quick workout as you exit the Beltway from a long day's grind, this area is a sweet spot in the local off-road scene. From here, cyclists less interested in mashing out their frustrations on technical track can instead leisurely pedal along a flat, dirt path, beneath Braddock Road and over to Lake Accotink Park. Here, a scenic woodland preserve, as well as an abundance of short, steep hills, tree roots, quick dips, and fast turns, awaits. Stop off after work and get out of traffic for this great mountain bike locale.

Sometimes it's interesting to see where you find singletrack. Typically, great mountain bike trails lie west or far north of the Washington suburbs. Out there— typically a "long drive" from where most of us live—singletrack and forest roads trace the landscape in all directions. The dirt's the limit. "If only we lived closer to the trails," goes the suburban cyclist's woeful anthem.

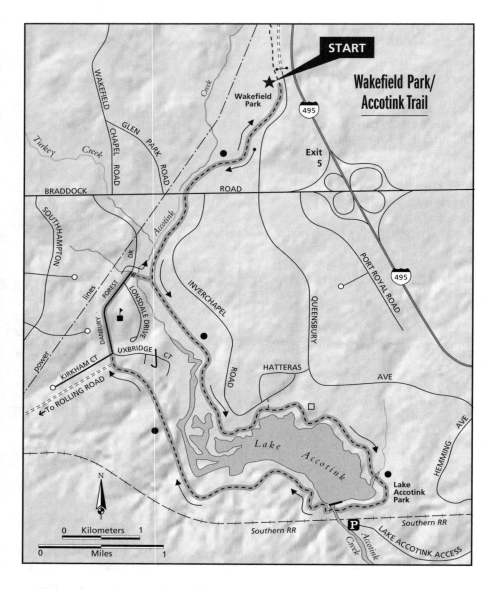

Wakefield Park/
Accotink Trail

But a closer inspection reveals we *do* live near the trails—thanks to the Fairfax County Park Authority. Wakefield and Lake Accotink Parks, less than half a mile from the Capital Beltway in Fairfax County, are filled with a network of fun, technical singletrack. Most of these singletrack trails are offshoots from the park's main loop, which is a scenic, wooded dirt trail around Accotink's scenic seventy-acre lake.

The Accotink Trail was once part of the Orange and Alexandria Railroad's original roadbed, built in the early 1850s. The rails and ties, of course, have since been removed, and a new rail was laid farther south along a straighter route.

Lake Accotink's history began in the 1930s, when the U.S. Army Corps of Engineers dammed Accotink Creek to create a reservoir for Fort Belvoir, nearly 5 miles downstream. In 1965 the lake and surrounding land was given to Fairfax County by the federal government for park and recreational use. The park's great trails, open to bicycling, have been "maturing" ever since.

This ride begins from Wakefield Park and travels south along the Accotink Trail around the lake, then back to Wakefield. There are even some great trails that go north from Wakefield and cross challenging routes beneath the power lines.

For thrill seekers, there is an abundance of short, steep hills, tree roots, quick dips, and fast turns. For the off-road cyclist with a lighter touch, Accotink Trail takes you through a scenic woodland preserve, quiet and relaxing in the spring and summer, breathtaking in the fall. Who says you have to drive far to get out of the gridlock and into the woods? For Beltway commuters, Accotink is less than a stone's throw away.

Miles and Directions

0.0 START at Wakefield Park Recreation Center near the big green recycling bins. The trail begins near the park entrance road and heads south through Wakefield toward Braddock Road.

0.2 Cross the athletic fields parking lot. Accotink Trail continues on the other side of the parking lot.

0.6 Cross under Braddock Road.

0.7 Just across Braddock Road, bear left, continuing on the main trail.

1.0 Stay left at the fork in the trail and follow the wooden Accotink Trail post.

2.1 Trail comes to a T. Turn right, following Accotink Trail. The creek should be on your right. This part of the trail winds up and down through the woods. A lot of fun.

2.9 Arrive at Lake Accotink's marina. You'll find concessions, food, drinks, putt-putt golf, canoe and boat rental, etc. Stay right, crossing the parking lot toward the dam.

3.0 Cross Lake Accotink Dam. Following the bike path, which parallels the train trestle, head toward the woods opposite the dam.

3.3 Reenter the woods, up a steep climb, on Accotink Trail.

Cruising downhill near Lake Accotink's dam.

4.5 Turn hard right off the dirt path on an asphalt trail, which takes you down Danbury Forest Drive in the neighborhood of Danbury Forest. Kings Glen Elementary School is on the right.

4.9 Reenter Accotink Trail on the right, just after Lonsdale Drive. This is a steep descent alongside the concrete steps into the woods.

5.0 Turn right off the asphalt path, following Accotink Trail across a wooden footbridge over Accotink Creek.

5.1 Turn left on Accotink Trail.

5.5 Cross under Braddock Road.

6.1 Arrive back at the parking lot of Wakefield's recreation center.

Ride Information

Local Information

Fairfax County Convention and Visitors Bureau, (800) 7FAIRFAX, www.visitfairfax.org.

Local Events and Attractions

The Athenaeum in Alexandria, (703) 548-0035.

Memorial Day Jazz Festival, Alexandria, VA, (703) 838-4844.

Torpedo Factory Art Center, Alexandria, VA, (703) 838-4565.

West End Dinner Theater, Alexandria, VA, (800) 368-3799; www.wedt.com.

23 Centreville Power Lines

Start: From Centreville Elementary School.
Length: 7.8 miles.
Approximate riding time: 1.5 to 2 hours.
Difficulty rating: Difficult, due to sections of very rugged terrain.
Trail surface: Rugged singletrack and paved bike paths.
Land status: Public and private rights-of-way.
Nearest town: Centreville.
Other trail users: Power line repairmen and four-wheel-drive motorists.
Canine compatibility: Leave the dog behind. This route follows some busy roads through busy suburban sprawl. No place for a dog.
Fees and permits: No fees or permits required.
Schedule: Accessible year-round.
Maps: USGS map: Manassas; ADC map: Northern Virginia road map.
Trail contacts: Virginia Power Company.

Getting There: From I-66: Take exit 53, heading south on Sully Road (Route 28).

Sully Road changes to Centreville Road across Lee Highway (U.S. Route 29). Follow Centreville Road for about 2 miles, then turn left into the Centreville Elementary School parking lot. *DeLorme: Virginia Atlas & Gazetteer:* Page 76, B-2.

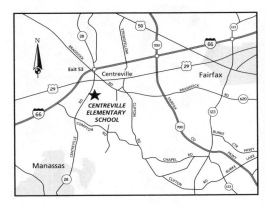

The Ride

Like so many communities in northern Virginia, Centreville has seen its share of suburban sprawl. In fact, in the past few years, this once small town has been all but swallowed by the ever-expanding behemoth of northern Virginia. Surprisingly, this incredible growth was once not so easy to come by, and Centreville struggled to get to where it is today.

Centreville had been trying to grow for some time, but for a while had an altogether tough time of it. Since its establishment in 1792, this small trading center, located nearly equidistant from Leesburg, Warrenton, Middleburg, Washington, Georgetown, and Alexandria, tried diligently to become more than just a rest stop along Braddock Road.

When construction began on Little River Turnpike in the late eighteenth century, for example, the town hoped this trade highway, stretching west from Alexandria, would pass through their community. At the time, Alexandria was the Potomac's largest market town. Developers, however, routed Little River Turnpike north in favor of smoother, more even terrain, bypassing the town altogether. The

Centreville Power Lines

town later tried to house the district court of Virginia, which served Fairfax, Fauquier, Loudoun, and Prince William Counties. This idea was also rejected in favor of Dumfries in Prince William County. Ever persistent, Centreville founded what it hoped would become a prestigious academy to attract outside scholars to take up residence in local homes. This effort also went without much success. At one time, Centreville was even known as a local center for slave rental and trade. But into the twentieth century, this small town remained nothing more than the unimposing rest stop it had always been.

As you pass through Centreville today, however, much of this history may seem very distant and unfamiliar, because the town has suddenly become a sprawling community of subdivisions, shopping centers, and Beltway commuters. And it continues to expand at a phenomenal rate farther and farther west.

Centreville is not unlike many communities surrounding the Washington-Baltimore area that have, in the last ten to twenty years, seen tremendous growth. This explosive growth has, in most cases, virtually wiped out the small-town flavor that dominated the region west of the cities. Towns and villages, desperate for so long to attract more people and new businesses, could never have anticipated the recent boom in development, which has transformed these small hamlets into huge bedroom communities for the Washington/Baltimore megalopolis.

With this growth, precious back roads and trails were permanently lost, forcing local off-road cyclists to look even harder for places to ride. Thus, the discovery of the power lines! They may not be scenic mountain roads or offer endless back-country exploration, but the rugged trails beneath these crackling wires make for the ultimate suburban off-road adventure. Power lines have it all—rocks, ditches, hills, dirt, and, most important, open land on which to ride. You'll find yourself crashing down rocky descents, slogging through muddy streambeds, then up and over steep, rutted climbs that snake back and forth beneath the supercharged black cables that bring power to the surrounding homes and neighborhoods.

The most important thing to remember when riding the power lines is that there is always a way through the obstacles. Sometimes you just have to find it. Have fun!

Miles and Directions

0.0 START at Centreville Elementary School. Travel south along the asphalt path parallel to Centreville Road. This leads you directly to the power lines.

0.2 Turn left off the asphalt path and hit the dirt trails beneath the power lines. Follow the trail on the left side.

0.75 Cross Bay Valley Lane.

Trails abound beneath the power lines.

0.8 Turn left at the small fenced-in substation, following the secondary power lines that run north along Little Rocky Run Creek to Braddock Road.

2.0 Pass a small park with tennis courts.

2.2 After passing the park, reenter the trail on the right side of the power lines.

2.4 Climb up the embankment at Braddock Road and turn right on the asphalt path. At this point, the trail beneath the power lines disappears as the power lines parallel Braddock Road.

2.8 Turn right on the asphalt bike path along Union Mill Road.

3.1 Centreville High School is on the left.

4.3 The bike path ends. Continue riding along the shoulder. Be careful of traffic.

4.8 At this intersection with Compton Road, go straight through the stop sign, continuing on Union Mill Road. Union Mill Road continues into a new housing development. Follow this to the power lines.

5.3 Turn right off Union Mill Road and ride to the power lines, heading west back to Centreville Road.

6.4 Cross Compton Road.

7.0 Pass the small fenced-in power station on the right. Continue straight. Cross Bay Valley Lane.

7.7 Reach Centreville Road. Turn right on the asphalt bike path back toward the school.

7.8 Arrive back at Centreville Elementary School.

Ride Information

Local Information

Prince William County/Manassas Conference and Visitors Bureau, (800) 432-1792; www.visitpwc.com.

Local Events and Attractions

Civil War weekends in Manassas, VA, July and August; (800) 432-1792.
Manassas National Battlefield Park, (703) 361-1339; www.nps.gov/mana/online.htm.
Splashdown Water Park, (703) 361-4451.

24 Great Falls National Park

Start: From the visitor center.
Length: 6.8 miles.
Approximate riding time: 1 to 1.5 hours.
Difficulty rating: Moderate, due to occasional steep, rocky singletrack.
Trail surface: Rocky, dirt trails and carriage roads.
Land status: National park.
Nearest town: McLean.

Other trail users: Hikers, equestrians, climbers, kayakers, and tourists.
Canine compatibility: Dogs will love it here—except that they must be kept on leashes. It's a busy park.
Fees and permits: $4.00 entrance fee.
Schedule: Open 7:00 A.M. to sunset.
Maps: USGS maps: Vienna, Falls Church; ADC map: Northern Virginia road map; National Park Service Official Trail Map and Guide.
Trail contacts: National Park Service, (703) 759-2915, www.nps.gov/gwmp/grfa.

Getting There: From the Capital Beltway (I–495): From exit 13 northwest of McLean, take Route 193 (Georgetown Pike) west toward Great Falls. Go about 4 miles, then turn right on Old Dominion Drive, which becomes the park entrance road. Go 1 mile to the end of this road and park at the visitor center. Telephones, water, food, rest rooms, and information are available inside the visitor center. *DeLorme: Virginia Atlas & Gazetteer:* Page 76, A-4.

The Ride

Great Falls is one of the United States's most popular national parks. How appropriate then for it to be located just 14 miles from our nation's capital. And what a thrill for cyclists to know that mountain biking is not only allowed at the park—it's welcome. Great Falls is a natural haven for thousands of Washingtonians seeking solitude from the daily grind of gridlock and government. Trails abound throughout this park on the river, offering cyclists, hikers, and equestrians alike rugged terrain. Some portions of the park's trails are wide dirt carriage roads dating back through history and meandering through the scenery, while others are steep, rocky, and narrow, keeping even agile cyclists on the tips of their seat.

There are more than 5 miles of designated trails to enjoy in this park. All of them conveniently intersect to create hours of off-road adventure. The trails vary in intensity, ranging from rolling forest roads beneath tall oaks and maples to steep, rocky singletrack, overlooking the dramatic Mather Gorge. The park's unequaled beauty,

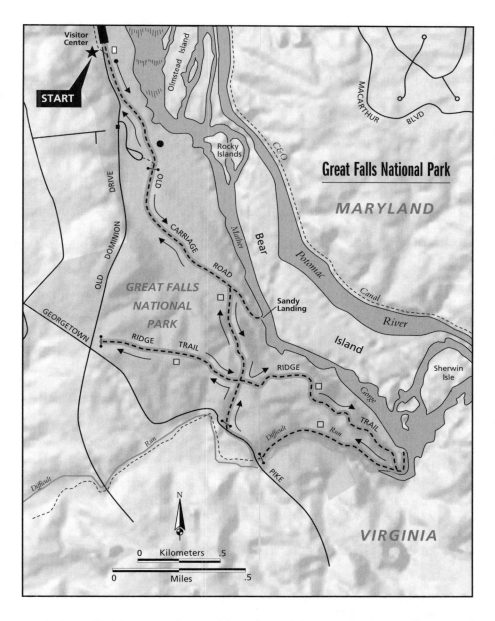

Great Falls National Park

MARYLAND

GREAT FALLS
NATIONAL
PARK

VIRGINIA

proximity to Washington, and accessible trails combine to make Great Falls National Park northern Virginia's most popular off-road cycling haven.

The ride begins at the visitor center parking lot and travels south along Old Carriage Road through the middle of the park. Old Carriage was used in the 1700s to carry settlers to their dwellings at Matildaville, ruins of which still stand today. Henry Lee, a Revolutionary War hero and friend of George Washington's, developed this small town. Named after Lee's first wife, Matildaville lasted only three decades before fading into history.

The route bends deep into the park and travels up and down the rocky pass along Ridge Trail. During the winter months, breathtaking views of the gorge show through deciduous trees. The trail then descends quickly to the Potomac (another great view) and follows along Difficult Run before heading north again back toward the start.

Great Falls has always been a popular place to visit for locals and international tourists alike. Some have come to survey the river's rapids, including George Washington, who formed the Patowmack Company in 1784 to build a series of canals around the falls. Theodore Roosevelt came to Great Falls to hike and ride horses during his presidency. Today, thousands come to enjoy Great Falls as well. But they don't come to build canals, develop towns, make trade, or seek solitude from the presidential office. They come only to ride the park's great trails, kayak the rapids, climb the steep cliffs, and bear witness to the magnificent scenery at Great Falls National Park.

Miles and Directions

0.0   START at Great Falls Visitor Center. Follow the Horse/Biker Trail south along the entrance road.

0.4   Bear right at the rest rooms and go around the steel gate on Old Carriage Road (unpaved).

1.1   Bear left down the trail to Sandy Landing.

1.3   Arrive at Sandy Landing, a beautiful spot along the river, great for viewing Mather Gorge. Return to Old Carriage Road.

1.5   Turn left, continuing on Old Carriage Road. Begin a steady uphill.

1.9   Turn left near the top of this climb on Ridge Trail.

2.7   Turn left after the steep descent on Difficult Run Trail. Head toward the Potomac.

2.9   Arrive at the Potomac River. This is another great spot to view Sherwin Island, where Mather Gorge and the Potomac River converge. Turn around.

3.1   Turn left on Difficult Run Trail west along Difficult Run Creek toward Georgetown Pike.

3.6   Turn right on Georgetown Pike. Be careful with traffic and ride on the dirt shoulder.

Cruising along Ridge Trail.

3.8 Turn right on Old Carriage Road. This is the first dirt road you come to along Georgetown Pike. Go around the gate and begin climbing.

4.0 Turn left on Ridge Trail. Follow this toward the entrance road.

4.7 Reach Great Falls's entrance road (Old Dominion Drive). Turn around and continue back on Ridge Trail.

5.4 Turn left on Old Carriage Road.

5.7 Bear left at the Sandy Landing Trail junction.

6.4 Go through the gate at the beginning of Old Carriage Road and head back to the parking lot at the visitor center.

6.8 Arrive back at the visitor center and parking lot.

Ride Information

Local Information
Fairfax County Convention and Visitors Bureau, (800) 7FAIRFAX; www.visitfairfax.org.

Local Events and Attractions
Colvin Run Mill, (703) 759-2771.
Wolf Trap Farm Park for the Performing Arts, (703) 255-1800.

Restaurants
Evans Farm Inn and the Sitting Duck Pub, (703) 356-8000.

25 Middleburg Vineyard Tour

Start: From the Middleburg Elementary School.
Length: 23.1 miles.
Approximate riding time: 2 to 3 hours (not counting stops at vineyards).
Difficulty rating: Moderate to difficult (due to length).
Trail surface: Unpaved dirt and gravel roads.
Land status: Public roads.
Nearest town: Middleburg.
Other trail users: Motorists and wine tasters.
Canine compatibility: Your dog will hate you if you take him on this ride. So don't.

Fees and permits: $3.00 to $5.00 per winery for wine tastings. Call in advance for current prices.
Schedule: Meredyth Vineyard, 10:00 A.M. to 5:00 P.M., seven days a week; Piedmont Vineyard, 10:00 A.M. to 4:00 P.M., seven days a week; Swedenburg Vineyard, 10:00 A.M. to 4:00 P.M., seven days a week.
Maps: USGS maps: Rectortown, Middleburg; ADC map: Loudoun County road map; Fauquier County road map.
Trail contacts: None.

Getting There: From the Capital Beltway (I–495): Take I–66 west 8.5 miles to exit 57, U.S. Route 50 West. Go 23 miles on U.S. Route 50 into Middleburg. John Mosby Highway (U.S. Route 50) becomes Washington Street within the Middleburg town limits. From Washington Street, turn right on Madison Street (Route 626). Go 0.1 mile and turn right into the Middleburg Elementary School parking lot. *DeLorme: Virginia Atlas & Gazetteer:* Page 75, A-7.

The Ride

This ride travels through some of Virginia's finest wine country, where visits to the vineyards are always welcome, and wine tasting is just part of the tour. Virginia is quickly becoming renowned worldwide for its wine. And Loudoun County is home to a number of the Old Dominion's finest wineries. This mostly unpaved (gravel and dirt road) ride is set up to lead cyclists through the area's beautiful rolling horse country, connecting (or passing nearby) a number of northern Virginia's most productive vineyards. Make plenty of time for this trip and stop often to taste the latest wine.

Start in the historic town of Middleburg, a small, touristy outpost in the middle of hunt country. Horses abound in this magnificent countryside. A town with a rich history, Middleburg has enjoyed its share of good fortune. Established in 1787, this centuries–old town was even graced by a U.S. president when the John F. Kennedy family attended the local Catholic church and built a home just outside town.

You'll pass more than just vineyards and automobiles along this ride.

The ride starts on a route toward Piedmont Vineyard but breaks off from the main road onto backcountry dirt, perfect for an off-road tourist. This first section rolls comfortably past small estates and low-key horse farms. But when you turn east, the roads lift you into the hills. You'll pass some of the old and new—abandoned stone houses and state-of-the-art homes—then head toward Meredyth Vineyard to lavish in the land of the well-to-do. Gorgeous estates rest on acres of open land, where thoroughbreds graze in the warm sun. What a wonderful place to ride and dream. But don't forget to stop at the vineyard. (Hours are from 10:00 A.M. to 4:00 P.M.) The rest of the ride rolls up and down below Bull Run Mountain, taking you past one more vineyard, the Swedenburg Estate, before leading you back into Middleburg.

If the wine doesn't get the best of you, then enjoy the endless dirt roads scattered throughout this region. This is excellent off-road riding for cyclists looking for a change of pace and scenery.

Miles and Directions

0.0   START at the Middleburg Elementary School parking lot. Turn left on Madison Street (Route 626, paved).

0.1   Turn right on Washington Street (U.S. Route 50, paved).

0.3   Turn left on Plains Road (Route 626, paved). Follow the purple vineyard sign.

1.1   Turn right on Route 705 (paved).

1.2   Route 705 changes to dirt (unpaved).

3.2   Stay straight on Route 705 at this intersection. Route 706 turns right.

Middleburg Vineyard Tour

3.4 Stay right on Route 705 at this intersection. Route 706 turns left.

4.2 Turn left at the T, continuing on Route 705. Route 708 goes right.

5.3 Turn left at the stop sign on Route 702 (unpaved).

7.6 Turn left on Route 626 (paved).

7.9 Bear right on Route 679 at the bottom of the descent. This turns into Route 628.

9.1 Turn left on Route 628 (unpaved). This turn is slightly hidden. The turn comes after a long rock wall on the left, just past a large brick house with three chimneys.

9.4   Meredyth Vineyards is on the left. Stop in for a tour. Hours are 10:00 A.M. to 4:00 P.M.

11.5   Turn right on Landmark School Road (Route 776, paved). (**Bailout:** For those who have had enough, you can turn left on Landmark School Road and take the shortcut back to Middleburg [2.4 miles].)

13.2   Turn left on Champe Ford Road (Route 629, unpaved).

17.1   Turn left on John Mosby Highway (U.S. Route 50, paved). Be careful of traffic.

17.5   Turn right on Cobb House Road (Route 629, unpaved).

18.5   Turn left on Snickersville Turnpike (paved).

18.8   Turn left at the bottom of the hill on Carters Farm Road (Route 627, unpaved).

21.3   Turn right on John Mosby Highway (U.S. Route 50, paved). Pass Swedenburg Estate Vineyard. Stop for a sip of wine before continuing on.

21.5   Turn left on Parsons Road (Route 627, unpaved).

22.6   Turn right on Landmark School Road (Route 776, paved).

23.0   Arrive back in Middleburg. Cross Washington Street to Madison Street.

23.1   Turn right into the school parking lot. Drink too much wine?

Ride Information

Local Information

Loudoun Tourism Council, (800) 752-6118.

Local Events and Attractions

Meredyth Vineyard, (540) 687-6277.

Piedmont Vineyard, (540) 687-5528; www.piedmontwines.com.

Swedenburg Estate Vineyard, (540) 687-5219.

In Addition

Mountain Biking and Wine

If my assumption is correct, many of you are like me and have never really refined your tastes in good wine. After all, we're mountain bikers for heaven's sake! If such is the case, then you may also find yourselves feeling about as silly and uneducated as I have when the proprietor of a winery serves samples of the vineyard's great variety of wines. You may understand little to none about what this person is talking about, and if you're like me, you politely sip the wine, nod your head at each flavor's description, and wonder how they can arrive at so many names for such similar tastes. Before subjecting yourself to this unnecessary display of embarrassing ignorance and vacant wine tasting, educate yourself a bit and enjoy tasting some of the vineyard's fine products. Hopefully, after reading some of the following information before cycling up to a winery's door, you may quite miraculously understand some of what the proprietor is telling you about his latest flavors and enjoy the samples that much more.

Wine is the fermented juice of grapes. Nearly all the wine made throughout the world comes from one species of grape—*Vitis vinifera*. As many as 4,000 varieties of grape have been developed from this one species. Each differs, sometimes only slightly, in size, color, shape of the berry, juice composition, ripening time, and resistance to disease. Only about a dozen of the 4,000 or more varieties of grapes are commonly used for wine making. Chief among them are Chardonnay, Riesling, Cabernet Sauvignon, Sauvignon Blanc, Pinot Noir, Gewurztraminer, and Muscat.

The main reason the varieties of *Vitis vinifera* are used throughout the world in wine production is because of their high sugar content when ripe. Wine with an alcohol content of 10 percent or slightly higher is produced from the grapes' natural sugar content after fermentation. Wines with less alcohol are unstable and subject to bacterial spoilage.

Wine Colors

We're all familiar with colors of wine: white wine, rosé, and red wine. But why the different colors and what's the big deal anyway?

- White wine is produced when only the juice from the grape is used. The skin is removed before fermentation begins. The juice is normally colorless, though some varieties have a pink to reddish color. Because only the grape's juice is used, white wine tends to be much sweeter and thus much easier on the palate for most people unfamiliar with drinking wine.

- A rosé is produced when the skins of red or black grapes are removed after fermentation has begun.
- Red wine is produced when whole, crushed red or black grapes are used, including the skins. Red wine is often more bitter and has a stronger taste than white wine.

What Are We Supposed to Eat with This Stuff Anyway?

It's suggested that we drink white wines with light foods such as salads, chicken, and fish. Red wines are recommended for heavier flavored foods such as red meat. The reasons are strictly for the palate. A strong tasting red wine may overwhelm the light flavors of chicken or fish, while the sweeter, lighter flavor of white wine may get lost on a hearty, juicy steak. What should cyclists drink with their spaghetti? Either one is fine. Heck, who cares. It's wine!

Where Does It Come From?

Although Italy produces more wine, the world's leading wine producer in terms of quality is France, with outstanding products from Bordeaux and Burgundy, the Loire and Rhone Valleys, and Alsace. Other major producers are Spain, the United States, Germany, Chile, Argentina, South Africa, and Australia. In the United States, California is the leading wine-producing region. Central Virginia is a close second.

The Process of Making Wine—in a Nutshell

White wine: Red and white grapes are stemmed and crushed before going into a horizontal press for more crushing (end plates in the horizontal press move toward each other and crush the grapes). The juice (sans the skin) then flows to a vat for fermenting. The juice has not had time to pick up color from the skins, leaving it white.

Red and rosé wines: The crushed grapes go directly into fermenting vats with their skins. After fermenting, the unpalatable red press wine is mixed with free-run wine. The dry skins and pulp (called marc) can be distilled into cheap brandy.

Fermentation starts when wine yeast on the skins of ripe grapes comes in contact with the grape juice. After running off into casks, the new wine then undergoes a series of chemical processes, including oxidation, precipitation of proteins, and fermentation of chemical compounds. Each of these processes creates the wine's characteristic bouquet (aroma). After periodic clarification and aging in casks, the wine is ready to be bottled.

Honorable Mentions

Northern Virginia

Compiled here is an index of great rides in northern Virginia that didn't make the list this time around but deserve recognition. Check them out and let us know what you think. You may decide that one or more of these rides deserves higher status in future editions, or, perhaps, you may have a ride of your own that merits some attention.

⊢ Burke Lake Park Ride

It's called Burke Lake Park Ride, but this 7.3-mile route starts from South Run District Park and follows a scenic, paved bike and hike path through the woods along South Run to Burke Lake. Obviously, cyclists don't have to go this route and can choose to start from Burke Lake Park directly, but the section from South Run Park adds a bit more dimension to the overall cycling experience.

This ride isn't designed for thrill seekers and singletrack lovers. Instead, it reveals the lighter side of off-road bicycle riding, leading cyclists on a pleasant off-road trip past flower gardens and lakeside vistas. The route is mostly flat and smooth, traveling along well-maintained dirt paths around Burke Lake or meandering along South Run on a paved bicycle path. If you get eager to take on some rough stuff, simply cut out from the South Run bicycle path near South Run District Park and take on

Burke Lake as seen from the bicycling and hiking path that surrounds it.

the rugged, hilly singletrack beneath the power lines. There's plenty for off-road cyclists to do along this easy route to and from Burke Lake, so bring the family and enjoy the ride.

To get there from the Capital Beltway, take I–95 south toward Richmond. Go only about 0.5 mile and take Springfield exit 57, Old Keene Mill Road (Route 644 West). Follow Old Keene Mill Road west 3 miles, then turn left on Huntsman Boulevard. Follow Huntsman Boulevard 1.5 miles to the Fairfax County Parkway (Route 7100). Turn right on the Fairfax County Parkway, travel about 0.3 mile, and turn left into South Run District Park. Parking, water, phones, rest rooms, and showers are available at the South Run Recreation Center. (*DeLorme: Virginia Atlas & Gazetteer:* Page 76, B-3. Also see *Mountain Biking the Washington, D.C./Baltimore Area.*)

| Difficult Run Trail (Glade to Great Falls)

This 12-mile point-to-point route from the Twin Branches Trail in Reston, Virginia, to Great Falls National Park on the Potomac may define what could someday become a new breed of unpaved trail system through the ever-growing and increasingly paved suburban landscape of northern Virginia. Combining a mixture of clay-surfaced singletrack, bike paths, public parkland, and creek corridors, this ride follows what is perhaps the longest, most unusual trail system in the Washington/Baltimore region. Mountain bikers will love it.

To get to the start of this ride from the Capital Beltway, take the Washington-Dulles Access Road (toll road) west for 7 miles to exit 5, Hunter Mill Road. Go south on Hunter Mill Road to Sunrise Valley Road and turn right. Go half a mile and turn left on South Lakes Drive. Turn left on Twin Branches Road. Follow Twin Branches Road to Glade Drive and park. Twin Branches Trail starts here. (*DeLorme: Virginia Atlas & Gazetteer:* Page 76, A-3. Also see *Mountain Biking the Washington, D.C./Baltimore Area.*)

⌡ C&O Canal Towpath

Here's a ride for those slow-twitch muscle types who can ride on and on and on and on without much more than a need to stop and fill up the water bottle once or twice. With 185 miles of off-road riding in one fell swoop (and that's just one way), the C&O canal towpath is one ride sure to challenge those who thrive on endurance activities. But few (in fact, almost none) of the cyclists who take to the canal each year attempt to ride the entire distance at once. However, anyone looking for a great trip along the Potomac River (leaving right from Georgetown) with virtually no elevation gain in sight should love this ride. Try it in sections, camp overnight, stay at some of the inns along the way to Cumberland, Maryland, or just ride up and down the canal near the city. Either way, it's a jewel for cyclists looking for an endless trip off the beaten path that leaves right from town.

A linear oasis through northern Virginia for off-road cyclists.

To get there from downtown D.C., start from the White House and head toward Georgetown. Take Pennsylvania Avenue N.W. toward Georgetown. Go 11 blocks to M Street, turn left into Georgetown, then go 2 blocks to Thomas Jefferson Street. Turn left on Thomas Jefferson Street. The Georgetown C&O Canal Visitor Center is here. This is the beginning of a great adventure. (*DeLorme: Maryland Atlas & Gazetteer:* Page 46, C3. Also see *Mountain Biking the Washington, D.C./Baltimore Area.*)

Western Virginia

George Washington National Forest

Jefferson National Forest

26 Elizabeth Furnace

Start: From the small gravel parking area opposite the Elizabeth Furnace Recreation Area and overnight campground.

Length: 13.3-mile loop (20-plus miles of trails total).

Approximate riding time: 3 to 5 hours.

Difficulty rating: Difficult. Bring extra tubes, extra water, and a lot of fitness. Full suspension (or at least front suspension) is also highly recommended.

Trail surface: Mountainous, rocky singletrack and forest roads. Some pretty tough hike-a-bike sections as well.

Land status: National forest.

Nearest town: Front Royal.

Other trail users: Hikers and equestrians. Warm weekends and holidays can bring crowds. Local cyclists are always complaining that northern Virginia mountain bikers should just stay home—all the more reason to hop in your car and make the drive.

Fees and permits: No fees or permits required.

Schedule: Public land; accessible year-round.

Maps: USGS maps: Strasburg, Toms Brook; George Washington National Forest topo map; National Forest Service trail map.

Trail contacts: Lee Ranger District, George Washington National Forest, (540) 984-4101 or (540) 984-4102; George Washington National Forest Headquarters, (703) 564-8300; Potomac Appalachian Trail Club (PATC), (703) 242-0693, www.patc.net.

Getting There: From Front Royal: Take Route 55 approximately 5 miles west to Waterlick. From Waterlick take Fort Valley Road (Route 678) southwest for 4.5 miles to a gravel parking area on the right, opposite the Elizabeth Furnace Recreation Area and overnight campground (just after you pass the large Bear Wallow parking area). Turn right into the gravel parking area. *DeLorme: Virginia Atlas & Gazetteer:* Page 74, A2.

The Ride

I won't lie to anyone out there. This is a tough ride. It features mountains, steeps, huge singletrack, amazing views, and killer descents. And while it's all the way out past Front Royal, Washingtonians can still make it here in under one hour. Cyclists from northern Virginia, Maryland, and West Virginia come here year-round to tame the steeps and conquer the rocky descents on their high-end full-suspension bikes. They usually fail.

So why do so many keep coming back, winter, spring, summer, and fall? Simply put, Elizabeth Furnace is home to some of the best all-around mountain bike trails

Just grin and bear it!

in all of northern Virginia. Bar none. It's steep. It's dangerous. It's long. It's fast. Enough said. Make the drive. You won't be sorry.

Located about one hour west of Washington, D.C., just outside Front Royal, Virginia, the tall, northern ridge of Massanutten Mountain stands alone, high above the Shenandoah Valley. Mountain bikers come in droves to this northeastern piece of the George Washington National Forest to test their skills, endurance, and patience on its tricky ridgelines, rocky singletrack, and brutal climbs. It's easy to understand why this piece of mountain is northern Virginia's Marilyn Monroe of mountain bike destinations. Cyclists just love it.

Its proximity to Washington makes it the closest ridable mountain for peak-starved northern Virginia off-roaders. Elizabeth Furnace's many trails travel along

Elizabeth Furnace

and through small creeks, up and down mountain ridges, and to paths where even the most hard-core rock huggers have difficulty keeping the rubber side down. But let's not overlook the softer side of Elizabeth Furnace. This off-road cycling sanctuary is not all difficult. There are a bunch of forest roads that travel through Fort Valley, the scenic hollow cradled between the east and west ridges of Massanutten Mountain (had he been defeated at the Battle of Yorktown, George Washington would have used this valley as a retreat). And most of the steep sections can be avoided by turning back at Strasburg Reservoir before committing yourself to the tortuous climbs to Signal Knob or the top of Green Mountain. Most of the ride up to Strasburg Reservoir is only moderately difficult, and if you're not feeling particularly adventurous, just turn around and follow the trails back to the start.

The ride starts from the gravel parking lot opposite the Elizabeth Furnace Recreation Area and overnight campground and progresses rather easily along Forest Road 1350. Past the gates, the forest road becomes overgrown, rolling up and down the ridgeline as it makes its way over Green Mountain. There are some wonderful views of Fort Valley and Massanutten Mountain from this road. Approximately 3 miles later, FR 1350 ends in what resembles a large dirt cul-de-sac overrun with small pines and tall grass.

You'll notice a worn trail descending into the woods at the end of the cul-de-sac. This trail takes you to Little Passage Creek. Turn right and follow the creek to Massanutten Mountain Road. You'll cross through the creek five times, so be prepared to get wet. This road leads to Strasburg Reservoir, a good place to turn around if you'd prefer to avoid the steep, rocky ascents and blistering downhills that follow.

For those with a conquering spirit, though, I absolutely recommend making the push to reach Signal Knob. You may end up hiking it most of the way to the top, but it's worth it.

Signal Knob's 2,106-foot peak reveals a sweeping panoramic view of the Shenandoah Valley. During the Civil War, Confederate soldiers used the peak to spot Union troops moving south

HUNTING SEASON Be very careful when riding here during hunting season, which begins in the fall. For opening and closing dates for the current hunting season, call the Virginia Department of Game and Inland Fisheries at (540) 248-9360 or go to www.dgif.state.va.us.

from Winchester. Soldiers hiked what is now the orange-blazed Massanutten Mountain West Trail and searched the valleys below for troop movement. Any information was subsequently flagged from Signal Knob to points farther south. This information would eventually reach the Confederate capital of Richmond. This system didn't stop Union troops from making Fort Valley a regular target, wreaking havoc on its mines, iron-producing furnaces, and farmland.

Most of the Massanutten Mountain West Trail up to Signal Knob is challenging but still very ridable. It isn't until the climb's final 500 feet that pedaling a bike becomes something more akin to hallucination than reality. Walking, for some, becomes the only alternative. But keep going! The view from the top and the subsequent descent are worth the effort.

On the return trip from Signal Knob you have two options: Head back down the orange-blazed Massanutten Mountain West Trail or follow the yellow-blazed Signal Knob Trail along the ridge toward Meneka Peak. If you choose to take the yellow-blazed trail toward Meneka Peak, be sure to turn right on the white-blazed Meneka Peak Trail before reaching the Shenandoah Valley Overlook. Otherwise, the rest of the trip down the yellow-blazed trail will be a downhill hike through scree and unridable misfortune. Your ultimate goal, whether you head back down the way you came along the orange-blazed trail or take the Meneka Peak Trail, is to hook up with the blue-blazed Bear Wallow Trail. The rewards for cycling Bear Wallow Trail over Green Mountain are enormous. A relatively smooth, quick, and exhilarating descent leads you all the way back to the Bear Wallow parking area along Route 678. If you've still got some steam, follow the white-blazed trail from this parking area back to your car, about a half mile through the woods. Otherwise, jump onto Route 678 and cruise back to the end of your ride.

Be prepared to spend anywhere from three to five hours on these trails. Bring plenty of food and water. Tools and extra tubes may also be necessary baggage, as well as extra clothing in case the weather shifts without warning and you're caught on the wrong side of the ridge when the sky opens up. Ride hard and have fun!

Miles and Directions

0.0 START from the gravel parking lot opposite the Elizabeth Furnace Recreation Area and overnight campground. Ride west through the first gate out of the parking lot and follow FR 1350 to the right.

0.1 Go through the second gate, continuing up FR 1350.

0.2 Pass the Bear Wallow Trail trailhead on the right. This takes you up to Signal Knob. Continue on FR 1350.

1.4 Reach the end of the first steady climb. FR 1350 starts to roll more. From this old wagon trail, once used in the 1840s to transport pig iron to Elizabeth Furnace, you can see across Fort Valley to the eastern ridge of Massanutten Mountain. Fall colors are brilliant along this route.

2.6 Begin the fun descent toward Mudhole Gap and Little Passage Creek.

3.3 FR 1350 ends in what resembles a large dirt cul-de-sac overgrown with small pines and scrub. At the opposite end of this open area is a trail leading straight into the woods. Take this short, rocky trail downhill to Little Passage Creek.

3.35 Bear right along the creek, traveling upstream through Mudhole Gap. Stay on the trail that runs parallel with Little Passage Creek. There are five stream crossings along this trail between here and FR 66.

3.6 First stream crossing.

3.65 Second stream crossing.

3.8 Third stream crossing.

3.9 Fourth stream crossing.

4.1 Fifth stream crossing. Go around the gate after this last stream crossing, then turn right on FR 66 (orange blaze). This dirt road heads north toward Strasburg Reservoir and Signal Knob.

6.1 Pass a trailhead for a trail traveling to Signal Knob on the left. Both FR 66 and this wet, slightly overgrown trail lead to Strasburg Reservoir and meet again on the west bank of the lake.

6.3 Following FR 66, reach the Strasburg Reservoir. Turn left and cross the dam.

6.4 Once on the other side of the dam, bear right with the shoreline. Go another 20 yards along the western shoreline until the trail next to the reservoir appears to end at an embankment. Hop over a large rock, push the bike up the embankment, and discover yourself on the Massanutten Mountain West Trail (orange blaze).

7.0 Pass Bear Wallow Trail (blue blaze) on the right. From this point up to Signal Knob, things get pretty steep and difficult.

8.1 The trail goes vertical! It becomes little more than a rock slide, scaling up to the top of the mountain toward Signal Knob. If you can, push yourself to get to the top. Signal Knob is well worth this extra effort.

8.3 Reach Signal Knob (2,106 feet). Whew! Catch a sweeping view of the Shenandoah Valley. The town of Strasburg is on the left. Return back down the Massanutten Mountain West Trail toward Bear Wallow Trail. **(Option:** For an alternate route down from Signal Knob, follow Signal Knob Trail (yellow blaze) from the radio tower to Meneka Peak Trail (white blaze), which then cuts back over to Bear Wallow Trail (blue blaze) and heads back to the start. Beware of the Yellow Trail from top to bottom. This trail becomes mostly unridable, and shouldering your bike will get really old after all the riding you've already done.)

8.5 Steep, rocky section ends. Trail becomes a more negotiable singletrack.

9.6 Turn left on Bear Wallow Trail (blue blaze). Begin a grueling switchback climb to the top of Green Mountain.

10.3 Reach the top of Green Mountain. To the left is Meneka Peak Trail (white blaze). Start the descent back down to Elizabeth Furnace, continuing on Bear Wallow Trail (blue blaze).

10.7 Nice view of Fort Valley to the left.

12.1 Pass the Glass House Trail on the right. Continue straight on Bear Wallow Trail (blue blaze).

12.9 Reach the bottom of a wild descent at the intersection with the blue- and white-blazed trails. Turn right, following the white-blazed trail back to FR 1350. The blue-blazed trail travels left across a small creek to the Elizabeth Furnace picnic grounds.

13.1 Turn left on FR 1350, heading back to the car.

13.2 Go around the gate.

13.3 Arrive at the parking lot. Hope you survived the climb over Green Mountain.

Ride Information

Accommodations

Camping is available at the **Elizabeth Furnace Recreation Area.** Primitive camping is available in the surrounding George Washington National Forest.

27 Massanutten Mountain

Start: From the steel gate on Route 636 at Runkles Gap.

Length: 30 miles out and back.

Approximate riding time: 2 to 3 hours.

Difficulty rating: Physically moderate due to length and extended climbing. Technically easy as most of the route is on well-maintained gravel and dirt roads.

Trail surface: Rolling gravel forest roads.

Land status: National forest.

Nearest town: Harrisonburg.

Other trail users: Motorists (very few, if any).

Canine compatibility: Not good. This long gravel road may tear up a dog's pads.

Fees and permits: No fees or permits required.

Schedule: Public land; accessible year-round.

Maps: USGS maps: Elkton West, Tenth Legion; George Washington National Forest topo map: Lee Ranger District.

Trail contacts: Lee Ranger District, George Washington National Forest, (540) 984-4101; George Washington National Forest Headquarters, (703) 564-8300.

Getting There: From Harrisonburg: Take U.S. Route 33 east for 11 miles toward Massanutten Mountain. Just past the entrance for the resort area, turn left on Route 602 and go about 5 miles to Greenwood. At Greenwood, turn left on Cub Run Road (Route 636) and follow this 2 miles up Massanutten Mountain into George Washington National Forest. Start at the national forest boundary, where the road changes to gravel. *DeLorme: Virginia Atlas & Gazetteer:* Page 67, A-6.

The Ride

Massanutten is probably best known for its four-seasons resort, eighteen-hole PGA golf course, and sixty-eight acres of downhill skiing. Nonetheless, this private resort area, located fifteen minutes east of Harrisonburg, encompasses only the southern tip of this unique mountain that stretches along the Shenandoah Valley from Harrisonburg all the way north to Front Royal. The remaining land on Massanutten Mountain is contained within the boundaries of the George Washington National Forest and is full of great public land on which to explore. More than 90 percent of the mountain is open to mountain bikers, although much of the ridable terrain is along old forest roads and wide doubletrack. While it may not be the downhiller's mountain of choice or the extreme singletrack destination (very little extreme terrain is available unless you go north to Elizabeth Furnace or can somehow pedal along the singletrack at Massanutten Resort), it is nonetheless a great place for extended overnight trips and long, leisurely off-road rambles.

Much of your ride will be along Cub Run and Pitt Spring Run.

Massanutten Mountain is part of the 182,000-acre Lee Ranger District of the George Washington National Forest. The mountain covers roughly one-third of that land and stands apart from the rest of the national forest in the center of the Shenandoah Valley. Bordering Massanutten on the east are Shenandoah National Park and the Blue Ridge Mountains; to the west lie the Allegheny Mountains. Massanutten's lonely place within the Shenandoah Valley, its proximity to Harrisonburg, and its unique plow-headed shape make it a landmark for all who travel through Virginia's heartland.

In the late 1800s and early 1900s, much of Massanutten Mountain was mined for iron ore. During that time, most of the mountain's southern half was stripped bare of its trees. Later, during the mountain's recovery, a forestry official declared that he could not find a single tree more than 6 inches in diameter.

Since that time, the mountain has managed to recover quite handsomely, with thick forests now covering its craggy slopes. The legacy left by the mining operations is a myriad of old dirt roads and trails used to transport iron ore and supplies to the many different iron furnaces, including Catherine Furnace and Elizabeth Furnace. These roads and trails are now owned and maintained by the National Forest Service for public use.

This relatively nontechnical ride starts from the southern end of Massanutten Mountain near Harrisonburg and travels north through its core, revealing the

MASSANUTTEN FOUR-SEASONS RESORT

Cyclists on the southern edge of Massanutten Mountain looking for more of a challenge should consider Massanutten Four-Seasons Resort, which opens the property on its western slope during certain times of the year for off-road cyclists. Guests and residents of the resort are welcome to ride here year-round. Call the resort for more information about mountain biking on the property and ask for a schedule of events and a detailed map of the western slope trail system. Massanutten has recently held such prestigious events as the Grundig/World Cup Downhill Race and various amateur cross-country mountain bike races. Contact (800) 207–MASS or www.massresort.com.

mountain's scenic beauty from a well-maintained gravel road. The route starts from the national forest boundary on paved Route 636. The road then becomes gravel and hard-packed dirt.

You begin with a moderate climb up the mountain through Runkles Gap. The route rolls up and down along Cub Run Road for approximately 1 mile before descending into the mountain's inner valley along the cascading Cub Run. Just before mile 9, Cub Run intersects with Pitt Spring Run and Roaring Run, both of which turn east and rush downhill before running into the Shenandoah River's south fork. Turn left at this intersection and follow Forest Road 375 uphill along the beautiful Pitt Spring Run (toward the radio tower).

The climb is a workout, but the scenic waterfalls and mountain cliffs provide a wonderful distraction along this route. Don't expect much of an overlook once you reach the radio tower. The trees are pretty thick, and you'll have to hike around to find the best view. However, if you do get a good glimpse through the trees, you can see to the west over the great Shenandoah Valley and the town of Timberville. To the east, Page Valley and the South Fork Shenandoah River are also visible.

The technical difficulty of this ride is fairly minimal. For cyclists wanting a peaceful ride, far removed from the motorized world, though, this is just the place

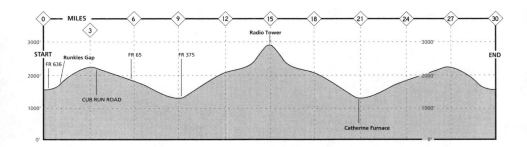

for a quiet and scenic afternoon. To further augment this leisurely ride, bring a lunch and relax along the cascades of Cub Run at one of the many small picnic areas or parking areas along the way.

Miles and Directions

0.0 START along Route 636 at the George Washington National Forest boundary. Park your car on the side of the road and head up the east side of Massanutten Mountain on Cub Run Road (Route 636).

0.1 Go through the gate. Cub Run Road turns to gravel and becomes Forest Road 65.

0.8 Pass through Runkles Gap.

2.3 Reach the top of the first climb (2,152 feet).

7.7 Pass a campground on the right.

9.2 Reach the intersection of Cub Run Road and Forest Road 375. Turn left on FR 375. **(Note:** Go straight for 0.25 mile to reach Catherine Furnace. This is one of the old iron furnaces used in the late 1800s to convert iron ore mined on Massanutten Mountain into usable plate iron.)

14.5 Reach the gate just before the radio towers. Go around this gate and continue up the mountain to the summit.

15.0 Reach the summit of Big Mountain (one of the peaks of Massanutten Mountain) at 2,962 feet. From this high point, you can peek through the trees and see parts of the Shenandoah Valley to the west and Page Valley to the east. The radio tower is owned and operated by WSVA-TV. From the summit, turn around, enjoy the descent to Catherine Furnace, and return to the start of the ride the same way you came.

Ride Information

Local Events and Attractions

Massanutten Four-Seasons Resort, (800) 207-MASS; www.massresort.com.

Bill's Barbecue is located on U.S. Route 33 just before the turn up Route 644 toward Massanutten Resort. Great barbecue!

28 Second Mountain

Start: From the intersection of trails on Forest Road 72, 6 miles uphill from Route 612.
Length: 6.6 miles point to point.
Approximate riding time: 1.5 hours, depending on your level of adventure for the day.
Difficulty rating: Moderate. The trails are wide due to use by four-wheel-drive vehicles and are very rocky.
Trail surface: There are several roller-coaster sections with terrific downhills.
Land status: National forest.
Nearest town: Rawley Springs.
Other trail users: Off-road vehicles (ORVs).
Canine compatibility: Dog friendly.
Fees and permits: No fees or permits required.
Schedule: Open year-round, weather permitting, but best from April through November.
Maps: USGS map: Rawley Springs.
Trail contacts: George Washington National Forest, Roanoke, VA, (540) 564-8300.

Getting There: From Harrisonburg: Drive U.S. Route 33 west toward Rawley Springs. Before Rawley Springs, turn right onto Route 612. Continue on Route 612 until you see a national park sign on the left for ORV access. Turn left onto Forest Road 72. Make sure your vehicle has adequate ground clearance to make this 6-mile climb to the trail intersection. *DeLorme: Virginia Atlas & Gazetteer:* Page 72, D-3.

The Ride

Second Mountain is a mecca for riders from the Harrisonburg area. Even though the grounds are shared with many motorcyclists and four-wheel-drive (4WD) enthusiasts, there is an ample amount of acreage to go around. Many of the trails are not as popular with motorized traffic, so these trails can be explored with great vigor. The roller-coaster theme weighs heavy, and the extent of damage is fairly minimal. These trails were transformed from their original function as fire roads into recreational access roads. This gives all-terrain-vehicle enthusiasts a chance to get on the trails but also limits their trail usage.

Make sure you have a vehicle with good ground clearance if you choose to drive the six-mile climb to the trail intersection where this ride begins. Also, make sure you pack plenty of water, because you'll be in a really remote area. Camping at the top can be rewarding if you've got a clear night and can take in the stars. The elevation affords spectacular views of the surrounding George Washington National Park.

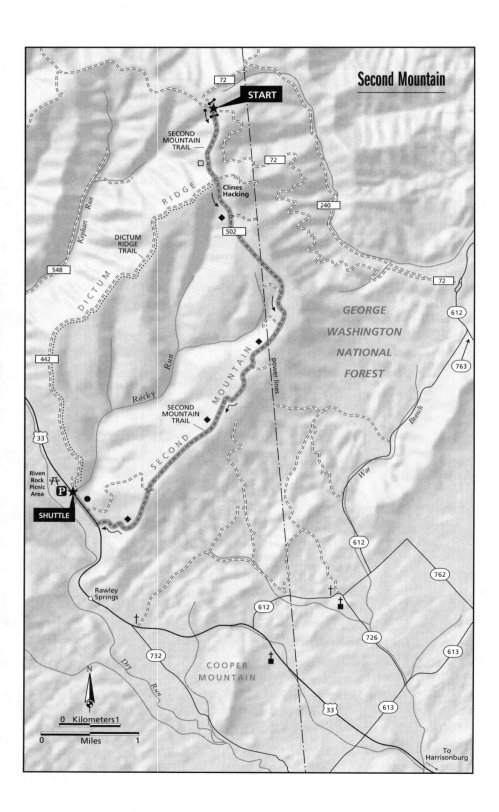

Second Mountain

START

SECOND
MOUNTAIN
TRAIL

Clines
Hacking

RIDGE

DICTUM
RIDGE
TRAIL

DICTUM

Kephart Run

72

72

240

502

548

442

33

Rocky   Run

SECOND
MOUNTAIN
TRAIL

SECOND   MOUNTAIN

power lines

GEORGE

WASHINGTON

NATIONAL

FOREST

612

763

72

War   Branch

Riven
Rock
Picnic
Area

P

SHUTTLE

612

612

762

726

613

Rawley
Springs

732

Dry   Run

COOPER
MOUNTAIN

33

613

N

0 Kilometers 1

0   Miles   1

To
Harrisonburg

When you arrive at the base of Forest Road 72, which takes you to the top, there will be a large brown sign with Smokey the Bear on it. From there, it's 6 miles to the top. Along the way you can experiment with any of the side roads. Most likely smaller motorized vehicles will occupy them. FR 72 is surprisingly smooth, but runoff has caused a few deep ruts that may not be cleared by low-profile vehicles. But if you can make it, it's a spectacular ride to the top. There's a mixture of exposed rock that consists of loose shale, limestone, and granite. Most of the switchbacks have steep inclines of worn rock that have obviously been scaled by trucks. Be careful while making your way around each bend, because you could unexpectedly meet one of these trucks.

The intersection of trails at the top are marked clearly with small, vertical brown signs that identify the trail names. As you venture onto the Second Mountain Trail, you'll notice a maintained gravel parking area for vehicles with trailers. This area has a directional sign and points of reference. This is where Forest Road 442 (Dictum Ridge) joins with U.S. Route 33.

Large granite boulders challenge your technical ability as you pass the power lines. The fine, sandy powder that coats most of the flat-rock sections can be very slippery. This rock exposure supplies an element of smoothness that keeps you on your toes. When passing through the roller-coaster-like sections, be observant of your speed. The excitement may tempt you to jump, but you can be sure that the other side hides a dangerous boulder or two. If you cling to either side of the trail, the passage should be much smoother.

Returning to the trailhead, you have the option of going into the Gauley Ridge Valley or riding north on FR 72 until you reach Feedstone Mountain. Even tooling around the parking area is enough to keep anyone occupied until the cows come home.

Harrisonburg is part of the Shenandoah Driving Tour and should be considered as a stop by those who are a long distance from home. Named after Thomas Harrison and established in 1780, Harrisonburg is home to James Madison University and Eastern Mennonite College and Seminary. There are many choices for nightly entertainment in the area, and many of the hot spots host live bands and a wide range of frothy refreshments.

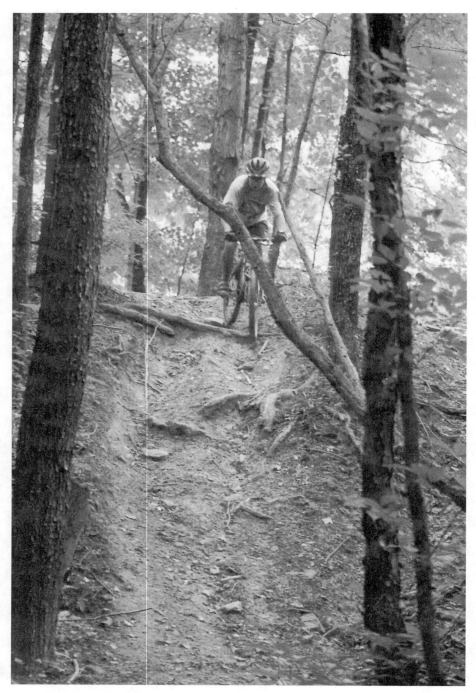

These ORV trails make mountain biking here on Second Mountain a real challenge. But it's a blast!

Miles and Directions

0.0 START by riding south on Second Mountain Trail (Forest Road 502). Go past the gate and climb an immediate but slight uphill section.

0.4 This area is full of technical sections of rolling uphills and downhills.

0.8 Come to a gravel parking lot for trucks with ORV trailers and a trail intersection called Clines Hacking. Continue straight on Second Mountain Trail. The spur on the right is Dictum Ridge Trail (FR 442).

1.5 Continue straight past the spur on the left.

2.1 Cross under power lines.

2.2 Continue straight past the spur on the right.

2.3 Continue straight past the spur on the right.

3.2 Cross under power lines again.

3.3 Continue straight past the spur on the left.

6.0 Reach the trail's end at U.S. Route 33. Take a right onto U.S. Route 33 to reach your shuttle vehicle. Be cautious of traffic.

6.6 Reach the parking lot and your vehicle.

(Loop Option: Instead of ending the ride at the Riven Rock picnic area, follow the signs and take a right off U.S. Route 33 onto Dictum Ridge Trail. Dictum Ridge Trail is a rutted, rocky, and reasonably steep forest road that leads back up to Clines Hacking. From Clines Hacking, it is less than a mile to the start of the ride.)

(Alternate Start: For those who don't have 4WD, here is a loop option. Park and start your ride from the Riven Rock picnic area off U.S. Route 33. You then have a choice of how to do the loop. Either start up the Dictum Ridge Trail and then fly down the Second Mountain Trail or do the opposite.)

Ride Information

Local Information

Harrisonburg-Rockingham Convention & Visitors Bureau, Harrisonburg, VA; (540) 433-2293.

Local Events and Attractions

Court Square Theater, Harrisonburg, VA; (540) 433-9188.

James Madison University, Harrisonburg, VA; (540) 568-6211; www.jmu.edu.

Eastern Mennonite University, Harrisonburg, VA; (540) 432-4159; www.emu.edu.

Accommodations

Boxwood Bed and Breakfast, Hinton, VA; (540) 867-5772.

29 Blueberry Trail

Start: From the signed trailhead on Route 742, west of Harrisonburg.
Length: 4.2-mile loop.
Approximate riding time: 1 hour.
Difficulty rating: Moderate. The few technical uphill sections are overshadowed by the superior downhill to the finish.
Trail surface: Relatively smooth, with technical uphills and a fast descent over water bars.
Land status: National forest.

Nearest town: Ottobine.
Other trail users: Hikers.
Canine compatibility: Dog friendly.
Fees and permits: No fees or permits required.
Schedule: Open year-round, weather permitting, but best from April through November.
Maps: USGS map: Briery Branch.
Trail contacts: George Washington National Forest, Roanoke, VA, (540) 564–8300.

Getting There: From Harrisonburg: Follow Route 42/Route 257 west toward Ottobine. At the intersection of Route 257 and Route 613, continue straight onto Route 742. This eventually turns into Route 933. Follow Route 933, a gravel road, past the dam on the left until you reach the sign on the left that reads BLUEBERRY TRAIL. Once you are inside the George Washington National Forest, Route 933 becomes Forest Road 225. *DeLorme: Virginia Atlas & Gazetteer:* Page 66, A-2.

The Ride

Expect to encounter wildlife at some point along this ride. The porous soil and rock foundation provide ideal conditions for blueberry growth. And where there are berries, you'll find wildlife. Many black bears are tagged and monitored in this region, so springtime riders should use extra caution when traversing past the blueberries. If you think you saw a bear, you probably did. Even though bear sightings are rare, you can never be too careful.

This is also a popular trek for Harrisonburg locals. Visitors are attracted to its accessibility and relatively short track. Make sure to take a rest at the plateau above Mud Pond Gap, because the 1.6-mile downhill will toss you if you're sleeping. There are many houses along the road, so make sure you are within legal limits. Multiple trails will provide ample entertainment.

The light sand color of the rocks is due to wear by vehicles and exposure to rain and altitude. The rainfall in this area is above average, so erosion can be extreme in some places. Most of the sloped sections have water bars that stand about 3 feet high

Blueberry Trail serves as a training ground for local cyclists.

by 3 feet wide. They provide speed control for larger vehicles and mountain bikes as well. The temptation to jump the bumps is high. However, the terrain on the back side can be treacherous and requires prior assessment.

Starting at the trailhead, the gradual climb takes you through groves of wild blueberries that grow in shrub form about 2 feet off the ground. In the spring, Mud Pond provides a delightful spot to eat some berries and take a break. Make sure to bring some "bug juice" because the pond hosts many insects during warmer seasons. Rattlesnakes especially like this area. The unique combination of small brush, granite terrain, and a water source creates the natural habitat for the rattler.

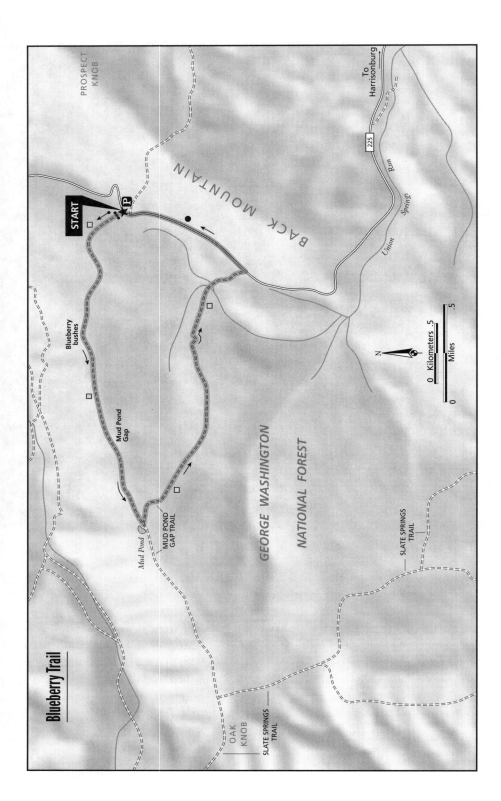

Blueberry Trail

START

P

PROSPECT KNOB

BACK MOUNTAIN

Blueberry bushes

Mud Pond Gap

Mud Pond

MUD POND GAP TRAIL

GEORGE WASHINGTON

NATIONAL FOREST

SLATE SPRINGS TRAIL

OAK KNOB

SLATE SPRINGS TRAIL

Union Springs Run

225

To Harrisonburg

N

0   Kilometers   .5

0   Miles   .5

When you reach the plateau and trail intersection at mile 2.4, you have the option of continuing uphill to Oak Knob or taking the dramatic downhill adventure back to FR 225. If you choose to continue on to Oak Knob, you are presented with a number of options, all of which will surely take up the remaining amount of daylight available to you. Find Oak Knob on the eastern portion of the ride map for Flagpole (Ride 31) to see all the other trails that connect there.

Most of the ride will cover terrain that requires middle gears. Clipless pedals are a bonus because the upward crank motion allows you to get through some of the technical and rocky uphill sections. Don't be discouraged by the uphill sections. The flatter sections will allow for your recovery. The trail began as a fire road and is still used for that purpose, but it seconds as a training ground for local cycling enthusiasts.

Try your hand at the numerous joining trails to Mud Pond and Blueberry Trail. When you visit the area, make sure to join some of the group rides that are offered through the local bike shops. The other cyclists are sure to add some local history to your adventure and technical advice about your riding.

Miles and Directions

0.0 START at the Blueberry Trail gate and sign, located across the road from a limited parking area. A smooth section just before a gradual uphill will start off your ride.

0.2 The first switchback goes left.

0.4 A right switchback points you toward a steeper uphill.

1.1 The gradual incline continues through sections of blueberry bushes.

1.6 This is where you reach Mud Pond Gap.

2.4 The trail makes a Y. Ride directly left on Mud Pond Gap Trail to start the downhill back to FR 225.

3.4 A flat traverse allows you to pedal for speed.

3.5 An extremely short and steep section of trail hides a slick rock face that should be taken with caution.

3.9 A large, wide creek crossing is sure to get your feet wet.

4.0 A white gate with candy-cane reflectors marks the road intersection. At the Y intersection, ride left and uphill onto FR 225.

4.2 Arrive back at your car.

Ride Information

Local Information
Harrisonburg-Rockingham County Visitors Center, Harrisonburg, VA; (540) 434-2319.

Accommodations
The Village Inn, Harrisonburg, VA; (800) 736-7355.

30 Reddish Knob

Start: From Briery Branch Dam.
Length: 20.5-mile loop. This would be a very good shuttle ride as well.
Approximate riding time: 2.5 to 3 hours.
Difficulty rating: Most difficult if ridden to the top. Timber Ridge is both technically difficult and physically draining.
Trail surface: Mountainous singletrack, gravel forest roads, and pavement.
Land status: National forest.
Nearest town: Harrisonburg.
Other trail users: Hikers and hang gliders.

Canine compatibility: Bring a dog only if you're doing a shuttle.
Fees and permits: No fees or permits required.
Schedule: Open year-round, weather permitting, but best from April through November.
Maps: USGS maps: Briery Branch, Reddish Knob (Virginia and West Virginia); George Washington National Forest topo map: Lee Ranger District.
Trail contacts: Lee Ranger District, George Washington National Forest, (540) 984-4101; George Washington National Forest, Roanoke, VA, (540) 564-8300.

Getting There: From Harrisonburg: Take Route 42 south for 4.5 miles to Dayton. From Dayton, turn right on Route 257 heading west. Go about 6 miles and reach the small town of Ottobine. Bear left, continuing on Route 257. Go about 3 miles to Briery Branch and turn left on Route 731. In less than a quarter mile, turn right on Route 924 toward the mountains. Follow Route 924 about 5 miles into the George Washington National Forest to Briery Branch Dam on the left. Park here. *DeLorme: Virginia Atlas & Gazetteer:* Page 66, A-2.

The Ride

Many years ago, when I first came through here looking for good rides in the Harrisonburg area, one of the guys at a now-defunct bike shop called Cool Breeze Cyclery & Fitness raved on and on about a backwoods mountain bike adventure he took with some fellow cyclists into the George Washington National Forest just west of town. After more than eight hours of cycling virtually endless unexplored trails, he explained, they chose to end their epic adventure. The sheer magnitude of ridable terrain in the mountains and national forest land just west of Harrisonburg was just too much for one day. That was all I needed to hear. I pulled my bike from the roof rack, eyed the tall Allegheny Mountains to the west, and set out to explore this land of mystic mountain bike terrain. I was not disappointed.

Mountain laurel lines the smooth singletrack down California Ridge.

Augusta County was founded in 1736 and at its greatest size embraced land as far west as the Mississippi River. What is now West Virginia, Kentucky, Ohio, Indiana, Illinois, Michigan, Wisconsin, and much of western Pennsylvania was once part of Augusta County. So that frontier residents could more easily access America's court of law and system of justice, Virginia's Augusta County Court was placed in what is known today as Pittsburgh, Pennsylvania.

Although Augusta County no longer contains the land it once held more than two centuries ago, it remains Virginia's second-largest county and includes land from the Blue Ridge to the Allegheny Mountains and much of the Shenandoah Valley. With its thousands of acres of national forest land, it is no wonder such singletrack bounty exits within its boundaries.

My first mountain bike ride into Augusta County's backwoods took me skyward through the George Washington National Forest into the Allegheny Mountains of western Virginia. The ride began up an unforgiving paved climb to the famed Reddish Knob. As the second-highest peak in Augusta County, Reddish Knob measures in at nearly 4,400 feet above sea level, and the climb to the summit (albeit along a paved road to the top) is relentless. But the views this peak offers are nothing short of spectacular. Locals claim that on the clearest days it's possible to see into five states. So far, in all the times I've been back to this ride (one of my all-time favorites), I've been hard-pressed to see that far through summer haze or winter gray. But the 360-degree view from the top of Reddish Knob is certainly one of Virginia's greatest treasures.

The ride begins at the Briery Branch Dam along Route 924, west of Harrison-burg. The climb to Briery Branch Gap, a 4.4-mile stretch of pavement, never eases up. Plan a shuttle if you'd rather spend time tearing it up on endless descents than climbing the endless road up Route 924. For a shuttle, park one vehicle at the Briery Branch Dam, then hop in the next vehicle for a drive to the top of Reddish Knob (a paved parking lot is on top). The descent down Timber Ridge may take well over an hour. Going down California Ridge will take less time but is a smoother descent through mountain laurel and soft singletrack.

If you ride your bike to the top, though, be sure to notice the tombstone a little more than one-quarter mile from the summit of Route 924 marking the death of Samual Curry. His body was found December 23, 1922, on this very spot, and no explanation has ever been given. My guess is that he was trying to ride a bike up this climb and keeled over two-thirds of the way up.

Just beyond Curry's grave marker, the sight of which may deal a demoralizing blow to those of you brave enough to make this climb on a bike, you'll reach Briery Branch Gap. The road splits here. You'll need to bear a hard left, continuing up the paved road toward Reddish Knob. Forest Road 85 gives you the first break on this relentless mountain and reveals the height you've climbed. Views of the Shenandoah Valley to the east are breathtaking. At one point along FR 85, you will literally be riding along the Virginia/West Virginia state line. Pedaling on the left side of the road has you in Virginia; the right side of the road, West Virginia. A few more pedal strokes and you reach Reddish Knob (4,397 feet).

Views atop Reddish Knob are stunning. Getting there is another story.

Miles and Directions

0.0 START from the parking area next to Briery Branch Dam on Route 924 (paved).

0.1 Outdoor toilet on the left.

4.2 Pass Samual Curry's tombstone up the embankment on the left.

4.4 Reach the intersection at Briery Branch Gap. Turn hard left, continuing up the mountain on FR 85 (paved) toward Reddish Knob.

4.6 Cross over the county line into Augusta County.

5.5 Overlook on the left.

6.3 The road divides Virginia and West Virginia along this ridge. The ridge is only as wide as the road itself.

6.5 Bear left at the split in the road. Continue uphill toward Reddish Knob.

6.9 Reach the summit of Reddish Knob, clearly the top of the world in these parts. **(Alternate Start:** From the Reddish Knob parking area, head downhill to locate the trailhead on the right side of the road.)

7.1 Returning downhill from Reddish Knob, turn right on Timber Ridge Trail (yellow blaze). **(Note:** This trailhead is slightly hidden. Look for a yellow diamond marker on a wooden trail post. This trail starts out a bit sketchy, then crosses a small rock slide. Once past the rock slide, follow the power lines downhill to the trail split.)

7.4 Cross the rock slide. Vista overlooking Middle Ridge and Buck Mountain on the right.

7.6 Reach the trail split. There is a wooden trail sign pointing left to California Ridge Trail and right to Timber Ridge Trail. Turn right on Timber Ridge Trail (yellow blaze) and continue to follow the yellow diamonds toward Tillman Road (Forest Road 101). **(Alternate Route:** If you're not interested in the long, rugged descent down Timber Ridge, turn left here and follow California Ridge Trail directly back to Briery Branch Dam. California Ridge Trail has a smoother surface and easier terrain.)

10.0 Pass Wolf Ridge Trail on the left. Stay right, continuing on Timber Ridge Trail (yellow blaze) to Sandspring Mountain. Wolf Ridge Trail is 5 miles to Tillman Road (FR 101).

10.7 Reach Sandspring Mountain. Bear right at this split, continuing to follow Timber Ridge Trail (yellow blaze) to the bottom. Watch out for the steel bar across Timber Ridge Trail less than 20 yards from this split!

14.7 Reach the bottom of one of the best downhills on the planet! Turn left on Tillman Road (FR 101). This is a well-maintained gravel road, which is nearly all downhill to Route 924.

18.3 Turn left on Route 924 (paved). Head back to Briery Branch Dam. This uphill section is fairly moderate.

20.5 Reach Briery Branch Dam and the car.

Ride Information

Local Information

Harrisonburg-Rockingham Convention & Visitors Bureau, Harrisonburg, VA; (540) 433-2293.

Local Events and Attractions

Court Square Theater, Harrisonburg, VA; (540) 433-9188.

James Madison University, Harrisonburg, VA; (540) 568-6211; www.jmu.edu.

Eastern Mennonite University, Harrisonburg, VA; (540) 432-4159; www.emu.edu.

Accommodations

Boxwood Bed and Breakfast, Hinton, VA; (540) 867-5772.

The Village Inn, Harrisonburg, VA; (800) 736-7355.

31 Flagpole

Start: From Briery Branch Dam.

Length: 17.6-mile loop or shuttle.

Approximate riding time: 2.5 to 3 hours.

Difficulty rating: Most difficult if ridden to the top. Slate Springs Jeep Trail is an extremely fast and challenging descent that can last as long as an hour.

Trail surface: Mountainous singletrack, gravel forest roads, and pavement.

Land status: National forest.

Nearest town: Harrisonburg.

Other trail users: Hikers and equestrians.

Canine compatibility: Bring a dog only if you're doing a shuttle.

Fees and permits: No fees or permits required.

Schedule: Open year-round, weather permitting, but best from April through November.

Maps: USGS maps: Briery Branch, Brandywine (West Virginia and Virginia); George Washington National Forest topo map: Lee Ranger District.

Trail contacts: Lee Ranger District, George Washington National Forest, (540) 984–4101; George Washington National Forest, Roanoke, VA, (540) 564–8300.

Getting There: From Harrisonburg: Take Route 42 south for 4.5 miles to Dayton. From Dayton, turn right on Route 257 heading west. Go about 6 miles and reach the small town of Ottobine. Bear left, continuing on Route 257. Go about 3 miles to Briery Branch and turn left on Route 731. In less than a quarter mile, turn right on Route 924 toward the mountains. Follow Route 924 about 5 miles into the George Washington National Forest to Briery Branch Dam on the left. Park here. *DeLorme: Virginia Atlas & Gazetteer:* Page 66, A-2.

The Ride

This ride is one of the state's all-time greats. Its only drawback, perhaps, is the daunting 7.7 mile climb in the first 7.7 miles of the ride—not much of a warm-up. Of course, this can be avoided if you make it into a shuttle ride, leaving one car at Briery Branch Dam and taking another car up to the intersection at Briery Branch Gap. You can then start your ride much closer to the top and avoid the bulk of the brutal ascent up Route 924.

Otherwise, like the ride up to Reddish Knob, start from the parking area at Briery Branch Dam before climbing the relentless ascent up Route 924 to Briery Branch Gap. Once you reach the gap, rather than turning left toward Reddish Knob, continue straight, following the hard, rocky dirt road. This road quickly switches north along the top of the Shenandoah Mountain's ridgeline and travels parallel to

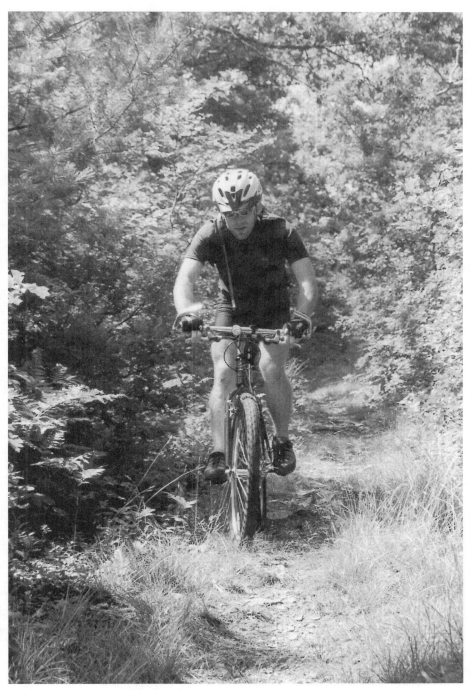

Carefully maneuvering down Slate Springs AA Jeep Trail.

Flagpole

WEST VIRGINIA

VIRGINIA

the Virginia/West Virginia border. You'll do another 3.3 miles of climbing before reaching Flagpole.

It hardly seems reasonable to spend the first 7.7 miles climbing. But like those long chairlift rides to the top of the nation's greatest downhill ski runs, you will reach the summit, take a deep breath, and launch yourself on an incredible journey to the bottom.

And what a journey this ride becomes! At mile 7.8, you'll need to bear right, off the main road through a hollow of trees, to reach the grassy mountaintop meadow called Flagpole. You may notice a pine tree on the edge of this meadow that is much taller than its neighbors. This wind-blown tree distinguishes itself because it can be seen from the roads below, resembling a flag on a flagpole blowing in the strong mountain gusts.

The view from Flagpole is spectacular, and on a clear day you can see east over the mountaintops into the Shenandoah Valley. Though the view is less dramatic than that from the summit of Reddish Knob, you will see the popular mountain peak not far to the south.

While enjoying the view from Flagpole, gather your wits and replenish your system. You'll need every ounce of courage and strength to negotiate what lies ahead. Just down the road is the orange-blazed Slate Springs trailhead and Slate Springs Trail, the path that will take you on a crazy downhill adventure to Hone Quarry Reservoir.

From Flagpole, get back on the dirt road and ride only one-tenth of a mile. Keep a sharp eye on the right side of the road for the bright orange diamond trail marker tacked to a tree. This marker is partially hidden, so if you pass a small camping area on the left and go sharply downhill on this main road, you've gone too far.

For nearly 7 long miles after turning onto Slate Springs AA Jeep Trail, you will descend, first along a twisting, narrow, off-camber goat trail of a singletrack that contours the mountain. Then you will descend, descend, and descend some more before being afforded a quick break as you pass a rocky little overlook. After this, the trail just drops, and down you go along a grassy path littered with out-of-control water bars that are more like moguls than trail maintenance. At this point, of course, your forearms are toast. If you're not careful, these larger-than-life water bars will throw you skyward. At last, just when your forearms are registering red, and your two-fingered brake levers now require both hands, the descent finally tapers off and follows the orange blazes across Hone Quarry Run. You then get a nice cruise along a fast dirt road back toward Route 924. Pass the Hone Quarry Reservoir, glide through a tunnel of tall pines, then coast up to the paved road (Route 924). Turn right on Route 924 and pedal back up to Briery Branch Dam and the start of the ride.

If you shuttled this one, get back in the car, grab your shuttle on top, and do it all over again.

Miles and Directions

0.0 START from the parking area next to Briery Branch Dam on Route 924 (paved).

0.1 Outdoor toilet on the left.

4.2 Pass Samual Curry's tombstone up the embankment on the left. Might this be a fore-shadowing of the day's ride?

4.4 Reach the intersection at Briery Branch Gap. Continue straight on the forest road, continuing to climb northeast toward Flagpole.

5.4 Pass Hone Quarry Ridge Trail on the right.

5.5 Nice view through a clearing in the trees on the right. A little trail on the right takes you to this view, then brings you back to the forest road.

7.7 Reach Flagpole! Bear right to get to the meadow. To continue this ride, get back on the forest road, heading northeast.

7.8 Just past Flagpole, from the forest road, turn right on Slate Springs AA Jeep Trail. This narrow singletrack clings to the edge of the ridge. Your brake pads will be smoking by the end of this descent. **(Note:** The trailhead for Slate Springs AA Jeep Trail is very hidden. Just before this trail, on the left, is a small clearing used for primitive camping. There is a stone campfire ring in the clearing. Past this campground, the dirt road drops downhill very dramatically. If you pass this primitive campground and begin a dramatic, rocky descent, you've gone too far. Look for a bright orange diamond trail marker stapled to a tree on the right, just below the forest road.)

8.7 Rock outcrop overlooking Hone Quarry Ridge. Stop and let your brakes cool. Prepare for a grassy, vertical descent.

10.4 Reach the bottom of the descent and bear to the right, continuing on the orange-blazed trail. Follow along Hone Quarry Creek downhill toward Hone Quarry Reservoir.

10.7 Slate Springs AA Jeep Trail ends at a dirt road. Turn left on this forest road. Note the metal multiuse trail post marking the trail you were just on.

11.1 Pass Hone Quarry Reservoir on the right.

14.9 Turn right on Route 924 (paved).

17.6 Reach Briery Branch Dam.

Ride Information

Local Information

Harrisonburg-Rockingham Convention & Visitors Bureau, Harrisonburg, VA; (540) 433-2293.

Local Events and Attractions

Court Square Theater, Harrisonburg, VA; (540) 433-9188.

James Madison University, Harrisonburg, VA; (540) 568-6211; www.jmu.edu.

Eastern Mennonite University, Harrisonburg, VA; (540) 432-4159; www.emu.edu.

Accommodations

Boxwood Bed and Breakfast, Hinton, VA; (540) 867-5772.

The Village Inn, Harrisonburg, VA; (800) 736-7355.

32 North Mountain Trail to Elliot Knob

Start: From the trailhead on Route 688, west of Staunton.
Length: 9.8-miles out and back.
Approximate riding time: 2.5 hours.
Difficulty rating: Mostly difficult. Many sections contain areas of loose rock.
Trail surface: The incline and flat sections are smooth and challenging. The sections toward the top become extremely rocky.
Land status: National forest.
Nearest town: Staunton.
Other trail users: Hikers.
Canine compatibility: Dog friendly.
Fees and permits: No fees or permits required.
Schedule: Open year-round, weather permitting, but best from April through November.
Maps: USGS map: Elliot Knob.
Trail contacts: Deerfield Ranger District, Staunton, VA, (540) 885–8028; George Washington National Forest, Roanoke, VA, (540) 564–8300.

Getting There: From Staunton: Follow Route 254 West. Bear left onto Route 42 South for 0.7 mile and then turn right onto Route 688 West in Buffalo Gap. Travel 4 miles until you reach the trailhead/intersection of North Mountain Trail and Crawford Mountain Trail. There is ample parking to the left in front of the white steel pole gate. *DeLorme: Virginia Atlas & Gazetteer:* Page 66, C-1.

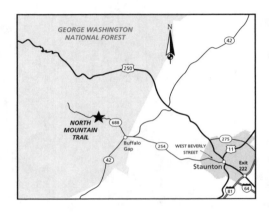

The Ride

In the 1730s, Scotch-Irish, Welsh, and German settlers began migrating down the Great Valley into western Virginia from Pennsylvania. The Augusta County area became a point of settlement for Scotch-Irish Presbyterians. In 1738, Augusta County was formed from Orange County and named after the wife of Frederick Louis, the Prince of Wales. Due to the county's small number of inhabitants, the local government did not convene until 1745. Today, a large portion of the county is protected within the George Washington National Forest and a small portion of the Shenandoah National Park, not to mention a few other state and national preserves.

The county saw a fair amount of action during the Civil War's valley campaigns. The ridges that frame the central valley provided cover and vantage for troops and ended up playing a key role in the war. On the way to North Mountain Trail, you'll see signs for Civil War attractions such as Fort Johnson, McDowell Battlefield, and Camp Allegheny. The hardwoods, pines, and rhododendrons along the trail create a scenic background by which to imagine the Civil War campaigns. Take the time to enjoy and engulf yourself in the history of this area.

CRAWFORD
MOUNTAIN
TRAIL

START

688

West Dry Branch

Dry Branch Gap

East Dry Branch

NORTH MOUNTAIN TRAIL
(ELLIOT KNOB TRAIL)

GEORGE WASHINGTON

Buffalo Spring

LEAD-OFF RIDGE

NATIONAL FOREST

688

Buffalo Gap

42

GREAT NORTH MOUNTAIN

Turnaround

ELLIOT KNOB
4,463 ft

HOGBACK

N

38

Little Calfpasture River

LITTLE NORTH MOUNTAIN

LITTLE

NORTH

MOUNTAIN

WILDLIFE

MANAGEMENT

AREA

Kings Gap

42

0 Kilometers 2

0 Miles 2

Visitors can stop at the Deerfield Ranger District office on Route 254 West, outside of Staunton, for advice and local maps of the Great North Mountain. The Deerfield office contains many animal specimens that have been recovered or donated to the Forest Service. The first one you'll see as you walk in is a barn owl with its wings reaching straight up. Some of the other exhibits include a baby deer, a screech owl, a hornet's nest, a falcon, and a big beaver.

The intersection of Crawford Mountain Trail and North Mountain Trail is the center of many mountain biking options. The trails that intersect this section of the North Mountain Trail are numerous and include Cold Springs Trail, Archer Run Road, Hite Hollow Road, and Ferris Hollow Trail. All of these trails extend southward as you ride past Elliot Knob. Consult a map and plan accordingly if you choose to go farther south or north on the North Mountain Trail. Riding north will eventually take you to the Ramsey's Draft Wilderness Area. Though off-limits to bikes, hikers will enjoy the virgin stands of hemlock trees—a rarity in Virginia. The distance from the start point of this ride to Ramsey's Draft is about 14 miles.

When you venture onto the Great North Mountain, make sure to pack some essential biking tools, including an extra tube and a pump. This trail is not for beginners, so don't be fooled. Physically, it can be downright exhausting. The trail starts on an old logging road and follows the Great North Mountain ridgeline to Elliot Knob. Plan to scramble over narrow paths and rugged terrain, attain high speeds on hair-raising descents, and climb stiff ascents to panoramic views. Riders not interested in taking this challenging ride can opt for another route that can be reached by staying on Route 42 (see Alternate Start in Miles and Directions).

Elliot Knob has many variations of flora and fauna. Hardwoods and spruce shade the hearty undergrowth of rhododendrons and young saplings. At 4,463 feet, the knob is one of the highest points in George Washington National Forest, and the views, especially of the Shenandoah Valley, are as glorious as you'd expect.

While in the Staunton area, take a drive along the Blue Ridge Parkway (no charge) or Skyline Drive (currently $10 for entry, but you can buy a $20 pass for the year). Staunton is very near to where these two scenic roads meet and extend south and north, respectively. Staunton was an important Confederate supply depot and railroad link. Make a stop at the historic train station, which was dubbed "the Breadbasket of the Confederacy." Thornrose Cemetery contains the graves of Confederate soldiers who defended Richmond from Union advances over the Shenandoah.

Miles and Directions

0.0   START at the parking area next to the gates (limited parking only). Facing west, take the trailhead that goes uphill to the left.

0.4   Reach the end of the first of many uphill climbs.

0.5   Begin the first downhill section, which contains many switchbacks.

0.6   A technical rocky section of singletrack and steep trail sloping to the right will take you uphill.

At 4,463 feet, Elliott Knob is the highest point in the George Washington National Forest.

1.1 There is a gradual switchback left.

1.7 Please use caution here. This is a very rocky and technical section.

1.8 The trail heading west leads to Buffalo Spring.

1.9 Come to a large section that contains a series of switchbacks and inclines.

2.1 Reach the third section of technical rocky singletrack. Keep in mind that this is mainly a hiking trail. Most of the terrain is not meant for fast bike traffic.

4.0 Reach the intersection of a closed forest road (FR 38) and Elliot Knob.

4.4 Veer left. A side road on the right leads to Elliot Knob, 730 feet away.

4.9 Turn right onto the road that leads to Elliot Knob. From here, there are spectacular views of the Shenandoah Valley and beyond. Turn around and return by the same route.

9.8 Reach the parking area and your vehicle. **(Alternate Start:** Continue driving past Buffalo Gap toward Chapin on Route 42 West. The right after FR 38 will be a direct uphill to Elliot Knob (4,463 feet). It is a direct ascent to the peak, but the journey back down is a little sweeter.)

Ride Information

Local Information

Augusta County Visitors Center, Staunton, VA; (800) 332-5219.
Rockfish Gap Regional Visitors Center, Waynesboro, VA; (800) 471-3109.

Local Events and Attractions

McDowell Battlefield, Monterey, VA; (540) 468-2550.

Accommodations

Inn at Keezletown Road Bed & Breakfast, Weyers Cave, VA; (800) 465-0100 or (540) 234-0644; www.bbhsv.org/keezlinn.

33 Williamsville Loop

Start: From the Bullpasture Gorge suspension bridge parking area.
Length: 7.3-mile loop.
Approximate riding time: 2 hours.
Difficulty rating: Moderate. The first mile is a technical uphill and the rest is downhill.
Trail surface: Rocky uphill and a smooth singletrack downhill.
Land status: National forest.
Nearest town: Flood.
Other trail users: Hunters, anglers, and spelunkers.
Canine compatibility: Dog friendly.
Fees and permits: No fees or permits required.
Schedule: Open year-round, weather permitting, but best from April through November.
Maps: USGS map: Williamsville.
Trail contacts: George Washington National Forest, Roanoke, VA, (540) 564-8300.

Getting There: From Staunton: Drive west on U.S. Route 250 toward McDowell for approximately 30 miles. Turn left onto Route 678 at McDowell. Follow Route 678 a little over 10 miles to the Virginia Department of Game and Inland Fisheries parking area on the left. This parking area is right near the Bullpasture Gorge suspension bridge and Bullpasture River. Park here for the start of your ride. *DeLorme: Virginia Atlas & Gazetteer:* Page 65, C-6.

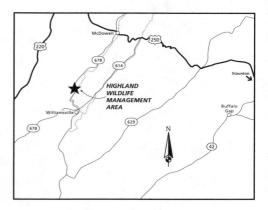

The Ride

The Hupman Valley Trail provides a challenging loop that ends at a beautiful bend in the Bullpasture Gorge. You'll likely find anglers catching trout here. Since hunters also enjoy the area, it's highly recommended that you not ride here during hunting season.

The ride starts from the parking lot and allows you a nice warm-up along the blacktop before you reach the Hupman Valley trailhead. From the Bullpasture Gorge suspension bridge, ride uphill on Route 678 until you pass through Williamsville. The spectacular view of the river will no doubt inspire you to continue on. Follow Route 614 east until the road turns to gravel. A green gate on the left marks the Hupman Valley trailhead. The trail begins with several switchbacks and rocky terrain. Keep a good line, and you can make it to the flatter sections, which allow you time to catch your breath and suck down some water. Try not to look west too much, because the view west of the Shenandoah Mountains could take your breath

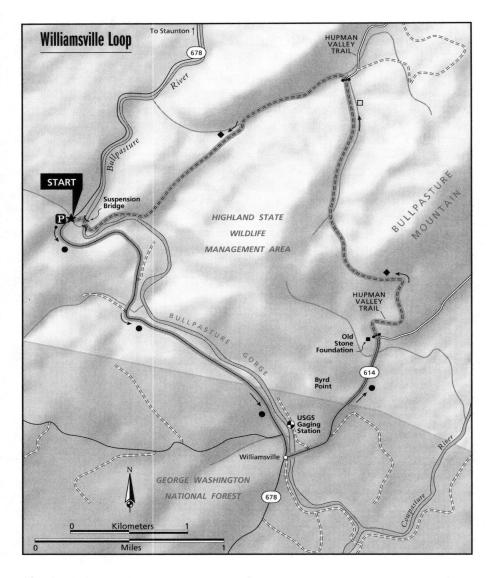

Williamsville Loop

To Staunton ↑

678

River

Bullpasture

HUPMAN VALLEY TRAIL

START

Suspension Bridge

P ★

HIGHLAND STATE

WILDLIFE

MANAGEMENT AREA

BULLPASTURE MOUNTAIN

HUPMAN VALLEY TRAIL

BULLPASTURE GORGE

Old Stone Foundation

614

Byrd Point

USGS Gaging Station

Williamsville

N

GEORGE WASHINGTON

NATIONAL FOREST

678

Cowpasture River

| 0 | Kilometers | 1 |
| 0 | Miles | 1 |

away. When you reach 2,420 feet, the ride becomes a roller coaster through hardwoods and high grasses. The singletrack is overgrown with marsh grasses and briars. Always use caution in this section because a hidden surface rock could do some damage to your tires—make sure you have a spare tube and pump.

The ride itself does not take that long, and the scenery is spectacular. This spot is very remote though. Make sure you have plenty of gas, because Williamsville doesn't have a gas station. The nearest stations are in McDowell and Flood.

The Bullpasture Gorge suspension bridge parking area is central to a number of recreational options. Camping is permitted free-of-charge in the parking area. The suspension bridge allows access to the trail, fishing, and a small cave. The bridge entrance can be found by walking up the rock slide, left of the trail as you leave the parking lot. Crossing the blacktop road from the parking lot will take you to the underground origin of the joining river. You'll find a beach inside the cave, if you can stand the chilly temperature of the water and hold your breath long enough. This area is quite popular with locals, so weekends can be crowded during the warmer months. Bullpasture Gorge is a very private and wonderful escape from the greater world.

The Bullpasture River is located in the heart of the Appalachian Mountains and runs for approximately 5 miles. The highest elevation on Bullpasture Mountain is 3,240 feet. The mountain provides many opportunities for caving. One of these cave openings is located uphill to the right as you reach the river. Local officials advise seeking professional guidance when caving if you've never done it before. Contact the George Washington National Forest office if you're interested, and they should be able to find you a professional guide.

West of McDowell, you'll find wonderful accommodations at the Ginseng Mountain Lodge. The Ginseng Country Store is sure to please with local arts and crafts such as woodworking, sheepskins, maple syrup, and regional folklore. While you're in the area, make sure to check out all the events in the Staunton region. If you have the time to drive, indulging in the Shenandoah Driving Tour along U.S. Route 11 is definitely the way to go. The tour starts as far north as Winchester. Picking up the tour in Staunton allows you to visit historic places such as the Woodrow Wilson Birthplace and Museum, the Statler Brothers Mini-Museum, and the Museum of American Frontier Culture. Of particular interest to cyclists is the annual Shenandoah Fall Foliage Bike Festival.

Miles and Directions

0.0   START from the Bullpasture Gorge suspension bridge parking area. Ride the blacktop Route 678 through Williamsville.

2.0 After passing through Williamsville, turn left onto Route 614 and cross the gorge. The road will turn from pavement to gravel in 0.5 mile.

3.0 Turn left through the first green gate, leading to Hupman Valley Trail. There is an old stone foundation in the woods to the left of the gate.

3.1 The first switchback left will be on a gradual slope.

3.4 The first switchback right swings you around to face the Shenandoah Mountains.

3.5 Your second switchback left heads back in an eastern direction.

3.9 This level section is rocky and places you within visible distance of the top.

4.1 The plateau of the trail is not the highest part. Either side of the trail can take you to a higher elevation by foot.

4.2 There is a large area of fallen hardwoods on the left.

5.1 A green gate marks the Y intersection of Hupman Valley Road. Continue straight ahead and not down the maintained gravel jeep road.

5.2 Begin the downhill toward Bullpasture Gorge.

5.8 This switchback right brings you within audible distance of Bullpasture Gorge.

5.9 The last switchback right leads you along the gorge and back to the parking area.

7.1 A large and very flexible suspension bridge takes you across the gorge to the parking area.

7.3 Arrive at the parking lot, a wonderful place to cool your feet or jump off the rope swing.

Ride Information

Local Information

Highland County Chamber of Commerce, Monterey, VA; (540) 468-2550.

Shenandoah Valley Visitor Center, New Market, VA; (540) 740-3132; www.svta.org.

Local Events and Attractions

Shenandoah Fall Foliage Bike Festival, Williamsville, VA; (757) 229-0507; www.bikevirginia.org.

Museum of American Frontier Culture, Staunton, VA; (540) 332-7850; www.frontiermuseum.org.

Statler Brothers Mini-Museum, Staunton, VA; (540) 885-7297.

Woodrow Wilson Birthplace and Museum, Staunton, VA; (540) 885-0897; www.woodrowwilson.org.

Accommodations

Mill Gap Ruritan Camp Ground, Monterey, VA; (540) 499-2435.

Ginseng Mountain Lodging, Highland County, VA; (540) 474-5137.

34 Ellis Loop Trail

Start: From the Dun's Gap Road parking area.
Length: 5.6-mile loop.
Approximate riding time: 1 hour.
Difficulty rating: Moderate. You'll need a moderate degree of technical bike-handling skills to bump your way through the sections of rocky, rolling singletrack and ATV ruts. The ride isn't very long, but there are a couple of steep rollers that will keep you huffing.
Trail surface: Dirt roads and singletrack.
Land status: National forest.
Nearest town: Hot Springs.
Other trail users: Hikers, equestrians, and ATVs.
Canine compatibility: Dog friendly.
Fees and permits: No fees or permits required.
Schedule: Public land; accessible year-round.
Maps: USGS map: Warm Springs; George Washington National Forest topo map: Warm Springs District.
Trail contacts: Warm Springs Ranger District, (540) 839-2521; George Washington National Forest Headquarters, (540) 564-8300.

Getting There: From Hot Springs: Take U.S. Route 220 north for approximately 1.5 miles. Just before Mitchelltown, turn left on Route 618. Follow this uphill for nearly 2 miles to the gate. The pavement ends here. Bear left, continuing on Dun's Gap Road (Route 618). This is now a dirt road. Follow Dun's Gap Road a little more than 2 miles along Cowardin Run. There's a small gravel parking area on the left. Park here. The ride starts on the right side of Dun's Gap Road, across from the parking area. *DeLorme: Virginia Atlas & Gazetteer:* Page 64, D-4.

The Ride

In this land of bubbling high-mountain spas, where hot springs well up from the earth at an average temperature of 104 degrees, where diplomats, presidents, world travelers, and tired Virginians come to rejuvenate their weary bodies, and where the luxurious Homestead Resort has resided for more than two centuries, a new kind of recreation has taken shape. Near Hot Springs, Virginia, in the hills of the Allegheny Mountains, lie hundreds of miles of open mountain biking trails.

Mountain bikers throughout the region are making tracks to the Warm Springs Valley of Virginia's western slopes. They come to explore the off-road avenues of picturesque hillsides and pleasant hidden valleys, test their wits on rugged single-track, or pedal slowly through mountain-rimmed meadows. Then, after trekking exhaustively through the backcountry, these active vacationers can visit one of the area's many hot mineral spas and "take the cure," soaking their tired bodies in natu-rally heated springs. Does it get any better than this? Well, sure, if you never leave.

There are plenty of places to stay in the Warm Springs Valley. The region has several campgrounds, and primitive camping in the George Washington National Forest is virtually limitless. But why bother sleeping under the stars after a long ride when you can stay where the stars sleep? The Homestead, Virginia's five-star mountain resort, pulls out all the stops for weary travelers and makes a visit to the Warm Springs Valley a world-class event. For cyclists staying at the resort, The Homestead now offers off-road guided tours and rents bikes from the ski lodge.

As for the ride itself, this exciting 5-mile loop is close enough to Hot Springs that cyclists interested in a nice little pre-ride warm-up can pedal from The Homestead to the ride's start (less than 4 miles). Get on U.S. Route 220 and head north toward Mitchelltown. After a little over 1 mile, bear left up a narrow paved road (the only left turn before Mitchelltown). This is Route 618 (Dun's Gap Road). Follow Route 618 uphill for nearly 2 miles to a gate where the road turns left and changes to dirt. Follow this a little more than 2 miles along Cowardin Run to the start of the ride. Parking is available if you choose to drive.

Ellis Loop Trail starts at a small gravel parking area on Route 618. From here, turn right on Route 618, traveling less than 20 yards, then turn hard left through a gate and ride uphill on an old jeep road. Be sure to look up at the top of this climb to see the view of Warm Springs Mountain. The jeep road winds through a little valley along mostly flat terrain until a swift descent carries you down toward Jerry Run. Be sure to keep your eyes peeled for a black wooden arrow that points left into the woods (the trailhead for Ellis Trail). You've gone too far if you cross a creek along the jeep road. Once you locate the trailhead, notice that Ellis Trail is marked with large red wooden arrows all the way back to Dun's Gap Road.

Because Ellis Trail is a multiple-use trail, you will probably notice lots of horse tracks and possibly some ATV tracks. Chances are, though, you will be alone in this secluded wilderness as you roll along the often challenging trail. Just before Ellis Trail ends, there is one last steep climb before a very fast descent to the road. Be careful on this descent; there's a gate at the bottom that's usually closed, which may catch you off-guard.

Turn left on Dun's Gap Road and head back along Cowardin Run toward the start of the ride. The soothing sounds of Cowardin Run's cascading water may remind you of the hot mineral baths awaiting you back at the resort.

Miles and Directions

0.0 START at the parking area on Dun's Gap Road (Route 618). Turn right on Dun's Gap Road.

0.05 Turn hard left through the gate on the dirt jeep road. This dirt road carries you uphill for a spectacular view of the area.

0.3 Reach the top of this climb.

1.0 Great view to the left of the distant mountains. This is a very leisurely, scenic road through this valley.

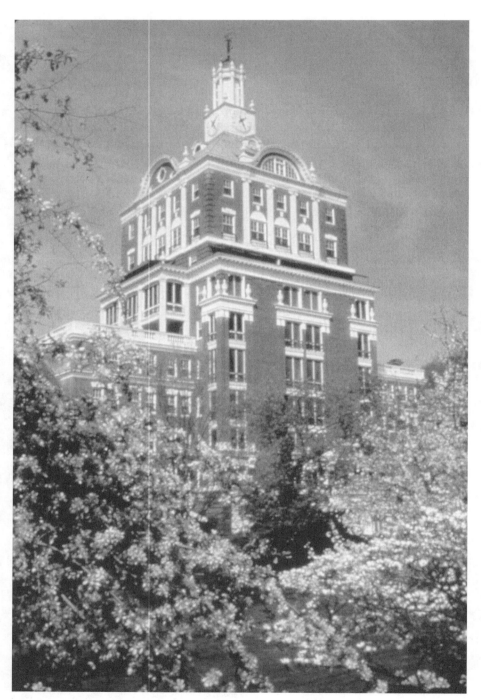

The Homestead, Virginia's five-star resort.

2.1 Reach the bottom of a fun descent. Turn left on Ellis Trail. **(Note:** Ellis Trail is marked with a black wooden arrow nailed to a tree and marked "#20." This arrow points into the woods. Once in the woods, Ellis Trail is marked with large red wooden arrows.) If you cross the stream at the bottom of this descent, then you've missed Ellis Trail. Turn around and hunt for these arrows.

2.7 Lake Bacova is visible through the trees on the right.

4.9 Go down a very steep descent and through a gate, then turn left on Dun's Gap Road. Follow Dun's Gap Road upstream along Cowardin Run to the parking area.

5.6 Reach the parking area.

Ride Information

Local Information

Bath County Chamber of Commerce and the Forest Place Visitor Center, (800) 628-8092 or (540) 839-5281.

Local Events and Attractions

The charming town of **Warm Springs** has a museum called Gristmill Square, restaurants, shopping, and the famous Warm Springs Pools, complete with separate nineteenth-century bathhouses for men and women.

Accommodations

In Warm Springs:
Anderson Cottage B&B, (540) 839-2975.
Meadow Lane Lodge, (540) 839-5959.

In Hot Springs:
The Homestead (shuttle service available to Roanoke Airport or to the Clifton Forge Amtrak station for registered guests), (800) 838-1766 or (540) 839-1766; www.thehomestead.com.
King's Victorian Inn, (540) 839-3134; inngetaways.com/va/kingsvic.html.

In Addition

Bicycle Camping

If you consider your mountain bike saddle the most comfortable seat in the house and crave an opportunity to prove your self-sufficiency, try bicycle camping. It does require more planning and preparation than a standard day trip, but the particular satisfaction gained from reaching a campground or a remote outdoor destination on two wheels, knowing you're ready for a cozy night outdoors, makes the extra effort worthwhile.

If you plan on doing a lot of bicycle camping and touring, it's a good idea to invest in quality equipment. Everyone should have a pair of sizable panniers that can be mounted on a rear rack (if you are planning a long trip, you might also consider a front rack). A lightweight backpacking tent, sleeping pad, and sleeping bag can be attached to the rear rack using two or three bungie cords. We all have a tendency to overpack, and the extra weight of unnecessary equipment may cause you to tire more easily. Here are some tips to help you find the appropriate amount of gear:

- Bring a multipurpose tool that includes a can opener, bottle opener, scissors, knife, and screwdriver.
- Pack only one extra change of clothes, plus any necessary layers such as a polypropylene shirt and tights, polar fleece, wool socks, and rain gear. If you are on a multi-day trip, bring extra shorts and T-shirts. If it's winter, bring an extra pair of polypropylene tights and a shirt, as well as a few extra pairs of wool socks.
- Bring a tin cup and spoon for eating and drinking and one lightweight pot for cooking.
- Invest in a lightweight backpacking stove, tent, and sleeping bag.
- Bring along freeze-dried food. You can buy many prepackaged rice and noodle mixes in the grocery store for half of what you'll pay at backpacking stores.
- Bring the minimum amount of water needed for your intended route. Find out if there will be water available. Invest in a water filter that can be used to filter water from sources along the trail.

Equipment List

Use the checklist of equipment below when you are planning for a single or multi-day trip. You can develop your own equipment list based on the length of your trip, the time of year, weather conditions, and difficulty of the trail.

Essentials
bungie cords
compass
day panniers
duct tape
fenders
pocket knife or multipurpose tool
rear rack
front rack
trail map
water bottles
water filter
tool kit
patch kit
crescent wrench
tire levers
spoke wrench
extra spokes
chain rivet tool
extra tube
tire pump

Clothing
rain jacket/pants
polar fleece jacket
wool sweater
helmet liner
bicycle tights
T-shirts/shorts
sturdy bicycle shoes/boots
swimsuit
underwear
bike gloves
eye protection
bike helmet/liner

First-Aid Kit
bandages (various sizes)
gauze pads
surgical tape
antibiotic ointment
hydrogen peroxide or iodine

gauze roll
ace bandage
aspirin
moleskin
sunscreen
insect repellent

Personal Items
towel
toothbrush/toothpaste
soap
comb
shampoo

Camping Items
backpacking stove
tent
sleeping bag
foam pad
cooking and eating utensils
can opener
flashlight/batteries
candle lantern
touring panniers
pannier rain covers
zipper-lock bags
large, heavy-duty plastic garbage bags
citronella candles (to repel insects)
small duffels to organize gear

Miscellaneous Items
camera/film/batteries
notebook/pen
paperback book

Tip:
Zipper-lock bags are a great way to waterproof and organize your gear. Large, heavy-duty plastic garbage bags also make excellent waterproof liners for the inside of your panniers.

35 Hidden Valley

Start: Past campgrounds on Forest Road 241.
Length: 11-mile loop.
Approximate riding time: 1.5 to 2 hours.
Difficulty rating: Moderate.
Trail surface: Jeep trails, singletrack, and dirt roads.
Land status: National forest.
Nearest town: Warm Springs.
Other trail users: Hikers, equestrians, and ATVs.
Canine compatibility: Dog friendly, but make sure he can swim.

Fees and permits: No fees or permits required.
Schedule: Public land; accessible year-round.
Maps: USGS maps: Warm Springs, Sunrise (Virginia and West Virginia); George Washington National Forest topo map: Warm Springs District.
Trail contacts: Warm Springs Ranger District, (540) 839-2521; George Washington National Forest Headquarters, (540) 564-8300.

Getting There: From Hot Springs: Take U.S. Route 220 north about 15 miles to Warm Springs and turn left on Route 39 West. Follow Route 39 West about 10 miles and turn right on Route 621 to the Hidden Valley Campground. Route 621 splits in 3 miles. Bear left, following FR 241. Pass Hidden Valley Campground in 5 miles. FR 241 turns to dirt. Go another 1.5 miles past the campground until it dead-ends at the cul-de-sac. There is a portable toilet here. The trail starts at the steel gate on the right. *DeLorme: Virginia Atlas & Gazetteer:* Page 64, D-4.

The Ride

Deep in the Allegheny Mountains of western Virginia is a quiet little place called Hidden Valley. This peaceful hollow is situated just west of Warm Springs, cradled within the green mountains of the George Washington National Forest.

Warm Springs is renowned for the natural hot springs that well up from deep below the ground on which the town is built. As you drive through Warm Springs, notice the large white spring boxes (bathhouses) containing the relaxing and therapeutic mineral baths. Perhaps this is just the thing you'll need after an arduous mountain bike ride in the nearby mountains.

If you have the time and money, reserve a night at the Homestead and spend a five-star evening wining and dining at this world-class resort. The Homestead Resort in Hot Springs is less than 6 miles from the secluded pastures and farmland

Hidden Valley.

of Hidden Valley. Hit the trails for an early-morning ride, treat yourself to a five-course lunch and mineral bath back at the resort, then head back to the mountains to explore some of the hundreds of miles of trails and dirt roads that crisscross the area.

The Hidden Valley Loop starts at the end of the road beyond the Hidden Valley Campground. Just across the Jackson River is the historic Warwick Mansion, which was the site of the motion picture *Sommersby,* starring Richard Gere and Jodie Foster. Some of the buildings from the movie set are still there. The restored mansion is now the Hidden Valley Bed and Breakfast, which may serve you well if the Homestead doesn't fit your budget.

The loop travels along flat terrain for the first half of the ride and parallels the clear waters of the Jackson River. There are three occasions that call for you to cross the river to continue on the old jeep road. Only once, however, do you have the option of crossing *over* the river (the first crossing can be made by walking across the swinging bridge). Just before the trail leads you to FR 241, you must ford the river twice more with your bike over your shoulder. The water is only knee-deep, and the currents aren't too strong, but be careful during the rainy seasons. The river can swell its banks, becoming too dangerous to cross by foot.

After crossing the river for the third and final time, you'll follow a jeep road through a thick grove of pines to a well-maintained gravel road with a choice of directions. To continue the Hidden Valley Loop, you must take a hard left off the gravel road around a metal gate. This leads you onto an overgrown dirt road that goes up and around a short incline (FR 241 West). The road's appearance improves dramatically as soon as you crest this small hill. From here, follow this rolling dirt road all the way back to Hidden Valley. You'll pass the entrance to the Hidden Valley Bed and Breakfast on your way down the last hill on FR 241, then cross over the Jackson River before arriving back at the start of the loop. Consider cycling over to the

Warwick Mansion (Hidden Valley Bed and Breakfast) and pedaling through the *Sommersby* movie set before leaving this beautiful valley.

Miles and Directions

0.0 START at the cul-de-sac on FR 241 past the Hidden Valley Campground. Go through the steel gate (marked ROAD CLOSED) on the east side of this parking area and follow the Hidden Valley Trail along the wagon track through the fields of Poor Farm.

0.1 Pass a tree with a brown arrow directing you through the field along the Jackson River.

0.5 Pass another brown arrow directing you away from the Jackson River to the middle of this field. Follow the wagon trail across the field.

0.6 Pass beneath a grove of trees and an overgrown wooden gateway. The trail continues straight through the field.

0.9 Leave the open fields of Poor Farm and enter into the thick woods on a flat jeep road paralleling the Jackson River. Two wooden posts mark the entrance. This section of the Hidden Valley Trail is blue-blazed.

1.5 There is a trail sign on the left of the jeep road. Turn left at this sign, following the Hidden Valley Trail (Forest Road 481, blue blaze). Cross over a little wooden footbridge toward the Jackson River. If you were to continue bearing right on what appears to be the main trail, you would end up on Muddy Run Trail (Forest Road 481B), which takes you to Forest Road 220.

1.6 Reach the swinging bridge, which spans the Jackson River. **(Note:** You can either ford the Jackson River straight ahead of you and get on the Hidden Valley Trail directly (the wet way) or go the roundabout way and walk across the swinging bridge to the other side. Once across the bridge, turn right on a little grassy foot trail that scales the hillside above the river. Follow this overgrown path back toward the river. This little trail takes you to the same spot on the blue-blazed Hidden Valley Trail (FR 481) that you would be on had you waded across the river. Choosing the bridge route keeps you dry, but only for the moment. You will still have two more river crossings without bridges. FR 481 continues along the left side of the Jackson River.)

3.4 FR 481 becomes a grassy doubletrack. Cross a small stream.

3.6 FR 481 returns to a jeep road.

3.8 Cross the Jackson River. You must get wet here! The river is only ankle- to knee-deep and about 40 to 50 feet across. You can see the road continuing on the other side. Walk carefully. The bottom may be slippery.

3.9 Cross the Jackson River again. The river is about knee-deep here. Be careful of the slick rocks on the river bottom.

4.0 Follow FR 481 through a small pine forest. Go up a little hill then around a steel gate. The road now becomes FR 241, which will take you all the way back to the start.

4.1 FR 241 comes to a split. Take a hard left around the steel gate. Bearing right on the well-maintained gravel road takes you north. Don't do this! Go under the gate and start climbing this overgrown dirt road. At first, this road may appear to lead nowhere. But once you reach the top of the small incline, the crushed-stone, shale-surfaced road opens up and reveals itself to be very ridable and well maintained.

6.7 Go around a gate.

10.3 Go around a gate. It's all downhill to Hidden Valley from this last gate.

10.8 Reach the bottom of a wild descent along FR 241 and pass the Warwick Mansion (Hidden Valley Bed and Breakfast) on the right. Bear to the left on this road. Cross over the river on a small concrete bridge.

11.0 Arrive back at the parking area.

Ride Information

Local Information

Bath County Chamber of Commerce and the Forest Place Visitors Center, (800) 628-8092 or (540) 839-5281.

Local Events and Attractions

The charming town of Warm Springs has a museum called Gristmill Square, restaurants, shopping, and the famous Warm Springs Pools, complete with separate nineteenth-century bathhouses for men and women.

Accommodations

Hidden Valley Bed and Breakfast, (540) 839-3178.

In Warm Springs:
Anderson Cottage B&B, (540) 839-2975.
Meadow Lane Lodge, (540) 839-5959.
In Hot Springs:
The Homestead (shuttle service available to Roanoke Airport or to the Clifton Forge Amtrak station for registered guests), (800) 838-1766 or (540) 839-1766; www.thehomestead.com.
King's Victorian Inn, (540) 839-3134; inngetaways.com/va/kingsvic.html.

36 Douthat State Park

Start: There are multiple trailheads on either side of Route 629 and from the various parking areas throughout the park. One of the more popular starting points is the Stony Run Trail. It begins at a small parking area just off Route 629, south of the main office.

Length: There are more than 40 miles of wooded trails to choose from throughout the year. Nearly all of them are open to bikes.

Approximate riding time: Varies depending on routes chosen.

Difficulty rating: Easy to difficult. Several sections throughout the park have fast, rocky downhills filled with switchbacks and hidden corners. Other areas have creek crossings that can be wide and require patience to cross, unless you don't mind getting your feet wet. The easier trail sections tend to be located along or near the lake.

Trail surface: There are smooth sections, exposed roots, creek crossings, and technical inclines.

Land status: State park.

Nearest town: Clifton Forge.

Other trail users: Hikers, backpackers, and anglers.

Canine compatibility: Dog friendly. Dogs love it here, but they must be kept on leashes.

Fees and permits: $2.00 per car on the weekend, $1.00 per car during the week.

Schedule: Open year-round, weather permitting.

Maps: USGS maps: Healing Springs, Nimrod Hall; Douthat State Park Mountain Bike Trail Map.

Trail contacts: Douthat State Park, Millboro, VA, (540) 862-8100, www.dcr.state.va.us/parks/douthat.htm.

Getting There: From Lexington: Drive west on I-64/U.S. Route 60 toward Clifton Forge. Take exit 27 and turn right onto Route 629, following signs to Douthat State Park. Route 629 is the only road that leads into the park from Clifton Forge. Follow the brown park signs. Parking for the Stony Run Trail is located on the left. *DeLorme: Virginia Atlas & Gazetteer:* Page 52, A-4.

The Ride

Douthat State Park (pronounced "dowthat"), listed on the National Register of Historic Places, opened on June 15, 1936, and continues to be a model for parks across the country. In fact, editors of the *1999 Outside Family Vacation Guide* named Douthat State Park one of the nation's ten best summer vacation spots (listing it among sites in such enviable locations as California and British Columbia).

Douthat was one of the first five parks created under the Civilian Conservation Corps (CCC) and was designed to provide visitors of all types with multiple recreational opportunities. As many as 600 men lived and worked here between 1923 and 1942, building the park's camps and facilities. Nearly everything you'll find at Douthat was constructed by the CCC during this time, including the log cabins, a guest lodge, a full-service restaurant overlooking the lake (open throughout the summer season only), a gift shop and camp store, and the lake itself. The CCC built the dam across the cold mountain waters of Wilson Creek to form Douthat Lake, which covers fifty surface acres and is laden with trout (stocked twice a week from April through September). No motorized boats are allowed on the lake, so about all you might hear is the splashing of paddles on the water from a canoe, paddleboat, or rowboat.

The lake and its mountainous surroundings are sure to entice you to stay awhile. Camp in one of the three campgrounds or thirty-two rental cabins so you can explore as much of the 4,493 acres of splendor as possible. There is a centralized bathhouse with hot showers for campers in any of the seventy-seven campsites. And should you choose to stay in one of the thirty-two rustic log cabins (most of which are original CCC cabins), you'll be treated to just about everything you'll need for an extended stay. The cabins include electricity, central air, hot showers, fireplaces, and fully supplied kitchens (bring your own groceries). The cabins are typically booked solid throughout the year, so reserve early.

Douthat is a great place to introduce your children to camping, fishing, hiking, and mountain biking. And the park hosts countless programs and special events year-round, including (we're hoping) some upcoming mountain bike clinics. While fishing is still the park's most popular activity, hikers and mountain bikers may someday outnumber anglers. Nearly 200,000 visitors came to the park in 1999, and, according to park rangers, more visitors than could be counted rode in on mountain bikes. The remote location of Douthat State Park (surrounded by the George Washington National Forest) makes it a real treasure and a place you'll want to return to season after season—whether it's for one of the annual mountain bike races, some scenic hikes, or just an extended stay in one of the fully equipped log cabins overlooking the lake.

There are twenty-four different trails to choose from in the park, totaling more than 40 miles of ridable terrain. The variety of "magic" mountain bike trails, as some have called them, has lead to the park's nickname, Mountain Bike Disneyland. The trails in the park range in elevation from 1,400 to 3,200 feet, which allows plenty of opportunity to ascend to new and exhausting heights. Mountain bikers have access to all but three trails: the Heron Run Trail (blue), the YCC Trail (blue), and the Buck Lick Interpretative Trail (red). The park trail guide, available at the park office, details the distance and difficulty range of each trail in the park. And once

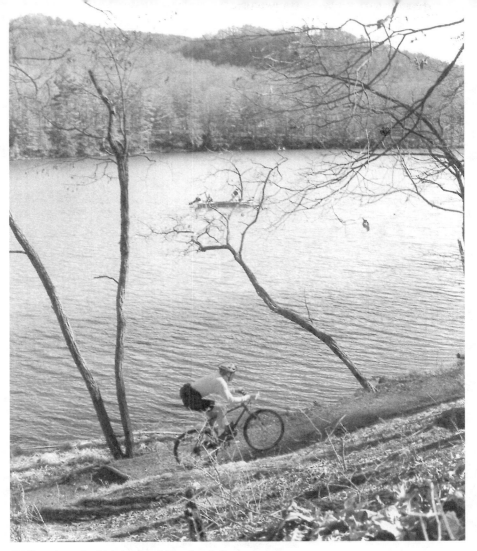

Riding along the high banks of Douthat Lake.

you're in the woods, you'll find that each of the trails is clearly marked with an abundance of signs and corresponding color blazes. It'll be tough to get lost and even tougher to decide which trail to take next.

The spring of 2002 marked the fourth annual Middle Mountain Momma Mountain Bike Adventure Race, put on by East Coasters, a local bike shop, and sponsored by Woods, Water & Wheels in Lewisburg, West Virginia. This race is usually included in the East Coasters' Virginia State Championship Mountain Bike Series. The name of the race was chosen in honor of folksinger John Denver and his song "Country Roads." Mountain bikers treasure Douthat State Park's 40 miles of glorious singletrack, 17 miles of which form the race.

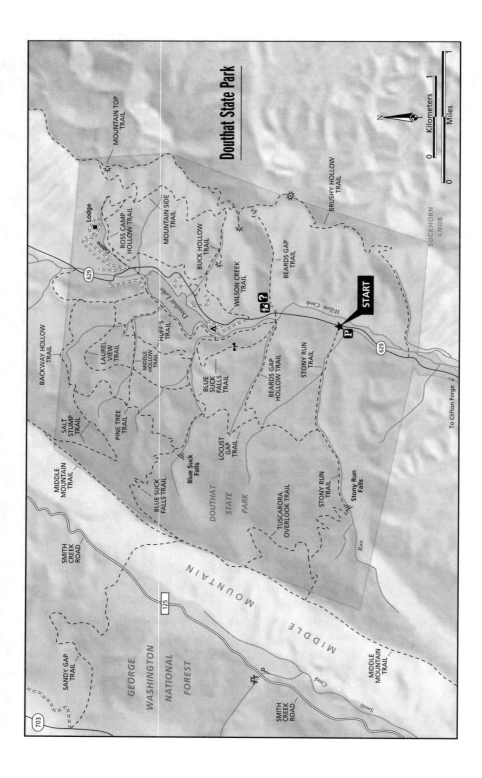

Douthat State Park

START

P

BUCKHORN KNOB

MOUNTAIN TOP TRAIL

ROSS CAMP HOLLOW TRAIL

Lodge

cabins

MOUNTAIN SIDE TRAIL

BUCK HOLLOW TRAIL

WILSON CREEK TRAIL

BEARDS GAP TRAIL

BRUSHY HOLLOW TRAIL

Wilson Creek

629

Douthat Lake

HUFF'S TRAIL

BACKWAY HOLLOW TRAIL

LAUREL VIEW TRAIL

MIDDLE HOLLOW TRAIL

BLUE SUCK FALLS TRAIL

BEARDS GAP HOLLOW TRAIL

STONY RUN TRAIL

To Clifton Forge

629

SALT STUMP TRAIL

PINE TREE TRAIL

LOCUST GAP TRAIL

Blue Suck Falls

TUSCARORA OVERLOOK TRAIL

STONY RUN TRAIL

Stony Run Falls

Run

MIDDLE MOUNTAIN TRAIL

BLUE SUCK FALLS TRAIL

DOUTHAT STATE PARK

MIDDLE MOUNTAIN

SMITH CREEK ROAD

125

MIDDLE MOUNTAIN TRAIL

GEORGE WASHINGTON

SANDY GAP TRAIL

NATIONAL FOREST

SMITH CREEK ROAD

Smith Creek

703

N

0 Kilometers 1
0 Miles

Miles and Directions

The most popular mountain biking trail in the Douthat trail system is Stony Run. Stony Run will exercise your full spectrum of abilities, as most of the terrain is consistently challenging. The trail forms a roughly 6-mile loop, passing by popular spots such as Tuscarora Overlook Trail, Blue Suck Falls, and Lookout Rock. Stony Run, like all of Douthat's trails, is well marked with clear signs at all of the major intersections. The beginning of the route is flat and fast, and there are exposed roots in several places. Crossing creeks is a regular practice, and the rocks can be quite treacherous—but riding next to the stream keeps you cool as you sweat your way up to Locust Gap. The transfer from Stony Run Trail onto Locust Gap Trail changes your ride from technical terrain to casually meandering inclines and downhills. Locust Gap is much narrower than Stony Run and will require the rider to use more caution on tight sections with high brush growth.

Along your ride, you'll pass under hickory, poplar, and tall oaks and alongside mountain laurel, rhododendron, and huckleberry bushes. Among the wildlife you might see are squirrels, lizards, snakes, rabbits, songbirds, deer, owls, and possibly an occasional black bear. The variety of trails and the diverse wildlife create the perfect environment in which to bike.

Ride Information

Local Information
Virginia Department of Conservation and Recreation, Richmond, VA; (804) 225-3867.

Accommodations
Seventy-seven campsites with centralized bathhouses cost $18 per night year-round. Thirty-two climate-controlled, fully stocked log cabins (minus the food) are available year-round. Prices vary depending on size of the cabin and time of year. A one-bedroom cabin will cost between $45 and $70 per night and can be rented nightly or weekly. Call ahead for current information on prices and for reservations: (800) 933-PARK.

Gift shop/camp store is located next to the Lakeview Restaurant (open seasonally).

Restaurants
Lakeview Restaurant is a full-service restaurant overlooking Douthat Lake, open throughout the summer season (Memorial through Labor Day).

Local Events and Attractions
Middle Mountain Momma Mountain Bike Adventure (field limit 150), held in late May, Douthat State Park, (540) 862-8100.
George Washington National Forest, Roanoke, VA; (540) 564-8300.

37 Sherando Lake Loop

Start: From the Turkey Pen Trail parking lot.
Length: 18.2-mile loop.
Approximate riding time: 2 to 2.5 hours.
Difficulty rating: Moderate to difficult, with one extreme climb and some lengthy descents.
Trail surface: Miles of singletrack, some wet and some rocky and dry, with a good section of the Blue Ridge Parkway thrown in for good measure.
Land status: National forest.
Nearest town: Waynesboro.
Other trail users: Hikers.
Canine compatibility: Don't bring 'em. You'll be racing down the parkway on this ride.
Fees and permits: Day use at Sherando Lake: $8.00 per carload for three or more persons; $6.00 a car for two persons; $4.00 a car for one person; $1.00 for a person on a bicycle.
Schedule: Main gate is open from 6:00 A.M. to 10:00 P.M.
Maps: USGS maps: Sherando, Big Levels; George Washington National Forest map: Pedlar Ranger District sportsman's map: $4.00, $5.00 if ordered by mail (call the park service for this map).
Trail contacts: Glenwood and Pedlar Ranger Districts, (540) 291-2188; George Washington and Jefferson National Forest Headquarters, (540) 564-5100.

Getting There: From I-64 near Waynesboro: Take exit 96 (Waynesboro-Lyndhurst exit). Follow signs to Sherando Lake. Follow Route 624 2.5 miles to Lyndhurst. At Lyndhurst, bear left on Route 664 South. Go approximately 5.3 miles on Route 664, through Sherando to Forest Road 42. Turn right on FR 42, called Coal Road, and go half a mile to the first parking area on your left. This is the Turkey Pen Trail parking area. Park here. The trail starts from the far left corner of the parking lot. When parking here, please don't block the forest service road gate. *DeLorme: Virginia Atlas & Gazetteer:* Page 54, A-3.

The Ride

A friendly face at Waynesboro's Rockfish Gap Outfitters pointed at the store topo map and revealed, tapping his finger amid the thick green contour lines, that this was where he sends off-road riders who come in search of alpine adventure. "You want great trails," he said coolly, "you go here."

"Here" turned out to be one of the largest slabs of mountain I had ridden in central Virginia. These massive levels of ancient orogeny are just south of the magnificent Shenandoah National Park. They tower above the fertile valley of Shenandoah,

Sherando's Upper Lake.

Sherando Lake Loop

nestling the riches of this eastern breadbasket between great ridgelines and the slopes of western Virginia's Allegheny Highlands.

I turned into the gravel parking lot off FR 42 (Coal Road) and contemplated my ascent into what is commonly known as Big Levels.

Big Levels has much more to offer than just rugged ridgelines and rocky terrain, however. Between such ominous-sounding peaks as Torry Ridge and Devil's Knob lie the peaceful upper and lower lakes of Sherando Lake Recreation Area. The CCC built the lower lake, the larger of the two, in 1930. The smaller upper lake was built in the 1960s for flood control. The lower lake is used for swimming, boating, and fishing; the upper lake is known primarily for its good fishing. Camping is also popular at Sherando Lake Recreation Area, which has more than sixty units and a large group camping area.

Other nearby scenic wonders include the Blue Ridge Parkway, which rolls along the summits of mountains south of Big Levels; Saint Mary's Wilderness, along the southwest slopes of Big Levels; and the cascades of Saint Mary's Falls.

From the parking lot off FR 42, Turkey Run Trail begins its slow ascent on an old logging road. After a mile, the trail narrows into a thick-foliaged singletrack, gaining elevation at such a mild rate that you may wonder at times if you're going uphill at all. This changes dramatically, however, at mile 5.5, when the trail lifts off and aims upward to Bald Mountain Overlook. You might not mention to anyone that you needed to push your bike up this section of the trail, but no one will believe you if you say you didn't. The trail is slightly more than handlebar-width, with little room for bike-handling errors (one side of the trail is a wall of earth, while the other side is an unnerving drop through hundreds of feet of rugged terrain). For some, this ride poses no challenge, but with more than 1,000 feet of vertical climbing and eight sharp switchbacks in less than 1 mile, the trail becomes truly an adventure. But please keep the adventure confined to the trail itself and do not shortcut the switchbacks.

The reward? A few aches in the legs, spectacular views, more than 10 miles of furious downhill (all the way back to the ride's start), and the satisfaction of completing a truly rigorous course.

The descent begins at the top of that climb and winds down a rocky fire road to Bald Mountain Overlook and the Blue Ridge Parkway. Turn left on the parkway (there is rarely any traffic to contend with along this well-maintained scenic highway) and let gravity pull you for more than 3 miles past a number of scenic overlooks. Turn left into the woods just before the parkway starts climbing and continue downward along White Rock Gap Trail (orange blaze) through an old pine forest. This fun singletrack trail glides downhill for more than 2 miles before depositing you at Sherando's Upper Lake.

There are rest rooms at the different campgrounds in the Sherando Lake area and ice and vending machines adjacent to the beach house pavilion near the lower lake. Outside the park (along Route 664, heading back to the start of the ride), there's a general store with food and drinks.

Another point of interest on the way back to the start of the ride is Mount Torry Furnace on Route 664. This old iron furnace was built in 1804 to process iron ore mined in the nearby mountains. It was destroyed in 1864 during the Civil War, then rebuilt and operated until 1884.

Miles and Directions

0.0 START at the Turkey Pen Trail parking lot just off Coal Road (FR 42). From the trailhead, follow the jeep trail into the woods, heading south toward Bald Mountain Overlook. There will be blue blazes to follow once you reach the rock barricade at the end of Turkey Pen Road, just over 1 mile into the ride.

1.2 Turkey Pen Trail narrows from an old jeep trail into singletrack. This is a gradual climb. Blue blazes mark the trail, which is now called Mills Creek Trail.

2.6 Mills Creek Trail splits. Turn right, crossing Mills Creek. The trail continues on the other side of the creek, following the blue blazes.

5.5 Begin the switchback ascent up Bald Mountain toward Forest Road 162. There are eight very narrow switchbacks to the top. Good luck!

6.5 Reach the end of this climb! You are now at 3,437 feet elevation. The trail exits into a clearing used for primitive camping. Bear right through this grassy field toward FR 162, then turn left onto FR 162 (dirt road).

6.8 Pass the dirt road that goes up to where the old fire tower used to be. There is a pit toilet at the end of this road.

7.3 Reach the Blue Ridge Parkway and Bald Mountain Overlook. Go through the gate and turn left on the Blue Ridge Parkway. **(Note:** This section along the Blue Ridge Parkway is downhill all the way to White Rock Gap Trail. If you find yourself on any significant climbs, then you've passed the White Rock Gap trailhead.)

10.3 Turn left off the parkway onto White Rock Gap Trail. This turn comes just before the Blue Ridge Parkway begins to ascend. You will notice, before this ascent, a small, grassy clearing on the left. Oftentimes, there are cars parked here. At the back of this clearing, there is a large tree with an orange diamond nailed to its trunk. The White Rock Gap Trail marker is just a few yards into the woods from this tree. **(Note:** Along the descent down White Rock Gap Trail, there is an interesting park sign that reads: THE OLD MOUNTAIN HOME-SITE: MUCH OF THE BLUE RIDGE WAS SETTLED IN THE EARLY 1700S AND CLEARED FOR AGRICULTURAL PUR-POSES. THE LAND WAS NOT ECONOMICALLY SUITED FOR SMALL FARMS. THESE FARMS WERE ABANDONED IN THE 1860S WITH THE OPENING OF WESTERN LANDS AND THE COMMENCEMENT OF THE CIVIL WAR.)

12.3 Reach the upper lake of Sherando. Turn right on Route 91. This takes you through the Sherando Lake Campground toward the lower lake and out of the park.

14.9 Turn left on Route 664.

17.8 Turn left on Coal Road (FR 42) and go through the gate.

18.2 Reach the Turkey Pen Trail parking lot.

Ride Information

Local Events and Attractions

Blue Ridge Parkway is a 470-mile linear park from Front Royal, Virginia, to Cherokee, North Carolina.

38 Big Levels

Start: From Sherando's upper lake at Sherando Lake State Park.
Length: 26.8-mile loop.
Approximate riding time: 5-plus hours.
Difficulty rating: Extremely difficult, thanks to endless, scree-covered climbs (half the ride is uphill), rocky terrain, and overall length.
Trail surface: Singletrack, jeep trail, dirt roads, and paved park roads.
Land status: National forest.
Nearest town: Waynesboro.
Other trail users: Hikers.
Canine compatibility: This is a very dog-friendly place, but the ride itself may be too long, rocky, and grueling for your pooch. Also, the ride along Route 664 is no good for a dog. Consider leaving him behind on this one.
Fees and permits: Day use at Sherando Lake: $8.00 per carload for three or more persons; $6.00 a car for two persons; $4.00 a car for one person; $1.00 for a person on a bicycle.
Schedule: Main gate is open from 6:00 A.M. to 10:00 P.M.
Maps: USGS maps: Sherando, Big Levels; George Washington National Forest map: Pedlar Ranger District sportsman's map: $4.00, $5.00 if ordered by mail (call the park service for this map).
Trail contacts: Glenwood and Pedlar Ranger Districts, (540) 291–2188; George Washington and Jefferson National Forest Headquarters, (540) 564–5100.

Getting There: From I-64 near Waynesboro: Take exit 96 (Waynesboro-Lyndhurst exit), following signs to Sherando Lake. Follow Route 624 2.5 miles to Lyndhurst. At Lyndhurst, bear left on Route 664 South. Go approximately 7.5 miles on Route 664 to the Sherando Lake State Park entrance. Turn right on the park entrance road (Route 91). Follow the park entrance road past the campgrounds, all the way to the upper lake and group camp parking area. Park here, at the end of the road. *DeLorme: Virginia Atlas & Gazetteer:* Page 54, A-3.

The Ride

Narrow singletrack trails along rocky ridgelines and steep, barren, sun-baked jeep trails characterize this grueling route, one of the most difficult rides in the book. It's important to remember on a ride like this to bring lots of water and food, because there aren't any 7-Elevens out in the woods where you can grab a tasty Big Gulp. Another suggestion before starting this ride is to invest in some type of suspension if you don't already have it. The steep and rocky nature of these trails will probably cause more shock to the body than arms and backs were meant to absorb. Without shocks, you may end this ride quite sore.

Oh no, Bryan! I think your wheel's hung up.

The Big Levels ride begins at the Sherando Lake Campground near Sherando's upper lake. **(Note:** It can also begin at the Turkey Pen Trail parking area off Coal Road [Forest Road 42], following this route in reverse. A lot of folks prefer this ride starting from Coal Road so they can climb up Big Levels, as difficult as that may sound, then descend White Rock Gap Trail back to the park. This is another great way to travel this route, so take your pick.) To get to Sherando's upper lake, follow the park access road through the park toward the group campgrounds. Immediately after the final turn, before the group camping area, there is a grassy meadow next to the upper lake dam. The White Rock Gap trailhead is on the far side of this meadow at the gate. You may leave your car in the parking area, just past the trailhead.

White Rock Gap Trail crosses the meadow and heads into the woods, following small orange plastic blazes tacked to the trees. The trail splits almost immediately, heading either straight on the jeep road paralleling the lake or right, climbing into the woods. Take the trail to the right off the dirt road, which leads down to the lake. This trail leads back to White Rock Gap Trail.

At about mile 2, White Rock Gap Trail junctures with the Slacks Trail, marked by a wooden milepost. Turn right, following the blue-blazed Slacks Trail toward Torry Ridge. The trail is a vertical climb through this first section, and you may have to walk. It soon levels out, however, threading its way along a scenic ridgeline and crossing a small ravine and two rock slides before intersecting with Torry Ridge Trail. Turn left here on the yellow-blazed trail and follow the sign toward Bald Mountain Overlook on the Blue Ridge Parkway.

The real challenge begins here, as the route becomes extremely steep and rocky at this point. Turning the pedals up this trail may result in futility. Then, just as you've convinced yourself that the trail can't get any steeper, you must shoulder your bike and scramble on foot up a rock wall to connect with the trail on top. Fortunately, only a few yards past the top of this wall is a small rock outcrop with a breathtaking view of Kelly Mountain. Roll along this trail, before the final grassy climb, which heads uphill to an open area that was formerly Bald Mountain Lookout Tower. Turn right onto Forest Road 162 (Big Levels Primitive Road) and battle the hot, scrubby terrain toward Big Levels. At this point, you have conquered a mere quarter of the battle.

Ouch!

You receive a well-deserved break from the past one and a half hours of climbing with a quick and exhilarating downhill along FR 162. Dirt, holes, rocks, and mud make for an exciting downhill. But soon you'll be ascending again to the top of Flint Mountain. Much of this fire road is unforgiving, as the path repeatedly switches toward the top. With little shade from trees, the sun typically beats on this dusty, barren route, giving the road a harsh character.

At the top of Flint Mountain, continue along Big Levels Primitive Road until you reach a four-way intersection in a fairly large clearing. You will notice a small wooden gate on the left, marking the trail into Saint Mary's Wilderness (bikes are not allowed past this gate). On the right is Kennedy Ridge Trail, which travels sharply downhill to FR 42 (Coal Road). Take this trail if you wish to cut the ride short and avoid the extremely difficult descent down Big Levels Primitive Road. Kennedy Ridge, however, is still very difficult in its own right.

You'll encounter one more intersection along Big Levels Primitive Road before making the descent down Big Levels. Loose dirt and sand make up the surface cover at the spot where you must bear right and begin crisscrossing down the ridge to Coal Road. This section of switchbacks down to the bottom can be extremely difficult and will take some time to maneuver. Large rocks, steep grades, and the elements of fatigue combine to make this a true mountain biker's challenge. Do not follow the trail that heads straight down—a straight-line descent through the switchbacks does not always make for a faster descent. This deteriorating jeep trail is little more than a two-lane rock slide clear to the bottom of the mountain.

At last, you'll reach the bottom, pass through a gate, and be rewarded with a mostly downhill ride on Coal Road's well-maintained gravel and hard-packed dirt surface. Once you reach Route 664, turn right and enjoy the feel of smooth pavement. Remember to keep some money on hand in case you need to stop at the convenience store (along Route 664 on your way back to Sherando).

This ride sequentially combines all types of mountain bike terrain imaginable. It begins with smooth singletrack up White Rock Gap, then changes to a rocky trail along the slopes of Torry Ridge. Rocky, barren forest roads pick up where the trails leave off, as you travel along the mountaintops of Big Levels. Once at the bottom, you ride on Coal Road, a well-maintained gravel road. This leads you to pavement, and you're back to where you started from.

Miles and Directions

0.0   START from the parking area at the group campgrounds near Sherando's upper lake. Follow White Rock Gap Trail (orange blaze) across the upper lake meadow into the woods. **(Note:** The trail starts at the gate on the lake side of the park entrance road.) There is a large wooden trail post with an orange marker at the wood's edge. The trail splits just within the woods. Follow the upper trail, which meets back at White Rock Gap Trail.

2.2   Reach another trail split, marked with a wooden trail post. Bear right at this split, following the Slacks Trail (blue blaze) uphill toward Torry Ridge. White Rock Gap Trail continues left toward the Blue Ridge Parkway.

3.0 Reach the top of the steep ascent. The rest of the Slacks Trail rambles along the contours of the mountain's ridgeline.

4.3 The Slacks Trail passes below Slacks Overlook on the Blue Ridge Parkway. The overlook can easily be reached by a short path on the left marked with an orange blaze. Continue on the Slacks Trail. There are two rock slides ahead that you must walk across.

4.8 Reach a three-way intersection where the Slacks Trail runs into Torry Ridge Trail. Turn left at the sign, following Torry Ridge Trail (yellow blaze) up to Bald Mountain.

5.2 Shoulder your bikes up this rock slab. Torry Ridge Trail continues at the top.

5.3 Nice view of Kelly Mountain through the trees on the right.

5.8 Reach the summit of Bald Mountain (3,587 feet) where the old fire tower used to be. Turn right down this dirt road toward FR 162.

5.9 Turn right on FR 162 (Big Levels Primitive Road). This dirt road travels along Bald Mountain Ridge to Flint Mountain, then to Big Levels.

7.8 Reach the top of Flint Mountain. Begin the descent to Big Levels.

8.7 Arrive at a four-way intersection in a large clearing. Kennedy Ridge Trail is on the right of this clearing. On the left is a small wooden gate leading into Saint Mary's Wilderness (bikes not allowed). Continue straight on FR 162 (Big Levels Primitive Road).

9.8 Bear right (north) at this large, sandy intersection, following a rocky jeep trail down Big Levels. Turning left (west) takes you along Bald Mountain Trail for 3.5 miles to FR 42.

10.3 Cross a small creek (John's Run).

11.3 The trail becomes very rocky and steep. Follow the switchback route rather than the straight route.

14.5 Reach the bottom of this treacherous descent! Go around the gate and turn right on FR 42 (unpaved). Follow FR 42 to Route 664.

21.8 Turn right on Route 664 (paved), heading back to Sherando Lake.

22.4 Convenience store on the right. Ahh, refreshments!

22.8 Mount Torry Furnace on the right.

24.2 Turn right into Sherando Lake State Park on Route 91. Remember to carry your receipt with you so you don't have to worry about paying a second time to get back into the park.

26.1 Pass the lower lake.

26.8 Reach the group campgrounds. Is your body devastated?

(**Alternate Start:** Start from the Turkey Run Trail parking area and travel this route in reverse, heading along FR 42 (Coal Road) to Kennedy Ridge. You'll climb Big Levels first and finish your ride flying down White Rock Gap Trail back into the park at Sherando's upper lake. This is a great way to approach this trail, so give it a try.)

Ride Information

Local Events and Attractions

Blue Ridge Parkway is a 470-mile linear park from Front Royal, Virginia, to Cherokee, North Carolina.

39 Henry Lanum Memorial Trail

Start: From the Appalachian Trail parking area on Route 775.
Length: 5.3-mile loop.
Approximate riding time: 1 to 1.5 hours.
Difficulty rating: Difficult, due to length and extreme climbs combined with rugged single-track.
Trail surface: Singletrack and jeep trails.
Land status: National forest.
Nearest town: Buena Vista.
Other trail users: Hikers and equestrians.
Canine compatibility: Dog friendly.
Fees and permits: No fees or permits required.
Schedule: Public land; accessible year-round.
Maps: USGS maps: Montebello, Forks of Buffalo; George Washington National Forest map: Pedlar Ranger District sportsman's map: $4.00, $5.00 if ordered by mail (call the park service for this map).
Trail contacts: Glenwood and Pedlar Ranger Districts, (540) 291-2188; George Washington and Jefferson National Forest Headquarters, (540) 564-5100.

Getting There: From I-81 near Lexington and Buena Vista: Take U.S. Route 60 east through Buena Vista to Route 634 (Daris Mill Creek Road) and Ham's County Store near Oronoco. Turn left on Route 634. In approximately 1.5 miles, bear right at the split on Route 755 (Wiggin's Springs Road), which changes to gravel. Follow this road approximately 3 miles to Hog Camp Gap, where the Appalachian Trail crosses the road. Park in the parking area on the left side of the road or continue a short distance ahead, taking the gravel road to the right. It becomes a trailhead parking lot for Henry Lanum Memorial Trail. *DeLorme: Virginia Atlas & Gazetteer: Page 54, B-2.*

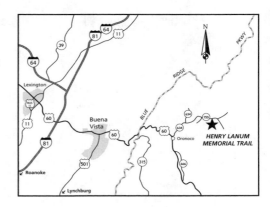

The Ride

Formerly known as the Pompey and Mount Pleasant Loop Trail, this 5.3-mile loop is well worth the trip to its somewhat remote location.

The Henry Lanum Memorial Trail has the reputation of being a "somewhere else to go" trail for outdoors people weary of the state's major trail systems and eager for a change of scenery. This well-marked course from start to finish is not so heavily traveled, and consequently it offers considerable solitude.

However, for off-road cyclists, the Henry Lanum Memorial Trail is not just a place to go when Virginia's other trails prove mundane. For daring and eager mountain bikers, this is a first-class loop of trails with more challenges and greater rewards than many trails more conveniently located and twice as long.

START

P

48

775

APPALACHIAN
TRAIL

HENRY LANUM MEMORIAL
TRAIL

Pompey Mtn
4,032 ft ▲

North

635

Fork

Henry Lanum Memorial Trail

Buffalo

N

☼ Mt Pleasant
▲ 4,021 ft

River

0   Kilometers   .5

0   Miles   .5

    The trail is located 9 miles east of Buena Vista, off U.S. Route 60. Its remoteness
is apparent as you drive along a number of back roads north of U.S. Route 60 to the
trailhead parking lot where this ride begins.

    The loop is something of a spur to the Appalachian Trail (hikers need simply to
follow the Mount Pleasant National Scenic Area signs to find this loop), which
crosses the dirt road at the trailhead parking lot. The lot itself is intended to be an
access point for the Appalachian Trail. However, when Henry Lanum designed the
Pompey and Mount Pleasant Loop, developing it for public use, his vision was to
create a beautiful diversion from the popular Appalachian Trail. He succeeded in
doing so, personally maintaining this loop year-round. In July 1991, Lanum died
while working on the Hidden Lake Trail in Idaho's Panhandle National Forest. In

memory of Henry Lanum Jr., the Pompey and Mount Pleasant Trail was renamed and dedicated in his name. Because the Henry Lanum Memorial Trail is not actually a part of the Appalachian Trail, cyclists are welcome to ride here.

This ride begins at the same trailhead parking lot that intersects with the Appalachian Trail. You could begin the loop by parking farther down the road at the Henry Lanum Trail parking area, but there is more space in this lot, and the ride to the loop's start is recommended.

Follow the dirt road downhill momentarily until you see a grassy trail on the right that zips up into the woods. Follow this path to another trail sign, where you'll turn left and find yourself at the parking area and trailhead for the Henry Lanum Memorial Trail.

After riding this loop, it becomes apparent that unbearably steep climbs can be avoided if you travel in a counterclockwise direction. Follow the trail on the right side of the parking area (marked MOUNT PLEASANT) around the wooden trail gate and pedal into the woods on a flat old logging road. This trail gradually ascends until it reaches the North Fork Creek and the cascades. At this point, the trail climbs rather abruptly toward Mount Pleasant. This climb lasts nearly 1 mile before you reach the top and pedal through a small meadow. You'll ascend another 0.5 mile of steep, rocky terrain to reach the summit of Mount Pleasant (4,021 feet). This prominent peak offers an outstanding view of the Appalachian Mountains, and its 3,000-foot drop-off yields a mostly unimpaired view. Traveling to the top of this peak adds an extra mile to the loop. (**Note:** The park service recently relocated 1 mile of this trail due to resource damage, so call ahead for the status on this trail should you be interested in riding it.)

The loop continues along the ridge top upward to Pompey Mountain. No startling views or sweeping panoramas are visible from this mountaintop, but the thrilling descent on the other side compensates nicely. Ride this descent with extreme caution—the trail is extremely narrow and steep and is loaded with obstacles that can throw you from your bike. As soon as this descent ends, you'll climb a bit before hitting a wild and deliriously fast downhill run to the trailhead parking lot at the beginning of this loop. Please be extra careful on this last descent so that you don't collide with other trail users. Much of this descent is quick and bumpy

If you make the extra 1-mile hike to Mount Pleasant, you won't be disappointed.

and is known to have some blind corners. From the trailhead parking area, follow the same route back to the Appalachian Trail parking area.

If you're interested in muscling this loop at a slower pace to capture its scenery, watch for patches of wildflowers, mountain laurel, blueberries, rhododendron, oak, hickory, and yellow birch. The trail winds through a garden of colorful flora.

(Attention: The park service is beginning to see a good deal of resource damage as a result of mountain bike use along this loop. Trail damage is caused primarily by bikers "braiding" the tread to avoid rocks. This results in the trail widening, which causes increased erosion. Park managers are monitoring the situation. A worst-case scenario would be that the trail could be closed to bikes if damage increases to unacceptable levels. Thankfully, it hasn't gotten to that point yet. Please do your best to help maintain this trail if you ride here. We don't want this trail closed to bikes.)

Miles and Directions

0.0 START from the trailhead parking area next to the Appalachian Trail. Go east on Route 48.

0.2 Just before Route 48 and Route 635 split, a little grass trail zips up the hill on the right side of the road. This is Grassy Trail. Marking this trail are three wooden posts with a blue square. Bear right off Route 48 on Grassy Trail and follow it into the trees.

0.3 Come to a trail sign and a small wooden trail gate. Turn left, continuing on Grassy Trail to the start of the Henry Lanum Memorial Trail.

0.35 Cross Route 635 and enter a small parking area at the start of the Henry Lanum Memorial Trail. Note two trailheads from this parking area. Both trails lead into the woods. Take the trail on the far right marked MT. PLEASANT 2.6 MILES. This will take you around the loop in a counterclockwise direction. You can go either way. However, traveling counterclockwise makes this loop much more manageable and fun. The loop starts off as a flat wagon trail along the creek. Go around the wooden trail gate to begin.

1.6 Arrive at the cascades. The trail continues up from here.

1.9 Start climbing toward Mount Pleasant.

2.7 The trail becomes level, crosses through a thick meadow, and reaches a wooden trail sign. From this sign you may either continue this loop toward Pompey Mountain or detour a half mile to the summit of Mount Pleasant. If you wish to make the 1-mile round-trip effort to the top of Mount Pleasant, be aware that the trail is very steep and rocky. From 4,021 feet, however, the view is well worth the trouble, revealing an incredible panorama of the surrounding mountains.

3.4 Crest Pompey Mountain (4,032 feet). There's no real view from this mountaintop, but the climb is rewarded with a wild descent down a challenging, narrow trail.

3.8 This descent ends. Start climbing again. This climb is moderate compared with those before it.

4.3 Reach the top of this climb. The trail levels off, then begins a final fast descent to the beginning of the loop. This descent is very quick. Watch out for other trail users on your way down.

5.0 Return to the Henry Lanum Memorial Trail trailhead. Ride back to the car the way you came.

5.3 Arrive at the parking area.

Ride Information

Local Information
Historic Lexington Visitor Center, Lexington, VA; (540) 463–3777; www.lexingtonvirginia.com.

Local Events and Attractions
Virginia Military Institute.
Washington and Lee University.

40 Blue Ridge Dirt Ride

Start: From the Buena Vista Overlook.
Length: 15.3-mile loop.
Approximate riding time: 2 hours.
Difficulty rating: This is a fairly easy to moderate ride along unpaved forest roads and the paved Blue Ridge Parkway. The climbing is moderate, but the nontechnical trail surface tempers the climbs well.
Trail surface: Forest roads and the Blue Ridge Parkway.
Land status: National forest.
Nearest town: Buena Vista.
Other trail users: Motorists.

Canine compatibility: Not good—too much road riding.
Schedule: Public land; accessible year-round. Parkway may be closed to vehicle traffic during heavy snow.
Maps: USGS map: Buena Vista; George Washington National Forest map: Pedlar Ranger District sportsman's map: $4.00, $5.00 if ordered by mail (call the park service for this map).
Trail contacts: Glenwood and Pedlar Ranger District, (540) 291–2188; George Washington and Jefferson National Forests Headquarters, (540) 564–5100; Friends of the Blue Ridge Parkway, (800) 228–PARK.

Getting There: From I–81 near Lexington and Buena Vista: Take U.S. Route 60 (Buena Vista exit) East. Pass through Buena Vista on U.S. Route 60 East and enter the George Washington National Forest. Climb up to the Blue Ridge Parkway. Cross beneath the parkway, then turn left on the entrance ramp to access the Blue Ridge Parkway. Turn left on the Blue Ridge Parkway heading south. Go approximately 0.5 mile to the Buena Vista Overlook on the right. *DeLorme: Virginia Atlas & Gazetteer:* Page 54, C-1.

The Ride

The Blue Ridge Parkway and Skyline Drive together form a scenic byway of some 570 miles of quiet, beautifully designed road, rolling atop the peaks of the Appalachian Mountains. Construction began on the project in 1935 near the Virginia–North Carolina border and continued north to Front Royal, Virginia. The parkway changes names at the top of Afton Mountain near Waynesboro, Virginia. The route south into North Carolina is the Blue Ridge Parkway (which is free to ride on), and the route north, which winds through the Shenandoah National Park all the way to Front Royal, is Skyline Drive (which currently costs $10.00 per car, $5.00 per bike). The first segment of the grand parkway opened in April 1939, while the final section opened in 1987 with the completion of the Grandfather Mountain

Hundreds of miles of dirt forest roads exist alongside Blue Ridge Parkway for cyclists to take advantage of.

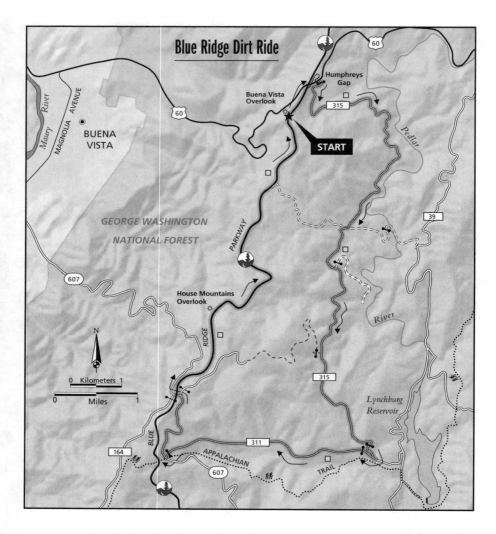

segment in North Carolina. Throughout their short history, nearly 600 million people have visited Skyline Drive and the Blue Ridge Parkway. That's almost 11 million visitors per year, or more than 30,000 per day.

From Front Royal, Virginia, to the Cherokee Indian Reservation near Cherokee, North Carolina, Skyline Drive and the Blue Ridge Parkway are the scenic links between Shenandoah National Park in Virginia and the Great Smoky Mountains of North Carolina and Tennessee. They follow the Appalachian's highest ridges, attaining altitudes of more than 6,000 feet while averaging between 3,000 and 4,000 feet. This magnificent national treasure was designed specifically for a leisurely and scenic route through this prominent mountain region.

The moderately difficult and extremely scenic loop included in this guide is meant to illustrate to mountain bikers an obvious but often overlooked asset of the Blue Ridge Parkway.

The parkway, from Front Royal to Cherokee, is well suited for both bicycle tourists and day cyclists alike. However, the smooth pavement and long, leisurely climbs may not appeal quite as much to the off-road rider. What many folks fail to realize is that along certain sections of the parkway, off-road cyclists can access hundreds of miles of both well-maintained and abandoned forest roads, all of which are open to the public. Virginia's main access is through the Glenwood and Pedlar Ranger Districts of the George Washington and Jefferson National Forests. The Blue Ridge Parkway extends more than 100 miles through this 147,000-acre section of public land and offers countless points of access into the national forest.

In addition to the dramatic change of scenery, from skyline views along the parkway to dense, old-growth forests surrounding the dirt roads, these forest routes afford cyclists the luxury to abandon their traffic woes and concentrate on nothing but the ride itself. There are seldom any vehicles to worry about, either in view or in earshot, and wildlife is often visible from every point of the ride. The lush green of the forest's thick undergrowth and splashy array of colorful wildflowers could hardly exist along the paved roads of the busy world beyond.

This loop starts from the Buena Vista Overlook on the Blue Ridge Parkway. As at most overlooks and access points, there's plenty of room to park the car. Pedal north up the parkway a bit, then exit west on U.S. Route 60. This takes you right down to Forest Road 315 (Panther Falls Road).

Through the gate, this well-maintained dirt road descends the mountain toward Pedlar River, for which this district of the forest is named. After a few ups and downs and more than 7 miles of forested serenity, FR 315 comes to an end at FR 311. Unfortunately, most of these dirt roads don't have any signs or road names, so it's important to follow the maps closely, know your distances, and carry a compass. There are so many miles of dirt roads back here that a wrong turn can get you completely spun around and heading in the wrong direction.

At FR 311, pass through a gate and begin climbing the slow but steady grade back toward the parkway. At the top of this climb, pass through another gate and come to another intersection (Route 607). Turn right on this dirt road and notice the Blue Ridge Parkway on your left. Route 607 travels along the ridge for just over 1 mile, then ducks under the parkway and heads down the west side of the mountain to Buena Vista. Unfortunately, at this point Route 607 doesn't directly access the parkway. You will have to walk your bike up the embankment at the underpass to get on the road. Once up the embankment, turn right and ride along the mountain peaks for more than 4 miles back to your car. Much of this section is downhill.

This ride is but one of the countless opportunities the Blue Ridge Parkway offers mountain bikers as it passes through this large segment of the George Washington National Forest. Please remember, of course, that while the Blue Ridge Parkway becomes Skyline Drive and travels through Shenandoah National Park just north of Afton Mountain, mountain bikes are not allowed within the park's boundaries. In Virginia, only national forest land is open to cyclists.

Miles and Directions

0.0 START at the Buena Vista Overlook on the Blue Ridge Parkway. Head north on the Blue Ridge Parkway to U.S. Route 60.

0.1 Cross over U.S. Route 60.

0.2 Exit the Blue Ridge Parkway to U.S. Route 60 East.

0.3 Turn left on U.S. Route 60 East through Humphreys Gap.

0.4 Turn right on FR 315 and go through the gate (this gate is usually open year-round). This dirt road winds up and down through the valley of the Pedlar River.

3.4 Cross over Roberts Creek. An unnamed dirt road intersects with FR 315 at this point. Continue straight on FR 315. Reach the low point along FR 315 (1,390 feet).

4.5 Cross over Shady Mountain Creek. This, like Roberts Creek, is a fairly small tributary of the Pedlar River.

6.9 Turn right on FR 311. Turning left would take you to the Lynchburg Reservoir. FR 311 travels along Little Irish Creek up the mountain to the Blue Ridge Parkway.

9.5 Reach the top of this climb, go through the gate, and turn right on Route 607. This dirt road climbs a little farther to reach the Blue Ridge Parkway.

10.5 Arrive at the Blue Ridge Parkway through Robinson's Gap (2,412 feet). Unfortunately, when Route 607 meets up with the parkway, it doesn't actually connect with it. Rather, Route 607 goes underneath the parkway to the other side, then descends all the way to Buena Vista. To get on the parkway, climb the embankment from Route 607 with your bike on your shoulder. This easy little hike gets you on the parkway. Turn right, heading north on the Blue Ridge Parkway. **(Note:** An alternative to climbing the embankment is to cross underneath the Blue Ridge Parkway heading west to Buena Vista. There is a dirt road to the left. Turn left on this road and follow it for about 1 mile. Turn left again over a steep bank. Less than a quarter mile ahead through the gate is the Blue Ridge Parkway.)

11.7 Pass House Mountains Overlook on the left.

15.3 Arrive at Buena Vista Overlook on the left.

Honorable Mentions

Western Virginia

Compiled here is an index of great rides in the western highlands region that didn't make the list this time around but deserve recognition. Check them out and let us know what you think. You may decide that one or more of these rides deserves higher status in future editions, or, perhaps, you may have a ride of your own that merits some attention.

K Duncan Hollow Trail

As I may have noted in the Massanutten Mountain chapter (see Ride 27), there are countless routes of singletrack, doubletrack, and forest roads on which mountain biking is superb. Most of the mountain is within the George Washington National Forest and is open to the public for multiple uses. This route, known as Duncan Hollow, leaves right from the Massanutten visitor center and takes cyclists through the heart of Massanutten Mountain. Located just 5 miles east of New Market, the visitor center gives people a chance to walk the quarter-mile Massanutten Story Trail to learn more about the history of the mountain. The ride heads north from the visitor center along Forest Road 274, taking you along Passage Creek all the way up to Camp Roosevelt. At Camp Roosevelt, you'll turn back around and follow the orange-blazed Duncan Hollow Trail, climbing your way up Middle Mountain to Scothorn Gap. From Scothorn Gap, follow the yellow-blazed trail all the way downhill back to FR 274. Turn left onto FR 274 and make your way back to the visitor center. This is a fairly long loop at just over 17 miles, so plan to bring along enough water and food, or even consider camping overnight at Camp Roosevelt.

To get to the Massanutten visitor center and the start of this ride, travel on I–81 to the town of New Market. From New Market, turn east on U.S. Route 211 and head up the mountain through New Market Gap to the visitor center. The trail starts from here. *(DeLorme: Virginia Atlas & Gazetteer:* Page 73 C-D7.)

L Edinburg Gap ORV Trails: Massanutten Mountain

The George Washington National Forest Service has, over the past number of years, recognized operating off-road vehicles in the national forests as a valid use of forest land and consequently has identified and constructed a number of all-terrain vehicle (ATV) and off-road vehicle (ORV) trails for four-wheel-drive vehicles, motorcycles, and motorbikes. These trails also provide excellent mountain biking, as cyclists will find miles of narrow twisting routes coupled with wide inviting paths, all of which are clearly labeled and easy to follow. Cyclists should be aware that there are motorized vehicles back here and should ride with their heads on a swivel in case a truck or motorcycle comes out of nowhere and needs to be avoided at an emergency's pace. Don't fool yourself. You won't be alone back here or find a peaceful place to ride. It can sometimes be noisy and downright crowded with traffic. But you will find tons of tough, rugged trails on which to ride, and an afternoon back here won't be hard to fill. Just stay away after a big rain, as the ruts and ridges created by the ORVs get really nasty and full of mud.

In the Lee Ranger District at Edinburg Gap, there are two ORV trail systems: Peters Mill Run ORV Trails and Tasker Gap ORV Trails. Both systems can be accessed from Route 675 southeast of Edinburg. Signs will direct you from Route 675 onto the ORV trails. To get there, take I–81 to the Edinburg/Route 675 exit. Go east (left) on Route 675 through Edinburg. When you see the Chrysler dealer, stay on Route 675 by turning right onto Edinburg Gap Road. Follow Route 675 up the mountain about 3 miles. The trailhead is at the very top on your right, just after a hairpin turn to your right. For more information on the ORV trails in the forest, visit www.fs.fed.us/gwjnf/orvtrails.html. For a detailed trail map of the Tasker Gap ORV Trails, go to the Northern Virginia Trail Rider's Web site at www.nvtr.org/taskers.html. *(DeLorme: Virginia Atlas & Gazetteer:* Page 73 B-7.)

M McDowell Battlefield Trail

Here's a great little ride for history buffs if you happen to be in the neighborhood for the Williamsville Loop ride (see Ride 33). This ride is located right next to the town of McDowell, just north of Williamsville. You can start at either the west end or the east end of this point-to-point ride, which take you up Bullpasture Mountain to the top of Sittlington Hill and the core of the McDowell Battlefield. Fought on May 8, 1862, this battle was the Jackson's Valley Campaigns' first victory. The trail isn't very long (just a little over 1 mile each way), but it takes you uphill to over 2,500 feet. To start from the eastern end of this trail, park at the battlefield parking area along U.S. Route 250, approximately 1 mile from the top of Bullpasture Mountain. If you want to start from the western end of this trail, park at the Presbyterian church at the junction of Route 678, right outside McDowell. To learn more about this trail and the area, visit the Sugar Tree Country Store in McDowell for interpretive information and details about the Civil War Trail. For more information, call (800) 396–2445. *(DeLorme: Virginia Atlas & Gazetteer:* Page 65, B-7.)

N South Pedlar ATV Trail

Situated in the Pedlar Ranger District of the George Washington National Forest, this is a looping network of nearly 20 miles of trails designed for the recreational

Riding through a forested area in the South Pedlar ATV Trail system.

all-terrain-vehicle rider. The routes here are open to ATVs, motorbikes, and mountain bikes and follow narrow twisting trails through the hilly terrain of the Blue Ridge Mountains. The South Pedlar ATV Trail system (also known as Terrapin and Rattlesnake Trails) is popular among mountain bikers from Lynchburg, Buena Vista, and Lexington and boasts some of the most difficult terrain around. Cyclists interested in heading out here should consider coming in the spring when the mountain laurel, thick around here, are in spectacular bloom. The forest is pretty dense in the summer, sheltering you from most of the summer heat. The trail is located 0.5 mile west of the Blue Ridge Parkway off Route 130. Signs for the trailhead parking are posted along Route 130. Once you arrive, there's a pay-as-you-park honor system in place. Please don't hesitate to drop in your $5.00 parking fee to support the forest service. For more information, go to www.fs.fed.us/gwjnf/orvtrails.html. *(DeLorme: Virginia Atlas & Gazetteer: Page 54, D-1.)*

○ North Mountain Trail Near Roanoke

This is a trail that Roanoke's hard-core mountain bikers often frequent when they're feeling aggressive. Fewer than 10 miles west of Roanoke on Route 311, you can access this trail in the New Castle Ranger District of the Jefferson National Forest. Narrow, rugged singletrack follows the North Mountain ridge nearly 12 miles north. There are some smaller trails that fall down the west side of North Mountain to Forest Road 224, a forest road that may give you the relief you need to get back to the start of this ride. *(DeLorme: Virginia Atlas & Gazetteer: Page 42, A-2.)*

Southwest
Virginia

George Washington National Forest

Jefferson National Forest

41 Brush Mountain

Start: From FR 188.2 off U.S. Route 460.
Length: 8.3-mile loop.
Approximate riding time: 2 to 2.5 hours.
Difficulty rating: Both physically and techni-cally, this ride is tough. There are long, fast singletrack descents and equally long, tough climbs. It's not all bad, but be prepared for a good workout.

Trail surface: Singletrack and gravel road.
Land status: National forest.
Nearest town: Blacksburg.
Other trail users: Hikers and equestrians.
Canine compatibility: Dog friendly.
Fees and permits: No fees or permits required.
Schedule: Open year-round, weather permit-ting.
Maps: USGS maps: Blacksburg, Newport; Jef-ferson National Forest topo map: Blacksburg District.
Trail contacts: Jefferson National Forest, Roanoke, VA, (540) 265–6054; Blacksburg Ranger District, Blacksburg, VA, (540) 552–4641.

Getting There: From Blacksburg: Take Main Street (Business U.S. Route 460) west toward Brush Mountain. Continue on U.S. Route 460 west for about 4 miles. At the top of the climb over Brush Mountain, turn left on FR 188.2 (dirt road). Park wherever you can along FR 188.2 or go 2 miles along FR 188.2 to the old lookout tower and park. *DeLorme: Virginia Atlas & Gazetteer:* Page 41, B-6.

The Ride

Brush Mountain has become, for nearly all off-road cyclists in this area, the quin-tessential mountain biking haven. Its proximity to town and campus—the mountain is cycling distance from Virginia Tech—makes Brush Mountain an ideal place for busy students and gnarly-seeking riders to mash. Cyclists can easily spend a long afternoon riding around the mountain's trails and still get back with plenty of time to hit the books at day's end (yeah, right—like that'll happen). There are tons of technical downhills, grueling uphills, rocks, more than 1,000 vertical feet, and dozens of miles of well-maintained trails from which to choose.

The Brush and Gap Mountain multiple-use trails have not gone underappreci-ated. Local clubs practice regular trail maintenance to preserve this mountain biking mecca. There are numerous water bars strategically placed along the steep descents

Even dogs love it here.

Brush Mountain

that protect the trails from excessive runoff and erosion. Trail corduroying, a method of repairing wet or muddy trails, is also evident throughout the mountain's trail system, further maintaining the trail's integrity despite so much use. If you want to become more involved with trail maintenance, or just want some fun people to ride with, contact the friendly family at the East Coasters Bike Shop, down the road from Brush Mountain.

The closest access to the trails on Brush Mountain is from Forest Road 188.2, just off U.S. Route 460. This is a great place to start if you're riding from town. Take U.S. Route 460 west out of Blacksburg and start climbing (this is the east side of Brush Mountain). At the top of this climb, on the left, is FR 188.2. Follow this gravel-surfaced road up the steep hill and along the ridge of Brush Mountain. This leads you all the way to the site of the old fire tower, a circular drive at the end of the state-maintained service road.

From this circular drive, continue along the ridge of Brush Mountain, on what is now an unmaintained jeep trail. Follow this trail along the ridge for 0.5 mile before reaching a three-way split. Notice at this point the red paint blazes on the trees. Turn right, following the red blazes into the woods, and begin your first wild descent down "The Beast," toward Poverty Creek. Hold onto your brake pads as you descend through four very tight switchbacks, then straight down the west side of Brush Mountain.

At the bottom of the descent, this red-blazed trail comes to a T, intersecting with the orange-blazed multiple-use trail. Turn right at this T and follow the smooth, flat singletrack trail alongside Poverty Creek. Be aware of hikers and equestrians who may also be using this trail, and always yield the right-of-way. The orange blazes will lead you all the way back to FR 188.2 if you choose to complete this loop.

In just under 1 mile along the secluded Poverty Creek Multiple-Use Trail, you'll reach a small opening. To follow this loop, you need to bear right into the woods, following the orange blazes. Bearing to the left will lead you to Gap Mountain, which has an entirely different network of great trails. To continue this loop, though, turn right and follow the orange blazes. These lead you toward Pandapas Pond. Please note that bicycles are not allowed within 300 feet of Pandapas Pond. There are a number of trails bordering the pond designed exclusively for hikers. Be careful not to stray too far on the Poverty Creek Multiple-Use Trail and wind up at Pandapas Pond.

Before the pond, the orange trail turns right and crosses over Poverty Creek into a thick growth of rhododendron. From this point, all the way back up to the ridge of Brush Mountain and FR 188.2, the trail weaves through heavy foliage, rolling up and down the mountain's western slope. This section is so exciting that you'll want to turn around at the jeep trail coming in on the left and grind it out a second time. Once at the jeep trail, turn right and climb your way back up to FR 188.2.

Because Brush Mountain is so close to town, the easiest way to get there may be by bicycle. There are few places to park aside from the circular drive at the old fire tower or along FR 188.2. Unfortunately, parking is severely limited on the mountain's peak. And FR 188.2, while accessible to cars, is a gravel road with some large potholes. You may prefer to leave your car near the East Coasters Bike Shop, then ride the 4 miles uphill to the start. Another great option is to park at the Pandapas Pond parking lot and walk your bike over to the main trail. This option will, of course, start you in a different place than the featured ride, but it will nevertheless lead you to the same trails. A lot of people prefer starting here so they can park their cars and avoid some of the huge climbs.

There are no camping facilities at the park, so make reservations in Blacksburg if you decide to stay in the area. The numerous trails here at Brush Mountain provide more than one day of riding, and staying overnight will allow you to explore all that Brush Mountain, Poverty Creek, and Pandapas Pond have to offer. Each switchback, incline, and singletrack has the potential of opening a new avenue of trails to explore. Enjoy the other trails such as Snake Root, Jacobs Ladder, Queen Anne, Prickley Pear, Skullcap, Trillium, and Indian Pipe. All of these trails lead to each other at some point along the ride, so pick up a map and some local advice from the East Coasters bike shop. Each trail here at Brush Mountain is guaranteed satisfaction as well as an opportunity for cyclists to ride premium singletrack.

Miles and Directions

0.0 START at FR 188.2, just off U.S. Route 460. Head up the steep climb to the top of the ridge.

0.9 Pass the first orange-blazed trailhead for the Brush Mountain Multiple-Use Trail. Continue on FR 188.2. This forest road is a well-maintained, gravel service road with some steep rolling hills.

1.9 Reach the remains of the old lookout tower at a large circular drive. State maintenance ends at this point. Go straight through this circular drive to the old jeep trail that continues into the woods.

2.5 The trail splits in a number of different directions. Turn right into the woods, following the red blazes. This trail leads to an incredible singletrack descent called The Beast. Watch out—it's fast! **(Note:** Along the trail between the old lookout tower and this turn, you will ride through two semipermanent mud holes before reaching the trail split. If you turn left at this split, you will drop down the south side of Brush Mountain through private property. Going straight takes you all the way to Boley Fields. Make sure to turn right (west) on the red-blazed trail.)

3.7 Reach the bottom of this descent.

3.75 Cross over Poverty Creek. This is a fairly dry creek crossing.

3.8 Turn right on the Poverty Creek Multiple-Use Trail (orange blaze). This is a well-maintained, flat, smooth singletrack trail that parallels Poverty Creek. The thick growth of rhododendron on either side of this trail gives it a deep, remote quality. You may feel very removed from the outside world along this peaceful trail.

4.6 Reach a small clearing. Bear right on the trail that leads into the woods and follow the orange blaze. At this point, if you bear left into the open area, you will end up following trails that lead to Gap Mountain and Forest Road 708 on the west side of Poverty Creek.

4.7 Arrive at a four-way trail intersection after a quick, muddy section. Go straight through this trail intersection, following the orange diamond blazes nailed to the trees in front of you.

5.2 Turn right (southeast) across Poverty Creek on a narrow singletrack trail that winds through trees and a thick grove of rhododendron. There are two orange paint squares nailed to a tree at this turn, but both are slightly hidden. If you reach Pandapas Pond, 0.2 mile away, you've gone too far. **(Caution:** Mountain bikers and equestrians are not allowed to ride within 300 feet of Pandapas Pond, so try not to miss the turn.)

5.6 Just past the thick grove of rhododendron, start climbing a steep hill with switchbacks.

5.85 This orange-blazed trail comes to a T intersection. Stay left, following the double orange blazes. The trail immediately comes to another T intersection. There are four orange blocks painted on a tree on the left. Take a hard right at this T intersection. Start climbing.

6.2 Descend a short but very steep hill with warning labels posted on the trees. The uphill on the other side is equally as steep.

6.5 Turn right on a wide jeep trail. This takes you uphill all the way back to FR 188.2.

7.4 Turn left on FR 188.2.

8.3 Reach U.S. Route 460.

(**Alternate start:** Pandapas Pond Park. Park in the first parking lot on the left. Trailheads abound.)

Ride Information

Local Information

For information on the area, go to the Web site www.blacksburg.va.us.

Local Events and Attractions

Smithfield Plantation, Smithfield Plantation Drive, Blacksburg, VA; (540) 231-3947.

Virginia Museum of Natural History at Virginia Tech, Blacksburg, VA, (540) 231-3001.

Group Rides

Saturday mornings, weather permitting. Rides start at 10:30 A.M. Sponsored by East Coasters, a local bike shop, (540) 951-2369.

42 Mountain Lake

Start: From Mountain Lake Resort.
Length: 21.4-mile loop.
Approximate riding time: 2.5 to 3 hours.
Difficulty rating: Moderate to difficult, due to the length of the ride and some long, gradual climbs. Technically, this ride doesn't pose a great challenge.

Trail surface: Hilly dirt roads and jeep trails, some of which can get rocky.
Land status: National forest.
Nearest town: Blacksburg.
Other trail users: Hikers and motorists.
Canine compatibility: Dog friendly, although the trip may be a little long for the pooch.
Fees and permits: No fees or permits required.
Schedule: Open year-round.
Maps: USGS maps: Eggleston, Interior (Virginia and West Virginia), Pearisburg, Lindside; Jefferson National Forest topo map: Blacksburg District.
Trail contacts: Blacksburg Ranger District, (540) 552-4641; Jefferson National Forest Headquarters, (540) 265-6054.

Getting There: From I-81 near Blacksburg: Take exit 118 to U.S. Route 460 West to Blacksburg. Take the U.S. Route 460 bypass (left fork) around Blacksburg to Route 700. Turn right on Route 700, going 7 uphill miles to Mountain Lake. *DeLorme: Virginia Atlas & Gazetteer:* Page 41, B-5.

The Ride

Mountain Lake, one of only two natural lakes in the state of Virginia (the other is Lake Drummond in the Great Dismal Swamp) and one of the highest lakes in the East, is home to the renowned Mountain Lake Resort. This romantic sandstone resort has been a luxurious year-round mountaintop getaway for nearly 200 years.

In 1986, the majesty of this grand old resort hotel was captured forever on film as the setting for the major motion picture *Dirty Dancing,* starring Patrick Swayze.

At nearly 4,000 feet above sea level, Mountain Lake is cool and pleasant in summer, and its winters can often register some of the coldest temperatures in the state. This climate helps make Mountain Lake ideal for outdoor recreation year-round, from mountain biking in the summer to cross-country skiing in the winter. Autumn brings with it an explosion of fall colors, such that few places can match. During the

Mountain Lake.

winters, when the mountains are filled with heavy snow, cross-country skiing and horse-drawn carriage rides keep visitors busy and entertained.

The resort offers many guest activities on its 2,600-acre lot, and it recently designated several miles of its wooded trails for mountain bikes. Tangent Outfitters of Dublin, Virginia, occupies a small shop at the resort and rents mountain bikes from the Lakeview Cottage. Guided mountain bike trips are also scheduled from the resort for those interested in exploring some of the area's more scenic spots. Maps detailing the trail systems are available from Mountain Lake Resort.

This fairly large loop, from Mountain Lake Resort to Butt Mountain, doesn't actually use any of the trails on the Mountain Lake Resort property. Instead, it leads cyclists on a more strenuous off-road journey deep into Jefferson National Forest. This is a great ride for anyone interested in spending an afternoon mountain biking who isn't afraid of a few hefty climbs along the way.

The terrain is hilly, and the surface is at times rather rocky. Be prepared for a long ride. When you arrive at Butt Mountain Overlook, you're greeted with a panoramic view of the New River Valley and the vast stretches of land nearly 2,000 feet below, making all the effort worth your while. Perhaps the only lookout comparable in the entire region is the fabled McAfee's Knob, located north of Roanoke on the Appalachian Trail.

If you have any remaining energy after Butt Mountain, take time to depart from the main route and check out the cascading falls along Cascades Trail. Otherwise, continue along the jeep road down through Little Meadows, then climb uphill toward Route 613. This incredibly steep road heads back to Mountain Lake and was used as a brutal climb in the mountainous stage four of the Tour DuPont professional bicycle race in both 1994 and 1995. Many of the world's greatest cyclists struggled up Route 613 before making the harrowing, high-speed descent back down Route 700. American world champion and Tour de France winner Lance Armstrong was first to crest this category-1 climb over Salt Pond Mountain at Mountain Lake Resort both years running, and in 1995 he won the 141-mile stage from Lynchburg to Blacksburg with a solo breakaway.

Chances are, after this ride you may want to pedal directly into the seventy-two-degree water of Mountain Lake. Afterward, taste the superb cuisine in Mountain Lake's formal stone dining room. If you're visiting in autumn, help celebrate a traditional German Oktoberfest, held the last two Saturdays in September and each Friday and Saturday in October. If you're interested in mountain biking on top of the world, Mountain Lake is, without question, the place to go.

Miles and Directions

0.0   START at Mountain Lake Resort. From the resort, follow the paved road (Route 613) around the west side of the lake.

0.6   Route 613 changes to a dirt road.

1.5   Pass the Mountain Lake Biological Station on the right. The University of Virginia sponsors this biological station. Bear left, continuing on Route 613.

3.2   Pass the parking area on the right for the War Spur and Chestnut Trail. These trails make a 4.5-mile loop through the Mountain Lake Wilderness of the Jefferson National Forest along Salt Pond Mountain Ridge. War Spur Overlook is less than 2 miles into this loop. Continue north on Route 613.

4.0   Start climbing Minnie Ball Hill.

5.3   Reach the top of this climb (3,972 feet). Turn left on Rocky Mountain Road at this intersection and follow the rocky jeep trail along the ridge of Big Mountain. There is a dirt parking area for the Appalachian Trail at this intersection.

8.6   Go through Bailey Gap (3,637 feet).

10.9 Go through Lybrook Gap (3,794 feet).

13.0 Reach Butt Mountain Overlook (4,210 feet). Check out the incredible view of the New River Valley. Continue following the main dirt road, now Forest Road 714. Get ready for a long, fast descent down to Little Meadows.

15.6 On the right is the trailhead for the Cascades Trail. Continue on FR 714.

16.0 Cross over Laurel Creek.

16.9 Pedal through Little Meadows.

17.1 Cross over Little Stony Creek. Get ready to start climbing again.

19.2 Go through Pacers Gap (3,635 feet).

20.1 Turn left on Route 613 (paved). This is a very steep section of road that takes you back to the summit at Mountain Lake Resort.

21.4 Arrive at Mountain Lake Resort. What a ride!

Ride Information

Accommodations

Mountain Lake Resort. Prices range from $75 to $335 per night; (800) 346–3334.

Local Events and Attractions

German Oktoberfest, September and October at Mountain Lake Resort.

43 Mount Rogers Loop

Start: From the pull-off on FR 90.
Length: 8-mile loop.
Approximate riding time: 2 hours.
Difficulty rating: This is a fairly difficult ride due to the elevation gains along the route. Cyclists will have to be ready to climb quite a bit and still be able to handle the technical descents on the other end.
Trail surface: Hilly fire roads and singletrack.
Land status: National forest.
Nearest town: Damascus.
Other trail users: Hikers and equestrians.
Canine compatibility: Dog friendly. Just watch out for the horses.
Fees and permits: No fees or permits required.
Schedule: Open daylight to dark year-round.
Maps: USGS map: Konnarock; Mount Rogers National Recreation Area topo map.
Trail contacts: Mount Rogers National Recreation Area, (540) 783–5196; Jefferson National Forest Headquarters, (540) 265–6054.

Getting There: From Abingdon: Take U.S. Route 58 east to Damascus. From Damascus, continue on U.S. Route 58 for approximately 6 miles to FR 90. Turn left on FR 90 (dirt road) and park along the side of the road at the small pull-off. *DeLorme: Virginia Atlas & Gazetteer:* Page 22, C-3.

The Ride

I was not the first to discover this ride. In fact, long before I arrived, countless hours had already been spent clearing the trails and marking this route. It's no accident, therefore, that this loop, used as the official race course for the Virginia Highlands Mountain Bike Club's Mountain Bike Challenge, is one of the finest mountain bike rides in Virginia.

Smooth singletrack, fast descents, spectacular overlooks and mountain meadows, winding dirt roads, and trails that grip the edges of steep ridges combine to form an extraordinary ride in the highlands of southwest Virginia, attracting Virginia's best off-road cyclists.

But this should come as no surprise, since this loop is located within the boundaries of Mount Rogers National Recreation Area. Mountain biking is both welcome and encouraged inside this 115,000-acre mountain wilderness. More than 400 miles of open trails in the Mount Rogers National Recreation Area wind over high mountain peaks, across wind-beaten meadows, and along rushing highland streams.

This is one of the East Coast's wildest and most rugged regions and includes a number of Virginia's loftiest mountains. It's no wonder mountain biking is taken seriously down here.

Mount Rogers National Recreation Area is named for Virginia's highest peak, Mount Rogers, which stands at 5,729 feet. Whitetop Mountain, a close second, stands nearby at 5,520 feet. It is often covered with snow long after the snow has melted away in the valleys (hence the name). The summit of Whitetop Mountain is also home to the highest vehicular road in the state. Route 89 takes cars from Route 600 on a spectacular uphill drive to the "balds," or open meadows, at the top of this lofty mountain.

Also near this loop is the Virginia Creeper Trail. This rail-trail travels 34 miles through the rugged landscape of Mount Rogers, from Abingdon to the Virginia–North Carolina border. If you're looking for a low-difficulty ride that passes over high river gorges, travels past waterfalls and rolling pastures, and crosses more than one hundred bridges and trestles, then stay an extra few days and fit this unique trail into your schedule.

This particular loop in the Mount Rogers National Recreation Area, just off U.S. Route 58, takes you up and over Iron Mountain. It begins on a well-maintained dirt road and eventually becomes complete singletrack. Though most of the dirt roads you will encounter on this loop travel uphill, there will be occasions of extreme speed on white-knuckled descents. The loop's singletrack stretches up and down the mountain's ridges and at times grips the side of the mountain with barely a bike-width of trail. Equestrians frequent these trails as well, so use caution when pedaling along these tight routes.

You'll also notice many different trails that branch farther into the national recreation area. Detailed area maps, useful for exploring the many trails in this vast off-road playground, can be found at the Highland Ski and Outdoor Center in Abingdon. Perhaps even set up a base camp at one of Mount Rogers National Recreation Area's many campsites and spend the weekend riding as many new trails as possible. Because of this area's inspiring scenery and its hundreds of miles of ridable trails, very few places in the state can compare to this mountain biking wonderland.

Miles and Directions

0.0 START from the pull-off on the right-hand side of FR 90, just off U.S. Route 58. Begin climbing this hard-packed dirt road.

0.5 To the right is a great view of Whitetop Mountain. Just up the road is a gated fire road.

0.6 Turn left, pedaling around the gate on this grassy forest service road. This jeep trail slowly winds uphill.

0.9 Turn right on a slightly hidden singletrack trail that climbs a short, steep hill. **(Note:** To find this trailhead, follow the grassy forest service road uphill for 0.3 mile from FR 90. As you round the third curve to the left, there is a large hickory tree and a small creek at the

Whitetop Mountain dominates the landscape.

apex on the right side of the road. The hickory tree marks the singletrack trailhead. The climb up this trail is very steep, but is less than a tenth of a mile.)

1.0 Reach the top of the steep singletrack climb and turn right on a wide singletrack trail.

1.4 Small clearing on the right. Continue straight (but bear left) on this wide singletrack trail.

1.5 Arrive at an intersection of trails. There is a shelter and picnic area on the left. To the right is a trail with man-made steps that heads up the mountain. Continue straight on the trail you're on and descend toward FR 90.

1.6 Arrive at an intersection between FR 90 and FR 615. FR 90 crosses from right to left. FR 615 bears a soft right and heads downhill. Turn left on FR 90 and follow this uphill to Iron Mountain Trail (yellow blaze). Note the Feathercamp Branch Trail on the far left, past the gate. Feathercamp Branch Trail will take you downhill along its grassy terrain for nearly 2 miles to U.S. Route 58.

1.7 Turn left on Iron Mountain Trail (yellow blaze). This trail gently climbs Feathercamp Ridge, skirting the ridgeline. The surface of this trail is smooth and well maintained.

2.4 Reach the top of the climb and begin a fun, quick descent.

2.7 Arrive at a T intersection. Turn right, continuing to loop clockwise around this route. A left turn would take you west along Iron Mountain Trail, traveling along the crest of Feather-camp Ridge. Note the large oak tree marked with a yellow blaze.

3.2 Cross Buzzard Den Branch. This section of trail at the bottom of the descent is often very muddy. Equestrians also use this trail, and you will notice the deep imprints of horse-shoes in the wet soil.

3.3 Reach the low point along this loop. Bear right up a very short trail. This takes you to a larger trail intersection.

3.35 At this trail intersection, turn hard left on the forest service road.

3.8 Nice view on the left.

4.6 Pedal across a small meadow.

5.0 Cross through a steel gate and turn right on FR 615. Start climbing.

6.1 Turn hard left on FR 90. This takes you back to the start of the ride. But you're not done climbing yet!

6.5 Reach the summit of this climb on FR 90. Get ready for a fast descent!

6.8 Spectacular view of Whitetop Mountain to the south.

8.0 Reach the start of the ride at the bottom of FR 90.

Ride Information

Local Information

Abingdon Convention and Visitors Bureau, Abingdon, VA; (800) 435-3440.
Mount Rogers National Recreation Area, (800) 628-7202.

Local Events and Attractions

Appalachian Trail Days (May), Damascus, VA; www.damascus.org.

Accommodations

Maxwell Manor Bed and Breakfast, Abingdon, VA; (888) 851-1100.
Summerfield Inn, Abingdon, VA; (800) 668-5905.
Silversmith Inn, Abingdon, VA; (800) 533-0195.
Victoria and Albert Inn, Abingdon, VA; (888) 645-5636.

44 Grayson Highlands State Park

Start: From Massie Gap parking area.
Length: 8-mile loop.
Approximate riding time: 2 hours.
Difficulty rating: Difficult. The excessive water crossings, teeth-rattling downhills, and length create a very challenging journey.

Trail surface: Flat sections, smooth uphills, and wet rocky downhills.
Land status: State park.
Nearest town: Volney.
Other trail users: Equestrians, hikers, backpackers, and anglers.
Canine compatibility: Dog friendly.
Fees and permits: $2.00 at the gate.
Schedule: April through November.
Maps: USGS map: Troutdale.
Trail contacts: Grayson Highlands State Park, Mouth of Wilson, VA, (540) 579-7092.

Getting There: From Marion: Follow Route 16 south for approximately 33 miles. Turn right onto U.S. Route 58 in Volney. Follow U.S. Route 58 for 8 miles, then turn right into Grayson Highlands State Park and onto Route 362. Park at the Massie Gap parking area, which is on the right, past Campground Road. *DeLorme: Virginia Atlas & Gazetteer:* Page 23, C-5.

The Ride

Virginia's highest state park, Grayson Highlands, lies adjacent to Mount Rogers (5,729 feet), Virginia's highest point, and ties together a unique collection of flora and fauna. A highly versatile recreational area, the park is one of the most picturesque spots you'll find in southwestern Virginia. You're likely to encounter some of the wild ponies that live and roam in the park year-round or catch the blooming of the Catawba rhododendron in the middle of June. Visitors are encouraged not to feed or spook the ponies, but they are relatively calm and will gladly pose for a photo. The large light pink blooms of the Catawba explode during the hot summer months and are accentuated by their clusters of shiny oval-shaped leaves. The aroma alone is worth the trip. Most of the Catawbas are around 4 feet high, but they can grow in excess of 8 feet.

The boreal forests in Grayson Highlands are the same as those found in Nova Scotia. This unique environment provides the perfect climate for moss, which has the ability to retain water almost all year. The presence of moss causes the area to be moist year-round. When combined with the elevation, this moisture makes the air temperature even cooler.

Pedaling along Virginia Highlands Horse Trail. Ride cautiously and quietly, so as not to spook the ponies.

A park sign at the trailhead reminds hikers and cyclists to take a sufficient supply of water if venturing into the backcountry. Within Grayson Highlands are a number of trails that connect with nearby landmarks like Whitetop Mountain and Mount Rogers. The park provides full camping facilities that make visiting the area a pleasure. Plan to spend some time here and explore the extensive trail system.

When you ride to Wilburn Ridge in the distance, you'll notice the Frasier firs, which are popular Christmas trees. There are many fir tree farms in this region, and some allow you to pick your own Christmas tree. Many trees are cut and sent throughout the nation.

The first uphill takes you through a short section of pines along a boulder-filled jeep trail. As you pass through the metal horse gate, you'll notice an adjoining trail to the right, which is your return path on this journey. This section has erosion logs to help decrease the amount of erosion on its steep slope. Entering the horse trail, you'll notice the adverse effects of erosion, which makes this first section challenging. Wilburn Ridge is an important landmark because it marks the intersection of the Appalachian Trail and the continuation of the horse trail. Make sure not to venture onto the Appalachian Trail, because only foot traffic is allowed.

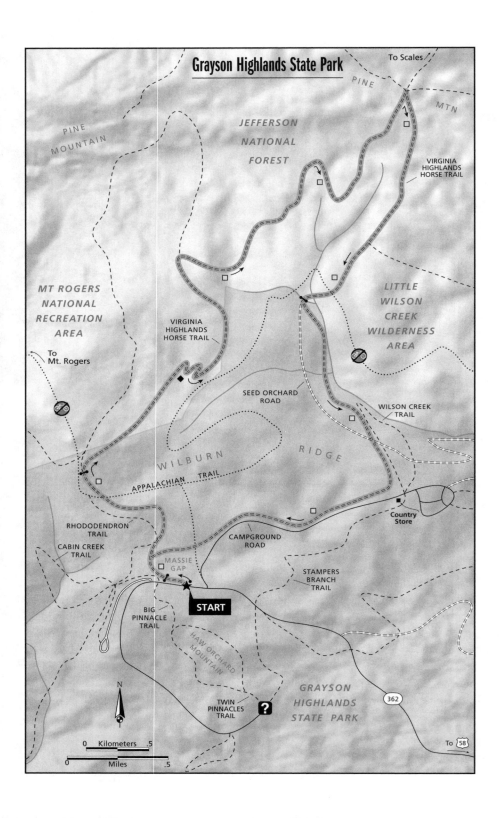

Grayson Highlands State Park

To Scales

PINE   MTN

PINE
MOUNTAIN

JEFFERSON
NATIONAL
FOREST

VIRGINIA
HIGHLANDS
HORSE TRAIL

MT ROGERS
NATIONAL
RECREATION
AREA

LITTLE
WILSON
CREEK
WILDERNESS
AREA

To
Mt. Rogers

VIRGINIA
HIGHLANDS
HORSE TRAIL

SEED ORCHARD
ROAD

WILSON CREEK
TRAIL

WILBURN   RIDGE

APPALACHIAN   TRAIL

Country
Store

RHODODENDRON
TRAIL

CABIN CREEK
TRAIL

CAMPGROUND
ROAD

STAMPERS
BRANCH
TRAIL

MASSIE
GAP

START

BIG
PINNACLE
TRAIL

HAW
ORCHARD
MOUNTAIN

GRAYSON
HIGHLANDS
STATE PARK

362

N

TWIN
PINNACLES
TRAIL

?

To 58

0   Kilometers   .5

0   Miles   .5

As you continue to ride north and northwest, you increase your chances of meeting the small population of wild ponies. You'll go through several metal gates throughout the ride. The second gate, at mile 1.3, contains a mileage sign and an Appalachian Trail register. This begins a glorious section of rocky, fast, switchback-filled downhill runs. Tighten your suspension and dial in your brakes. The remaining 6 miles offer repetitious creek crossings, switchbacks, and gradual elevation changes. Endurance plays a key part in completing the entire 8 miles.

Most of the terrain after the second gate is wooded. One area that extends into the valley is the last section without tree cover. As you begin the last leg that runs parallel to Campground Road, the Country Store will greet you with southern hospitality. It is visible from the trail and makes a wonderful intermission before the end of your journey. When you can see Massie Gap, you know that you're close to the finish. Take a hot shower, enjoy a campfire, and do it all again in the morning.

Miles and Directions

0.0 START from the Massie Gap parking lot and ride west toward the fence line. Several signs will inform you which trails do not permit mountain bikes.

0.2 Go through a metal horse gate and follow signs up to Wilburn Ridge.

0.3 Ride up the first incline.

0.4 The first plateau places you in the middle of the joining horse and jeep access.

0.5 This is Wilburn Ridge and a spectacular view.

0.7 The sign and intersection mark a crucial landmark. Continue straight ahead but note the following landmarks: the Appalachian Trail (AT) north goes right, the AT south goes left, Scales is 5 miles straight, Old Orchard Shelter is 8.1 miles straight, Mount Rogers is 3.8 miles.

1.0 A steady incline and likely place for a wild pony encounter.

1.2 The footpath for the AT goes directly uphill toward the fence line. You'll want to stay on the gravel road. This also marks the spot of the first creek crossing.

1.3 Dismount and open the gate manually. The trail register for the AT is on the facing side. The mileage sign is on the opposite side.

1.9 This is a section of technical traverses.

2.0 Encounter a very tight switchback right.

2.1 Encounter a steep downhill then a switchback left.

2.2 Encounter technical switchbacks right and left.

2.9 This marks a downhill traverse.

3.0 A flat section takes you into a valley.

3.1 The steep downhill is fairly treacherous.

3.2 Come to a large creek crossing (10 feet wide and 1 foot deep). This section opens up to a scenic part of the valley.

3.4 Another flat section allows you to catch your breath.

4.2 Encounter a creek crossing before a steady incline.

4.3 The extensive ridgeline is a great spot for photos of the valley.

4.4 Veer right downhill at the sign and intersection.

4.7 This creek crossing is very wide (about 15 feet) but can be crossed with care.

5.0 A large ravine requires you to gain a lot of speed.

5.2 A large steel gate marks the park boundary. A sign reads STATE PARK HORSE CAMP—2.5 MILES.

5.5 Come to another large creek crossing.

5.7 A sign directs you toward the campground.

5.9 A Y intersection is the pivotal point on the trail. Straight ahead is private property. Ride uphill to the right and continue along the Virginia Highlands Horse Trail.

6.3 Reach a gravel parking lot and the Country Store across the paved road. The road left will take you toward the camping area. Continue right on the trail that runs parallel to the road.

6.5 Continue up the steep incline before you reach the parking lot. This will take you along the camp road and back to the Massie Gap parking area.

6.6 Cross the access road and continue straight.

7.1 You will be in sight of Massie Gap Peak.

7.8 Continue straight toward the Massie Gap parking area. A foot trail to the left and marked by a blue blaze takes you back to Campground Road.

7.9 This is the intersection of the first incline. Turn left here, and the gate to reach the Massie Gap parking area will be in plain sight.

8.0 Arrive at your car and a descriptive park sign.

Ride Information

Local Events and Attractions

Jefferson National Forest, Roanoke, VA; (540) 265-6054.

Whitetop Mountain Maple Festival (Late March), Mount Rogers Fire Hall; (540) 388-3257.

Grayson Highlands Fall Festival (Late September), Grayson Highlands State Park; (540) 579-6423.

45 Hidden Valley Lake

Start: From the Hidden Valley Lake parking area and boat launch.
Length: 3.8-mile loop.
Approximate riding time: 1 hour.
Difficulty rating: Moderate due to the technicality of existing surface rocks and uneven trail transitions.
Trail surface: Most of the trail is smooth and flat with sections of surface rocks.
Land status: National forest.
Nearest town: Abingdon.
Other trail users: Hikers, backpackers, rock climbers, anglers, and hunters (in season).
Canine compatibility: Dogs not allowed.
Fees and permits: No fees or permits required.
Schedule: May through November.
Maps: USGS map: Brumley.
Trail contacts: Jefferson National Park, Roanoke, VA, (540) 265-6054.

Getting There: From Abingdon: Drive U.S. Route 19/U.S. Alternate Route 58 for 15 miles. Turn right onto Hidden Valley Drive (Route 690). Warning: This paved road is very steep, so make sure that your brakes and transmission aren't going to fail you. Use low gears going uphill and downhill. There are two switchbacks toward the top, so try not to lose momentum. When you reach the top, the road turns to gravel. (Rock climbers park here.) Continue straight until you reach the first right turn. Turn right here and park. *DeLorme: Virginia Atlas & Gazetteer:* Page 21, B-7.

The Ride

The Hidden Valley Lake loop will charm you and invite you back for more. This lazy roll through a section of Virginia's highlands has been known to make visitors want to stay forever. Anglers will rejoice at the great fishing to be had in the lake—species such as bass, northern pike, sunfish, and crappie. Rock climbing is another popular attraction. The land is privately owned, but as long as you sign in, respect the rock, and don't bring your dog, you're gladly welcome. The climber or other visitor, not the landowner, assume all risk. The exposed walls of limestone and sandstone are clearly visible as you drive toward the top of the ridge. Even if you don't climb, this trail offers a breathtaking view just the same.

Pass the peak of the ridge and continue onto the gravel jeep road straight ahead. There is ample parking at lakeside, and the ride should begin at this point. The beginning consists of a well-maintained jeep road until you reach the dam. At the dam the jeep road goes into tree cover and becomes slightly rocky. Some of the

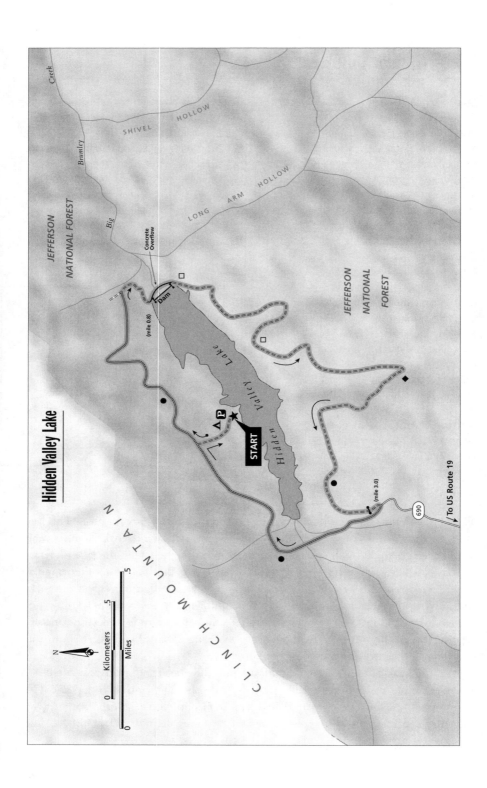

Hidden Valley Lake

N

Kilometers
0   .5

Miles
0   .5

CLINCH MOUNTAIN

JEFFERSON
NATIONAL FOREST

Creek

Bramley

Big

SHIVEL   HOLLOW

LONG ARM HOLLOW

Concrete
Overflow

Dam

(mile 0.8)

☐

☐

Hidden Valley Lake

JEFFERSON
NATIONAL
FOREST

◆

●

▲P
★

START

●

(mile 3.0)

690

To US Route 19

●

sharper edges of the exposed sandstone rocks can be potential hazards to your wheels. Consider staying in the worn path to avoid any mishaps. Extra tubes and tools are recommended on this trail.

After you finish several switchbacks and the two major inclines, the trail will plane out and the jeep road comes into sight. There's not much room for navigating around the boulder barrier that connects with the jeep road. A quick sprint back to the parking area is in order once you reach the road. Trail selection and variation is virtually nonexistent, but the run is short enough to be done in multiples. Facing east, toward the lake in the parking lot, provides the visitor with a dramatic sunset.

Since you're so deep into rural Virginia, you have the freedom of viewing stars and night swimming without the distractive glare of city lights.

Plan to camp but bring plenty of water. Even though the lake is always high, you'll need to bring potable water, unless you boil what you take from the lake. The drive back down is rougher than going up. Remember to use low gears while going both ways. This is a friendly area and has seen major improvements in recent years. Keeping the park clean has become an important part of the Forest Service's mission.

▶ Locals will tell you that the proper pronunciation of *Appalachian* is with equal stress on the first and third *a*'s: *Appalachian*.

If you don't care to camp, this ride is a mere thirty minutes from Abingdon. Book a room early and try to catch the Virginia Highlands Festival in mid-August. The festival is acclaimed nationwide and provides an assortment of crafts, food, and music. This weeklong extravaganza could be the perfect ending to a sweet ride at Hidden Valley.

Miles and Directions

0.0   START at the first parking area on the right. Go back up the road as if you were leaving. Turn right at the T intersection.

0.2   Continue straight and past the second gravel road on the right, which takes you to the camping area.

0.7   Follow the switchback to the right. The dam and lake are visible at this point.

0.8 Two steel gates are located at either end of the dam. Go down the concrete overflow and direct yourself right, toward the jeep road.

1.0 A switchback right begins a series of uphill sections.

2.1 There is a steady incline for the next 0.2 mile.

2.5 This flat section is overgrown and contains several surface rocks.

2.9 A steel barrier and entrance road are visible at this point. The barrier is straight ahead, and the entrance road will run from left to right. Continue right onto the gravel road.

3.0 Cross a stone barrier and ride right at the Y. Follow the road back to the parking area and beginning of the ride.

3.8 Arrive at the parking area.

Ride Information

Local Information

Abingdon Convention and Visitors Bureau, Abingdon, VA; (540) 676–2282.
Washington County Chamber of Commerce, Abingdon, VA; (540) 628–8141.

Local Events and Attractions

Virginia Highlands Festival (mid-August), Abingdon, VA; (800) 435–3440; www.va-highlands-festival.org.
Barter Theatre, Abingdon, VA; (540) 628–3991; www.bartertheatre.com.

Accommodations

Camberley's Martha Washington Inn, Abingdon, VA; (540) 628–3161; www.camberleyhotels.com.

Restaurants

The Tavern (reservations recommended), Abingdon, VA; (540) 628–1118.
The Starving Artist Café, Abingdon, VA; (540) 628–8445.

46 Seven Sisters Trail

Start: From the first gravel lot on the left as you head toward Stony Fork campsite on Route 717.
Length: 7.3-mile loop.
Approximate riding time: 2 hours.
Difficulty rating: Difficult due to a strenuous series of ascents.
Trail surface: Old established trail is well maintained and quite challenging.
Land status: National forest.
Nearest town: Wytheville.
Other trail users: Hikers, backpackers, and hunters (in season).
Canine compatibility: Dog friendly.
Fees and permits: $2.00 at Stony Fork campground. No fee for parking or biking at the parking area.
Schedule: All year, weather permitting.
Maps: USGS maps: Big Bend, Bland.
Trail contacts: Jefferson National Forest, Roanoke, VA, (540) 265-6054.

Getting There: From Wytheville: Drive I-77 North toward Bland. Take the exit for Route 717. Head south on Route 717 and park in the first marked lot on the left. A small square brown sign will mark the parking area. *DeLorme: Virginia Atlas & Gazetteer:* Page 39, D-7.

The Ride

Seven Sisters is not as kind as it sounds. This traverse will demand the very best of you. It is challenging from the very beginning. The seven peaks on Little Walker Mountain can surprise you and tantalize you. The series of gradual inclines in the beginning pump your legs so much they'll feel like rocks. Take the chance to refuel as you go down the back side of each peak. The last major incline at mile 2.6 is the climb of all climbs.

The delicious 1.7-mile downhill will leave you drooling for more, along with the spectacular view of Walker and Brushy Mountains. The Stony Fork camping area is a full-service facility that's a wonderful place to rest before you do it all again. If you are not fortunate enough to be able to stay, make sure to bring a camera and keep the ridge on Walker Mountain in mind. You won't be disappointed.

The trail begins with a subtle set of switchbacks before the sign at mile 1.0. This is a great warm-up for the next 7 miles. Rock exposure is not a great concern, except for one section when beginning the downhill at the end. This large bed of loose slate can prove to be tricky, due to the steep drop on the right that follows you all the way down. Most of the obstacles consist of fallen trees crossing the path and

Seven Sisters Trail

START

To Wytheville

WALKER MOUNTAIN

WALKER MOUNTAIN

JEFFERSON NATIONAL FOREST

Stony Fork Campground

Seven Sisters Trail

LITTLE WALKER MOUNTAIN

Highest point
on trail 3,310 ft

East Fork

Stony Fork

717

206

221

52

52

77

717

659

600

N

Kilometers

Miles

jagged turns through the trees. Navigating through vertical posts is kind of like skiing slalom on snow—you have to keep your rhythm.

Most of the trees are oak, red and yellow maple, pine, and white spruce. Common wildlife inhabitants are deer, squirrels, owls, red-tailed hawks, and the occasional black bear. As you enter the camping area, you pass through a fortress of hand-planted pines. These rows of symmetric pines appear to be a finishing gate as you blast through the last flat of Seven Sisters. There is one final man-made jump to clear when you reach the pine grove—perfect for pictures or a speed check. You may find that some of the tracks after the jump get uncomfortably close to the trees—ouch. By starting your ride from the first gravel lot on the left, you are granted a wonderful cool-down by taking the blacktop back to the parking area. The paved section is approximately 2 miles and is slightly inclined. From the road, you can see the Seven Sisters and Little Walker Mountain to the right and Walker Mountain to the left.

Seven Sisters is just minutes away from Wytheville. The rugged terrain has a reputation for making its visitors love it or hate it. After you are done, unwrap yourself from the pines and join everyone at the Pure Country Steak House and Saloon for some true southern soul food. Wytheville also hosts the historic Millwald Theatre, which is Virginia's oldest motion picture theater still in operation. Hospitality is as plentiful as the good food.

Miles and Directions

0.0 START at the gravel parking lot and trailhead.

0.1 You can cross the creek by either going through it or walking over the bridge.

0.3 The tight switchback left begins a steady incline.

0.6 Another switchback takes you to the right and up the ridge.

1.0 A sign and intersection mark a new direction. Turn right and uphill at the T intersection.

1.6 Come to the first major incline.

1.8 The second incline is steep but can be completed.

2.2 This begins the first of a series of tight tree sections and downhills.

2.6 A very challenging incline will most likely cause you to walk uphill.

3.2 A sign directing you to the campsite is located here at the highest point on the trail (3,310 feet).

Stopping to take in the views along Little Walker Mountain.

3.6 Ride carefully through this technical rock section and extremely fast downhill.

5.3 Reach the campsite. Turn right onto the blacktop (Route 717) to return to the parking area.

7.3 Return to the parking area after 2 miles of paved road.

(**Alternate Start:** Continue to Stony Fork campsite, park, pay, and ride to the trailhead 2 miles back as a warm-up.)

Ride Information

Local Information
Wytheville-Wythe-Bland Chamber of Commerce, Wytheville, VA; (540) 223-3315.

Local Events and Attractions
Big Walker Lookout, Wytheville, VA; (540) 228-4401.

Millwald Theatre, Wytheville, VA; (540) 228-5031.

Restaurants
Pure Country Steak House and Saloon, Wytheville, VA; (540) 223-7303.

In Addition

Rails-to-Trails

The mission of Rails-to-Trails Conservancy is to "enhance America's communities and countryside by converting thousands of miles of abandoned rail corridors and connecting open spaces into a nationwide network of public trails."

Every large city and small town in America, by the early twentieth century, was connected by steel and railroad ties. In 1916, the United States had laid nearly 300,000 miles of track across the country, creating the world's largest rail system. Since then, other forms of transportation, such as cars, trucks, and airplanes, have diminished the importance of the railroad, and that impressive network of rail lines has shrunk to less than 150,000 miles. Railroad companies abandon more than 2,000 miles of track each year, leaving unused rail corridors overgrown and idle.

It wasn't until the mid-1960s that the idea to refurbish these abandoned rail corridors into usable footpaths and trails was introduced. And in 1963, work began in Chicago and its suburbs on a 55-mile stretch of abandoned right-of-way that would become the Illinois Prairie Path.

It took nearly two decades for the idea of converting old railways into usable footpaths to catch on. Then, in 1986, the Rails-to-Trails Conservancy was founded, its mission specifically to help communities see their dreams of having a usable rail corridor for recreation and nonmotorized travel a reality. At the time the conservancy began operations, only 100 open rail-trails existed. Today, more than 500 trails are open to the public, totaling more than 5,000 miles of converted pathways. The Rails-to-Trails Conservancy is currently working on more than 500 additional rails-to-trails projects.

Ultimately, the goal is to see a completely interconnected system of trails throughout the entire United States. If you're interested in learning more about rails-to-trails and wish to support the conservancy, please write to:

Rails-to-Trails Conservancy
1400 16th Street NW, Suite 300
Washington, DC 20036–2222
or call (202) 797–5400

47 New River Trail State Park

Start: From the Pulaski Station.
Length: 51.5 miles.
Approximate riding time: Varies with distance.
Difficulty rating: Technically easy due to a flat gravel surface. Physically easy to moderate, depending on length of ride.
Trail surface: Rail-trail. Flat, hard-packed gravel surface.

Land status: State park.
Nearest town: Pulaski.
Other trail users: Hikers and equestrians.
Canine compatibility: Dog friendly.
Fees and permits: No fees or permits required.
Schedule: Open daylight to dark year-round.
Maps: USGS maps: Radford South, Dublin, Hiwassee, Fosters Falls, Max Meadows, Sylvatus, Austinville, Galax.
Trail contacts: New River Trail State Park Headquarters, (540) 699-6778, www.newrivertrail.org.

Getting There: From Roanoke: Take I–81 south to exit 94 and head north on Route 99 approximately 2 miles into Pulaski. Just before the first red light, there is a sign for the Northern Terminus, Dora Junction. Parking is available. *DeLorme: Virginia Atlas & Gazetteer:* Page 40, D-4.

The Ride

Virginia has always been a leader in park development. On June 15, 1936, for example, Virginia became the first state to open an entire park system on the same day. When Norfolk Southern Corporation donated a 57-mile section of railroad right-of-way between Pulaski and Galax to the Virginia Department of Conservation and Recreation in December 1986, the state again took the lead in park development and created its first linear greenway and certainly one of its most impressive parks.

Southwestern Virginia's New River Trail follows the 57-mile abandoned railroad bed from Pulaski to Galax, with a branch trail that leads to the town of Fries. For nearly 40 miles, this rail-trail parallels the banks of the New River, the great-grandfather of rivers. The New River is much older than its name might suggest. Flowing south to north, as very few rivers in North America do, the New River has the distinction of being the world's second-oldest river.

Along the trail, cyclists will cross more than thirty bridges and trestles and cycle through tunnels nearly 200 feet long. The longest bridge in the park, located at Fries

The New River is the oldest river in North America.

Junction, is more than 1,000 feet long and offers dramatic views of the ancient river that courses more than 40 feet below. Scenery unique to southwest Virginia is visible along the way. The area's rich history of an era long past, with the departure of the railroad, lives on wholeheartedly in the towns and communities that line the trail.

The railroad was built in the late 1800s by the Norfolk & Western Railway Company to transport what was believed to be a wealth of quality minerals in Wythe County, a cache larger than any other in the United States. Work on the railway began in Pulaski on December 10, 1883, and in 1890 much of the rail line reached well into Carroll County near Galax.

Blast furnaces were erected, massive supplies of minerals mined, thousands of tons of iron ore produced, and boom towns developed in numbers along the railroad as the industry prospered. Most of these towns still exist.

As the hills emptied and the mines played out their last supplies, the railway became less and less profitable for the Norfolk Southern Corporation. Finally, in 1986, the decision came to abandon this stretch of railroad and donate the right-of-way to the state for a new purpose.

With the help of volunteer groups throughout Virginia, the park was able to open 4 miles of trail in May of 1987. Today, all 57 miles of this rails-to-trails park is open to the public. With so many places along the route to park your car and access the trail, there's no need to attempt riding the entire trail in one day. Pick different

New River Trail State Park

New River Trail —●

START

sections with each visit and explore the beauty and history of one of Virginia's finest rail-trails and state parks.

Miles and Directions

(0.0 The New River Trail actually starts at the Pulaski Station, but due to parking issues, you'll be picking up the trail at mile 2.0, Dora Junction, where there is ample parking. I've adjusted the cues here so that this book agrees with the official mileage cues. In short, ignore this cue.)

2.0 START from Dora Junction, just off Route 99.

2.5 Peak Creek Trestle.

3.6 I-81 overpass.

OTHER TRAIL ENTRANCES

- Draper Station (mile 6.2)—From I-81, take Route 658 east through Draper. Parking is available across from Bryson's Store, less than 1 mile from I-81.
- Shot Tower Historical State Park (New River Trail headquarters, mile 25.2)—From I-77, take exit 24, go east on Route 69 to U.S. Route 52, and follow signs to Shot Tower.
- Buck Dam (mile 34.7)—Take Route 602 to Byllesby, then go north on Route 737 to the dam.
- Byllesby Dam (mile 37.3)—Go east on Route 602 off Route 94. Park at the dam.
- Gambetta and Chestnut Yard (mile 45.2)—Take Route 721 north past Cliffview.
- Cliffview Station (mile 49.5)—Take U.S. Route 58 to Galax, then go north on Route 887 to Cliffview Road (Route 721). Parking is on the left, across from Cliffview Mansion and Cliffview Trading Post.
- Galax Station (mile 51.5)—Parking is available where Route 58 crosses Chestnut Creek.

3.8 McAdam Trestle.

6.2 Draper Station. Parking, food, ranger station, rest rooms available.

6.5 Sloan Creek Trestle.

8.0 Delton Trestle.

8.1 Site of Clarks Ferry, which stopped operating in 1939.

9.0 Delton. Convenience store and campgrounds available.

10.2 Cross Hiwassee River Bridge (951 feet long) to the east side of the New River.

12.6 Allisonia Station. Convenience store located along trail.

12.8 Gauging station to measure the depth of the river.

13.2 Big Reed Trestle over Big Reed Island Creek.

14.2 Reed Junction.

17.4 Barren Springs Furnace. Built in 1883, it produced more than five tons of pig iron each day.

17.8 Barren Springs Station.

19.0 Lone Ash.

20.3 Bertha.

Some of the tunnels reach up to 200 feet long.

22.7   Pass over the stone arch. This was built over a local farmer's spring box so that he could continue refrigerating his food and milk.

24.3   Fosters Falls.

25.2   Shot Tower. New River Trail State Park headquarters. Parking, information, and rest rooms. Shot Tower was built in the early 1900s to make shot for guns used by local hunters and soldiers in the Civil War. Molten metal was dropped 150 feet from the top of the tower into a kettle of cooling water below. It was thought that 150 feet was the distance necessary to shape falling molten lead into shot.

28.9   Reach Austinville, named after Moses Austin. Moses was the father of Stephen Austin, for whom Austin, Texas, is named.

31.6   Ivanhoe Depot. Convenience store near the trail. (Ivanhoe Bridge is 670 feet long.)

32.6   Jubilee Park.

34.0   Junction with the Virginia Highlands Horse Trail.

34.7   Buck Dam.

35.5   Route 737 and New River Campground (sixteen sites).

37.3   Byllesby Dam.

38.6   Grayson sulfur springs, once a health resort touting its natural spa. The waters here were once thought to cure skin diseases and other ailments. The site of the old-time spa is now under water.

39.4 Grayson. Nearby rest rooms and picnic area available.

39.8 Fries Junction. The New River Trail splits here and heads to either Fries or Galax. (Longest bridge along this trail at 1,089 feet.)

43.3 Route 721 (Fries Branch).

45.3 Fries. Parking, information, and picnic area available (Fries Branch).

40.1 Site of 1928 train wreck that killed three people and injured nine.

40.3 Pass through a tunnel 229 feet long.

42.3 Gambetta.

45.1 Turntable site. The railroad line once ended here, before being extended all the way to Galax. The turntable was used to turn trains around so that they could head north again toward Pulaski.

45.2 Chestnut Yard.

46.3 Chestnut Creek Falls.

49.5 Cliffview Station. Parking, rest rooms, information, horse and bicycle rental, ranger station, and food available.

51.5 Galax Station. Located off the main trail. Parking available.

Ride Information

Local Events and Attractions

Wythe County Heritage Days (in June), Wythe County Parks and Recreation; (540) 223-6022; www.wytheville.org.

Accommodations

Hosteling International, Blue Ridge Mountains, Blue Ridge Parkway, Galax, VA; (540) 236-4962; www.hiayh.org.

48 Virginia Creeper Trail

Start: From the Abingdon Station.
Length: 33.4 miles.
Approximate riding time: Varies with distance.
Difficulty rating: Technically easy due to flat gravel surface. Physically easy to moderate, depending on distance.
Trail surface: Rail-trail. Flat, hard-packed gravel surface.
Land status: Linear right-of-way jointly owned by Abingdon and Damascus. Eastern segment is within Mount Rogers National Recreation Area.
Nearest town: Abingdon.
Other trail users: Hikers and equestrians.
Canine compatibility: Dog friendly.
Fees and permits: No fees or permits required.
Schedule: Open daylight to dark year-round.
Maps: USGS maps: Abingdon, Damascus, Konnarock, Whitetop Mountain, Grayson (Tennessee and Virginia), Park (North Carolina and Virginia); Virginia Creeper Trail map.
Trail contacts: Mount Rogers National Recreation Area, (540) 783-5196; Rails-to-Trails Conservancy, (202) 797-5400.

Getting There: From Roanoke: Take I-81 south to exit 8 in Abingdon. Go north on Alternate Route 58 to Main Street and turn right. Pass Martha Washington Inn and the historic Barter Theater before turning right on Pecan Street. The trail begins at the old locomotive on display at the trailhead. *DeLorme: Virginia Atlas & Gazetteer:* Page 22, C-1.

The Ride

For hundreds of years, this ancient route was used by Native Americans as a footpath through the high mountains of the Appalachians. In 1900, the first locomotive chugged along this course from Abingdon Station to Damascus. By 1914, the railroad extended over even more of this ancient foot trail, all the way to Elkland, North Carolina. For more than seventy-five years, the Virginia Creeper (locomotive 433) crept its way across rivers and gorges and up the steep grades of Virginia's highlands to collect timber, iron ore, passengers, and supplies. By 1977, due to economic hardships incurred as far back as the Great Depression, locomotive 433 could no longer survive. Salvage rights for the rail line were subsequently sold to willing bidders. A year later, after the U.S. Forest Service purchased the right-of-way from Damascus to the Virginia–North Carolina border, work began to restore this scenic pathway. A few years later, Damascus and Abingdon bought the rest of the old railway. Today, 34

OTHER TRAIL ENTRANCES

- Damascus (mile 15.5)—Take U.S. Route 58 east from Abingdon to Damascus. Once in Damascus, follow U.S. Route 58 through the town to the red caboose on the right. Parking available at this trailhead.

- Green Cove Station (29.3)—From the intersection of U.S. Route 58 and Route 91 outside Damascus, take U.S. Route 58 east. Stay right on U.S. Route 58 at the intersection with Route 603 and go 4.2 miles to Green Cove Road (Forest Road 600). Turn right on Green Cove Road and follow this to Green Cove Station. Parking available.

- Whitetop Station (mile 32.3)—Follow the above directions on U.S. Route 58 to Route 603. Stay right on U.S. Route 58 and go 6.2 miles to Fire House Road (FR 755). Turn right on Fire House Road and go approximately 2 miles to the Whitetop parking area.

miles of this ancient Native American footpath have come full circle and are, once again, open as a public trail for all to enjoy.

The Virginia Creeper Trail begins in Abingdon in southwest Virginia and stretches its 34 miles across striking scenery and over some of the state's most rugged land before ending at the Virginia–North Carolina border. The trail's waterfalls, deep river gorges, wildlife, rolling pastures, and one hundred bridges and trestles make it one of America's premier rail-trails.

Mountain biking happens to be one of the most popular activities on the trail. The surface is smooth and cinder covered, with a terrain that never exceeds a grade of more than 6 percent. The trail only becomes steep when it crosses Whitetop Mountain, Virginia's second-highest peak, and heads to its highest point of 3,600 feet at the Whitetop Station. One way to avoid this demanding aerobic workout is to take the Blue Blaze Shuttle (see "Ride Information") from Abingdon up to the Whitetop parking area. The shuttle will transport both you and your bike and allows cyclists a carefree and easy downhill ride from Whitetop Station all the way back to Abingdon. More information is available at Highland Ski & Outdoor Center in Abingdon, which also rents bikes.

One point to remember when cycling the Virginia Creeper is that the right-of-way passes through some private property. Local landowners ask that you shut gates behind you and respect their property as you ride along the trail.

Miles and Directions

0.0 START at the Abingdon Trailhead. There is limited parking here.

1.0 Cross under I-81.

1.3 Pass the Glenrochie Country Club.

2.9 Cross Route 677 in Watauga. Limited parking available here.

3.7 Walk or ride across the Dry Branch Trestle.

7.2 Walk or ride across the South Holston Trestle. This is a very scenic trestle. It spans the northern point of South Holston Lake, where the south and middle forks of the Holston River converge. This is the lowest point on the Virginia Creeper Trail (1,900 feet).

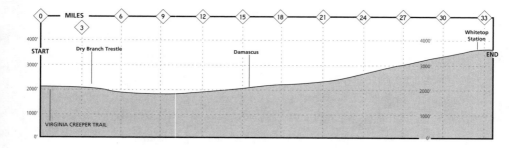

8.5 Arrive in the town of Alvarado. Limited parking available here.

15.5 Arrive in the town of Damascus. The big red caboose is a U.S. Forest Service information station. Limited parking available here. Rest rooms in the town park.

16.9 Cross Route 91. Be careful. Traffic is fast on this highway.

17.5 Ride across the Iron Bridge. Enter Mount Rogers National Recreation Area.

19.5 Reach the Straight Branch parking lot on the right. The Appalachian Trail goes off to the left. The Beech Grove trailhead is across U.S. Route 58 for those who wish to access the Iron Mountain Trail.

21.0 Arrive in Taylor's Valley. There is a vending area on the left. Go through the gate. The river is on your right. Limited parking available here.

21.4 Walk or ride across this trestle.

24.0 Pass through Konnarock Junction. Limited parking available here.

25.0 Walk or ride across High Trestle. Crossing this 550-foot-long trestle can be a bit unnerving as it is more than 100 feet above the ground!

25.4 The Appalachian Trail joins the Virginia Creeper Trail.

25.8 The Appalachian Trail goes left, deep into the Mount Rogers National Recreation Area.

27.2 Walk or ride across a small trestle.

29.3 Arrive at the old Green Cove Station. There is a seasonal U.S. Forest Service information station located here. There is also a portable toilet and limited parking available.

32.3 Arrive at Whitetop Station. This is the highest point on the trail at 3,576 feet. There is limited parking available.

33.4 Virginia–North Carolina border. This is the end of the Virginia Creeper Trail.

Ride Information

Local Information

Abingdon Convention and Visitors Bureau, Abingdon, VA; (800) 435–3440.
Blue Blaze Shuttle Service, Damascus, VA; (800) 475–5095 or (540) 475–5095; blueblaze.naxs.com.

Mount Rogers National Recreation Area, (800) 628–7202.

Local Events and Attractions

Appalachian Trail Days (in May), Damascus, VA; www.damascus.org.

In Addition

The Virginia Highlands Trail Network

Connections: It's a word you'll hear from rails-to-trails advocates over and over. Connections could mean a trail connecting a neighborhood to a park, or it could mean a trail connecting the suburbs to a subway line. On a larger scale, it may refer to connecting trails to create long traffic-free corridors. For example, volunteers are nearing completion on a series of trails that will connect Washington to Pittsburgh. Plans also call for an East Coast Greenway to extend from Maine to Florida.

In southwest Virginia, the connection has been made! Not long after the completion of the New River Trail, trail builders finished a connection to the trail network in the Mount Rogers National Recreation Area, which already connected with the Virginia Creeper Trail to the west. This distance, from Pulaski to Abingdon, is 134 miles. The bald mile-high peaks and rugged terrain of Mount Rogers give this ride the feel of a western odyssey rather than an eastern rail-trail ramble.

Before you start your journey, remember that it's important to contact the Mount Rogers Recreation Area for a comprehensive trail log, as there are four detours along parallel roads and trails that mountain bikers will need to follow. Starting at Pulaski, you proceed on the New River Trail. At mile 32.8 of the New River Trail, you reach a new extension of the Virginia Highlands Horse Trail (orange diamond blazes). Eventually, the trail connects with the Iron Mountain Trail (yellow blazes) near Route 16. The Iron Mountain Trail will take you to Beech Grove Trail, which takes you 1 mile farther to the Virginia Creeper Trail near Damascus. Follow the Virginia Creeper Trail for 19.7 miles, finishing your ride in Abingdon, where you can arrange a shuttle.

Allow four complete days for this trip, more if you plan on side trips or hikes in the wilderness areas. Numerous campgrounds convenient to the ride are located in the Mount Rogers Recreation Area and on the New River Trail. More traditional lodgings are also available in Galax as well as Abingdon and Pulaski. Greyhound offers one bus trip daily in each direction between Pulaski and Abingdon (see "Getting Around Virginia" in the Introduction). It may also be possible to utilize one of the bike shuttle services listed below, although none of the companies currently publish rates between the two cities.

Getting There

From Roanoke: Take I-81 south to exit 94 and head north on Route 99 approximately 2 miles into Pulaski. Just before the first red light, there is a sign for the Northern Terminus, Dora Junction. Parking is available. *DeLorme: Virginia Atlas & Gazetteer:* Page 40, D-4.

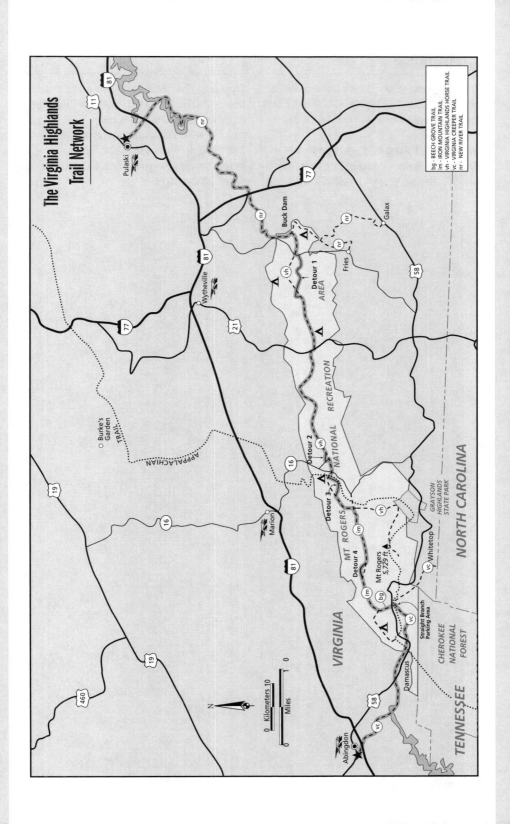

The Virginia Highlands
Trail Network

bg - BEECH GROVE TRAIL
im - IRON MOUNTAIN TRAIL
vh - VIRGINIA HIGHLANDS HORSE TRAIL
vc - VIRGINIA CREEPER TRAIL
nr - NEW RIVER TRAIL

Pulaski

Buck Dam

Galax

Fries

Wytheville

Detour 1
AREA

NATIONAL   RECREATION

Burke's
Garden

APPALACHIAN   TRAIL

Detour 2

vh

Marion

Detour 3

MT ROGERS

Detour 4

im

vh

GRAYSON
HIGHLANDS
STATE PARK

Mt Rogers
5,729 ft.

Whitetop

NORTH CAROLINA

bg

vc

Straight Branch
Parking Area

CHEROKEE
NATIONAL
FOREST

Damascus

VIRGINIA

Abingdon

TENNESSEE

N

0   Kilometers   10

0   Miles

81

11

77

81

77

21

16

19

16

81

19

460

58

58

vc

Ride Information

Trail contacts: Mount Rogers National Recreation Area, (540) 783-5196—Publishes a trail log for the entire route and trail brochures for each segment.

New River Trail State Park, (540) 699-6778.

Shuttle services: New River Trail: New River Bicycles, Draper, VA, (540) 980-1741;

VA Creeper Trail: Blue Blaze Bike and Shuttle, Damascus, VA, (800) 475-5095 or (540) 475-5095, blueblaze.naxs.com;

Adventure Damascus, Damascus, VA, (888) 595-BIKE or (540) 475-6262.

Maps: *DeLorme: Virginia Atlas & Gazetteer:* Pages 22 C-1, 40 D-4.

Honorable Mentions

Southwest Virginia

Compiled here is an index of great rides in southwest Virginia that didn't make the list this time around but deserve recognition. Check them out and let us know what you think. You may decide that one or more of these rides deserves higher status in future editions, or, perhaps, you may have a ride of your own that merits some attention.

P Mountain Lake Mountain Bike Trails

In 1994, Mountain Lake Resort (see Ride 42) designated nearly 10 miles of its trails for use by mountain bikes. Guests can rent mountain bikes from the Lakeview Cottage on a half-day or full-day rental basis and take guided trips to some of the Mountain Lake region's most scenic areas. All cyclists interested in riding the trails must get trail passes from the recreation office before heading out into the woods. A trail map is also available. For more information, call Mountain Lake at (800) 346–3334. *(DeLorme: Virginia Atlas & Gazetteer:* Page 41, B-5.)

Q Poverty Creek

The established nature and diversity of the trails between Gap and Brush Mountains just west of Blacksburg are what make riding at Poverty Creek so enjoyable. It's a virtual playground of terrain and intersections for cyclists around the area to enjoy for the better part of a day. The trails and roads are open to everyone. However, mountain bikers and equestrians are not allowed to ride within 300 feet of Pandapas Pond. The reason I'm including this ride as an honorable mention (you'll note I've already included a full-featured ride called Brush Mountain—Ride 41) is to highlight the diversity of what else exists just west of town. The Brush Mountain ride sends folks on a pretty hilly course up and down the western slopes of Brush Mountain. However, in the middle of the course, the ride follows the Basin Trail along Poverty Creek. This trail continues along Poverty Creek for nearly 7 miles to a loop around Boley Fields, offering cyclists the chance to go well beyond the Brush Mountain area. So the next time you head out to Brush Mountain, consider following Poverty Creek east for a while and see what else this area has to offer. Many local volunteers from the town of Blacksburg and Virginia Tech contribute to the maintenance of these trails, giving Poverty Creek and Pandapas Pond the distinction of being considered "scenic assets" by the U.S. Forest Service.

To get there from Blacksburg, drive northwest on U.S. Route 460 for 3 miles. You will pass over Brush Mountain. After you pass Route 621 on your right, turn left into the park entrance. Park signs mark the turn, and there is no fee for parking or biking. The large gravel parking lot is on your immediate left as you pass the sign. *(DeLorme: Virginia Atlas & Gazetteer: Page 41, B-6.)*

R Fairy Stone State Park

If you think Douthat State Park sounds great (see Ride 36), then check out Fairy Stone State Park, located in the foothills of the Blue Ridge Mountains near Martinsville, Virginia. The park is a little out of the way for most people, but those who find their way here always come home with pleasant memories. Fairy Stone State Park is one of six original state parks established in Virginia in 1933. The 4,868 acres of land were donated by Roanoke newspaper publisher Julius B. Fishburn, and to this day Fairy Stone remains one of the state's largest parks. The Civilian Conservation Corps built the twenty-four cabins and most of the facilities you'll find here back in the early 1930s, giving this park a sense of history not found in many other parks in Virginia. Nine of the park's 14 miles of trails are designated as multiuse trails and are open to horses, hikers, and mountain bikers. The rest are hiking-only trails. Similar in many ways to Douthat State Park, Fairy Stone is a great place to spend a weekend, bunking in one of the fully equipped rustic cabins, mountain biking during the day, and enjoying a Blue Ridge sunset over the 168-acre lake. For more information, call (540) 930–2424. To reserve cabins or campsites, call (800) 933–PARK. *(DeLorme: Virginia Atlas & Gazetteer: Page 26, B-2.)*

The Art of Mountain Biking

Within the following pages, you will find everything you need to know about off-road bicycling in Virginia. This section begins by exploring the fascinating history of the mountain bike itself, then goes on to discuss everything from the health benefits of off-road cycling to tips and techniques for bicycling over logs and up hills. Also included are the types of clothing that will keep you comfortable and in style, essential equipment ideas to keep your rides smooth and trouble-free, and descriptions of off-road terrain to prepare you for the kinds of bumps and bounces you can expect to encounter.

The mountain bike, with its knobby tread and reinforced frame, takes cyclists to places once unheard of—down rugged mountain trails, through streams of rushing water, across the frozen Alaskan tundra, and even to work in the city. There seem to be few limits on what this fat-tired beast can do and where it can take us. Few obstacles stand in its way, few boundaries slow its progress. Except for one—its own success. If trail closure means little to you now, read on and discover how a trail can be here today and gone tomorrow. With so many new off-road cyclists taking to the trails each year, it's no wonder trail access hinges precariously between universal acceptance and complete termination. But a little work on your part can go a long way to preserving trail access for future use. Nothing is more crucial to the survival of mountain biking itself than to read the examples set forth in the following pages and practice their message.

Without open trails, the maps in this book are virtually useless. Cyclists must learn to be responsible for the trails they use and to share these trails with others. This guidebook addresses such issues as why trail use has become so controversial, what can be done to improve the image of mountain biking, how to have fun and ride responsibly, on-the-spot trail repair techniques, maintenance hot lines for each trail, and the worldwide-standard rules of the trail.

Mountain Bike Beginnings

It seems the mountain bike, originally designed for lunatic adventurists bored with straight lines, clean clothes, and smooth tires, has become globally popular in as much time as it takes to race down a mountain trail.

Like many things of a revolutionary nature, the mountain bike was born on the West Coast. But unlike in-line skates, purple hair, and the peace sign, the concept of the off-road bike cannot be credited solely to imaginative Californians—they were just the first to make waves.

The design of the first off-road-specific bike was based on the geometry of the old Schwinn Excelsior, a one-speed, camel-back cruiser with balloon tires. Joe Breeze was the creator behind it, and in 1977 he built ten of these "Breezers" for himself and his Marin County, California, friends at $750 apiece—a bargain.

Breeze was a serious competitor in bicycle racing, placing thirteenth in the 1977 U.S. Road Racing National Championships. After races, he and friends would scour local bike shops, hoping to find old bikes they could then restore.

It was the 1941 Schwinn Excelsior, for which Breeze paid just $5.00, that began to shape and change bicycling history forever. After taking the bike home, removing the fenders, oiling the chain, and pumping up the tires, Breeze hit the dirt. He loved it.

His inspiration, while forerunning, was not altogether unique. On the opposite end of the country, nearly 2,500 miles from Marin County, East Coast bike bums were also growing restless. More and more old, beat-up clunkers were being restored and modified. These behemoths often weighed as much as eighty pounds and were so reinforced that they seemed virtually indestructible. But rides that take just forty minutes on today's twenty-five-pound featherweights took the steel-toed-boot- and blue-jean-clad bikers of the late 1970s and early 1980s nearly four hours to complete.

Not until 1981 was it possible to purchase a production mountain bike, but local retailers found these ungainly bicycles difficult to sell and rarely kept them in stock. By 1983, however, mountain bikes were no longer such a fringe item, and large bike manufacturers quickly jumped into the action, producing their own versions of the off-road bike. By the 1990s, the mountain bike had firmly established its place with bicyclists of nearly all ages and abilities. It now commands nearly 90 percent of the U.S. bike market.

There are many reasons for the mountain bike's success in becoming the hottest two-wheeled vehicle in the nation. It is much friendlier to the cyclist than a traditional road bike because of its comfortable upright position and shock-absorbing fat tires. And because of the health-conscious, environmentalist movement of recent decades, people are now more activity-minded and seek nature on a closer front than paved roads can allow. The mountain bike gives you these things and takes you far away from the daily grind—even if you're only minutes from the city.

Mountain Biking into Shape

If your objective is to get in shape and lose weight, then you're on the right track, because mountain biking is one of the best ways to get started.

One way many of us have lost weight in this sport is the crash-and-burn-it-off method. Picture this: You're speeding uncontrollably down a vertical drop that you realize you shouldn't be on—only after it is too late. Your front wheel lodges into a rut and launches you through endless weeds, trees, and pointy rocks before you come to an abrupt halt in a puddle of thick mud. Surveying the damage, you discover that, along with the layers of skin, body parts, and lost confidence littering the trail above, those unwanted pounds have been shed—permanently. Instant weight loss.

There is, of course, a more conventional (and quite a bit less painful) approach to losing weight and gaining fitness on a mountain bike. It's called the workout, and bicycles provide an ideal way to get physical. Take a look at some of the benefits associated with cycling.

Cycling helps you shed pounds without gimmicky fad diets or weight-loss programs. You can explore the countryside and burn 10 to 16 calories per minute or up to 600 to 1,000 calories per hour. Moreover, it's a great way to spend an afternoon.

No less significant than the external and cosmetic changes of your body from riding are the internal changes taking place. Over time, cycling regularly will strengthen your heart as your body grows vast networks of new capillaries to carry blood to all those working muscles. This will, in turn, give your skin a healthier glow. The capacity of your lungs may increase up to 20 percent, and your resting heart rate will drop significantly. The Stanford University School of Medicine reports to the American Heart Association that people can reduce their risk of heart attack by nearly 64 percent if they can burn up to 2,000 calories per week. This is only two to three hours of bike riding!

Recommended for insomnia, hypertension, indigestion, anxiety, and even for recuperation from major heart attacks, bicycling can be an excellent cure-all as well as a great preventive. Cycling just a few hours per week can improve your figure and sleeping habits, give you greater resistance to illness, increase your energy levels, and provide feelings of accomplishment and heightened self-esteem.

Be Safe—Know the Law

Occasionally, even hard-core off-road cyclists will find they have no choice but to ride the pavement. When you are forced to hit the road, it's important for you to know and understand the rules.

Outlined below are a few of the common laws found in Virginia as well as some common-sense ideas.

- In Virginia, you can pedal on any paved public road except urban freeways.
- Follow the same driving rules as motorists. Be sure to obey all road signs and traffic lights.
- Wear a helmet and bright clothing so that you are more visible to motorists. Bright colors such as orange and lime green are highly visible at night.
- Equip your bike with lights and wear reflective clothing if you plan on riding at night. When riding at night, the bicycle or rider must be equipped with a

white light visible at least 500 feet to the front and a red light or reflector visible at least 600 feet to the rear.

- Pass motorists on the left, not the right. Motorists are not expecting you to pass on the right, and they may not see you.
- Ride single file on busy roads so motorists can pass you safely.
- Use hand signals to alert motorists as to what you plan on doing next.
- Ride with the traffic and not against it.
- Follow painted lane markings.
- Make eye contact with drivers. Assume they don't see you until you are sure they do.
- Ride in the middle of the lane at busy intersections and whenever you are moving the same speed as traffic.
- Slow down and announce your presence when passing pedestrians, other cyclists, and horses.
- Don't ride close to the curb between parked cars unless they are far apart. Motorists may not see you when you try to move back into traffic.
- Turn left by looking back, signaling, getting into the left lane, and turning, or, in urban situations, continue straight to the crosswalk and walk your bike across the street when the pedestrian walk sign is illuminated.
- Never ride while under the influence of alcohol or drugs. Remember DUI laws apply when you're riding a bicycle.
- Avoid riding in extreme foggy, rainy, or windy conditions.
- Watch out for parallel-slat sewer grates, slippery manhole covers, oily pavement, gravel, wet leaves, and ice.
- Cross railroad tracks at a right angle. Be especially careful when it's wet out. For better control as you move across bumps and other hazards, stand up on your pedals.
- Don't ride too close to parked cars—a person opening the car door may hit you.
- Avoid riding on sidewalks. Instead, walk your bike. Pedestrians have the right-of-way on walkways. By law, you must give pedestrians audible warning when you pass. Use a bike bell or announce clearly: "On your left/right."
- Slow down at street crossings and driveways.

The Mountain Bike Controversy

Are Off-Road Bicyclists Environmental Outlaws?
   Do We Have the Right to Use Public Trails?

Mountain bikers have long endured the animosity of folks in the backcountry who complain about the consequences of off-road bicycling. Many people believe that fat tires and knobby treads do unacceptable environmental damage and that uncontrollable riding habits are a danger to animals and other trail users. To the contrary, mountain bikes have no more environmental impact than hiking boots or horseshoes. This does not mean, however, that mountain bikes leave no imprint at all. Wherever people tread, there is an impact. By riding responsibly, though, it is possible to leave only a minimum impact—something we all must take care to achieve.

Unfortunately, it is often people of great influence who view the mountain bike as the environment's worst enemy. Consequently, we as mountain bike riders and environmentally concerned citizens must be educators, impressing upon others that we deserve the right to use trails. Our responsibilities as bicyclists are no more and no less than any other trail user. We must all take the soft-cycling approach and show that mountain bicyclists are not environmental outlaws.

Etiquette of Mountain Biking

When discussing mountain biking etiquette, we are in essence discussing the soft-cycling approach. This term describes the art of minimum-impact bicycling and should apply to both the physical and social dimensions of the sport. But make no mistake—it is possible to ride fast and furiously while maintaining the balance of soft cycling. Here are a few ways to minimize the physical impact of mountain bike riding.

- **Stay on the trail.** Don't ride around fallen trees or mud holes that block your path. Stop and cross over them. When you come to a vista overlooking a deep valley, don't ride off the trail for a better vantage point. Instead, leave the bike and walk to see the view. Riding off the trail may seem inconsequential when done only once, but soon someone else will follow, then others, and the cumulative results can be catastrophic. Each time you wander from the trail, you begin creating a new path, adding one more scar to the earth's surface.

- **Do not disturb the soil.** Follow a line within the trail that will not disturb or damage the soil.

- **Do not ride over soft or wet trails.** After a rain shower or during the thawing season, trails will often resemble muddy, oozing swampland. The best thing to do is stay off the trails altogether. Realistically, however, we're all going to come across some muddy trails we cannot anticipate. Instead of blasting through each section of mud, which may seem both easier and more fun, lift the bike and walk past. Each time a cyclist rides through a soft or muddy section of trail, that part of the trail is permanently damaged. Regardless of trail conditions, though, always go over the obstacles across the path, not around them. Stay on the trail.

- **Avoid trails that, for all but God, are considered impassable and impossible.** Don't take a leap of faith down a kamikaze descent on which you will be forced to lock your brakes and skid to the bottom, ripping the ground apart as you go.

Soft cycling should apply to the social dimensions of the sport as well, since mountain bikers are not the only folks who use the trails. Hikers, equestrians, cross-country skiers, and other outdoors people use many of the same trails and can be easily spooked by a marauding mountain biker tearing through the trees. Be friendly in the forest and give ample warning of your approach.

- **Take out what you bring in.** Don't leave broken bike pieces and banana peels scattered along the trail.
- **Be aware of your surroundings.** Don't use popular hiking trails for race training.
- **Slow down!** Rocketing around blind corners is a sure way to ruin an unsuspecting hiker's day. Consider this: If you fly down a quick singletrack descent at 20 miles per hour, then hit the brakes and slow down to only 6 miles per hour to pass someone, you're still moving twice as fast as they are!

Like the trails we ride on, the social dimension of mountain biking is very fragile and must be cared for responsibly. We should not destroy another person's enjoyment of the outdoors. By riding in the backcountry with caution, control, and responsibility, our presence should be felt positively by other trail users. By adhering to these rules, trail riding—a privilege that can quickly be taken away—will continue to be ours to share.

Trail Maintenance

Unfortunately, despite all of the preventive measures taken to avoid trail damage, you're still going to run into many trails requiring attention. Simply put, a lot of hikers, equestrians, and cyclists alike use the same trails—some wear and tear is unavoidable. But like your bike, if you want to use these trails for a long time to come, you must also maintain them.

Trail maintenance and restoration can be accomplished in a variety of ways. One way is for mountain bike clubs to combine efforts with other trail users (hikers and equestrians) and work closely with land managers to cut new trails or repair existing ones. This work not only reinforces to others the commitment cyclists have in caring for and maintaining the land, but it also breaks the ice that often separates cyclists from their fellow trail users. Another good way to help out is to show up at your favorite off-road domain on a Saturday morning with a few riding buddies ready to work. With a good attitude, thick gloves, and the local land manager's supervision, trail repair is fun and very rewarding. It's important, of course, that you arrange a trail-repair outing with the local land manager before you start pounding shovels into the dirt. The land manager can lead you to the most needy sections of trail and instruct you on what repairs should be done and how best to accomplish the task. Perhaps the most effective trail maintenance, though, can be done by yourself and while you're riding. Read on.

On-The-Spot Quick Fix

Most of us, when we're riding, have at one time or another come upon muddy trails or fallen trees blocking our path. We notice that over time the mud gets deeper and the trail gets wider as people go through or around the obstacles. We worry that the problem will become so severe and repairs so difficult that the trail's access may be threatened. We also know that our ambition to do anything about it is greatest at that moment, not after a hot shower and a plate of spaghetti. Here are a few on-the-spot quick fixes that will hopefully correct a problem before it gets out of hand and get you back on your bike within minutes.

Muddy Trails. What do you do when trails develop huge mud holes destined for the EPA's Superfund status? The technique is called corduroying, and it works much like building a pontoon over the mud to support bikes, horses, or hikers as they cross. Corduroy (not the pants) is the term for roads made of logs laid down crosswise. Use small- and medium-size sticks and lay them side by side across the trail until they cover the length of the muddy section (break the sticks to fit the width of the trail). Press them into the mud with your feet, then lay more on top if needed. Keep adding sticks until the trail is firm. Not only will you stay clean as you cross, but the sticks may soak up some of the water and help the puddle dry. This quick fix may last as long as one month before needing to be redone. And as time goes on, with new layers added to the trail, the soil will grow stronger, thicker, and more resistant to erosion. This whole process may take fewer than five minutes, and you can be on your way, knowing the trail behind you is in good repair.

Leaving the Trail. What do you do to keep cyclists from cutting corners and leaving the designated trail? The solution is much simpler than you may think. (No, don't hire an off-road police force.) Notice where people are leaving the trail and throw a pile of thick branches or brush along the path, or place logs across the opening to block the way through. There are probably dozens of subtle tricks like these that will manipulate people into staying on the designated trail. If the tricks are executed well, no one will even know that the thick branches scattered along the ground in the woods weren't always there. And most folks would probably rather take a moment to hop a log in the trail than get tangled in a web of branches.

Obstacles in the Way. If there are large obstacles blocking the trail, try and remove them or push them aside. If you cannot do this by yourself, call the trail maintenance hot line to speak with the land manager of that particular trail and see what can be done.

We must be willing to *sweat for* our trails in order to *sweat on* them. Police yourself and point out to others the significance of trail maintenance. "Sweat equity," the rewards of continued land use won with a fair share of sweat, pays off when the trail is up for review by the land manager, and he or she remembers the efforts made by trail-conscious mountain bikers.

Rules of the Trail

The International Mountain Bicycling Association has developed these guidelines to trail riding. These "rules of the trail" are accepted worldwide and will go a long way in keeping trails open. Please respect and follow these rules for everyone's sake.

1. Ride only on open trails. Respect trail and road closures (if you're not sure, ask a park or state official first), do not trespass on private property, and obtain permits or authorization if required. Federal and state wilderness areas are off-limits to cycling. Parks and state forests may also have certain trails closed to cycling.

2. Zero impact. Be sensitive to the dirt beneath you. Even on open trails, you should not ride in conditions where you may leave evidence of your passing, such as on certain soils or shortly after a rainfall. Be sure to observe the different types of soils and trails you're riding on, and practice minimum-impact cycling. Never ride off the trail, don't skid your tires, and be sure to bring out at least as much as you bring in.

3. Control your bicycle! Inattention for even one second can cause disaster for you or for others. Excessive speed frightens and can injure people, gives mountain biking a bad name, and can result in trail closures.

4. Always yield. Let others know you're coming well in advance (a friendly greeting is always good and often appreciated). Show your respect when passing others by slowing to walking speed or stopping altogether, especially in the presence of horses. Horses can be unpredictable, so be very careful. Anticipate that other trail users may be around corners or in blind spots.

5. Never spook animals. All animals are spooked by sudden movements, unannounced approaches, and loud noises. Give the animals extra room and time so they can adjust to you. Move slowly or dismount around animals. Running cattle and disturbing wild animals are serious offenses. Leave gates as you find them, or as marked.

6. Plan ahead. Know your equipment, your ability, and the area in which you are riding, and plan your trip accordingly. Be self-sufficient at all times, keep your bike in good repair, and carry necessary supplies for changes in weather or other conditions. You can help keep trails open by setting an example of responsible, courteous, and controlled mountain bike riding.

7. Always wear a helmet when you ride. For your own safety and protection, a helmet should be worn whenever you ride your bike. You never know when a tree root or small rock will throw you the wrong way and send you tumbling.

Thousands of miles of dirt trails have been closed to mountain bicycling because of the irresponsible riding habits of just a few riders. Don't follow the example of these offending riders. Don't take away trail privileges from thousands of others who work hard each year to keep the backcountry avenues open to us all.

The Necessities of Cycling

When discussing the most important items to have on a bike ride, cyclists generally agree on the following four items.

Helmet. The reasons to wear a helmet should be obvious. Helmets are discussed in more detail in the "Be Safe—Wear Your Armor" section.

Water. Without it, cyclists may face dehydration, which may result in dizziness and fatigue. On a warm day, you should drink at least one full bottle during every hour of riding. Remember, it's always good to drink before you feel thirsty—otherwise, it may be too late.

Cycling shorts. These are necessary if you plan to ride your bike more than twenty to thirty minutes. Padded cycling shorts may be the only thing keeping your derriere from serious saddle soreness by ride's end. There are two types of cycling shorts you can buy. Touring shorts are good for people who don't want to look like they're wearing anatomically correct cellophane. They look like regular athletic shorts with pockets, but have built-in padding in the crotch area for protection from chafing and saddle sores. The more popular, traditional cycling shorts are made of skintight material, also with a padded crotch. Whichever style you find most comfortable, cycling shorts are a necessity for long rides.

Food. This essential item will keep you rolling. Cycling burns up a lot of calories, and no one is safe from the "bonk." Bonking feels like it sounds. Without food in your system, your blood-sugar level collapses, and there is no longer any energy in your body. This instantly results in total fatigue and light-headedness. So when you're filling your water bottle, remember to bring along some food. Fruit, energy bars, or some other forms of high-energy food are highly recommended. Candy bars are not, however, because they will deliver a sudden burst of high energy, then let you down soon after, causing you to feel worse than before. Energy bars are available at most bike stores and are similar to candy bars, but they provide complex carbohydrate energy and high nutrition rather than fast-burning simple sugars.

Be Prepared or Die

Essential equipment that will keep you from dying alone in the woods:

- Spare tire
- Tire irons
- Patch kit

- Pump
- Money (spare change for emergency calls)
- Spoke wrench
- Spare spokes: Tape these to the chain stay.
- Chain tool
- Allen keys: Bring appropriate sizes to fit your bike.
- Compass/GPS
- Duct tape
- First-aid kit (See "First-Aid Kit" section)
- Rain gear: For quick changes in weather.
- Matches
- Guidebook: In case all else fails and you must start a fire to survive, this guidebook will serve as excellent fire starter!
- Food and water
- Jacket

To carry these items, you may need a bike bag. A bag mounted in front of the handlebars provides quick access to your belongings, whereas a saddlebag fitted underneath the saddle keeps things out of your way. If you're carrying lots of equipment, you may want to consider a hydration backpack or a set of panniers. Panniers are larger than other types of bags and mount on either side of each wheel on a rack. Many cyclists, though, prefer not to use a bag at all. They just slip all they need into their jersey pockets and off they go.

Be Safe—Wear Your Armor

While on the subject of jerseys, it's crucial to discuss the clothing you must wear to be safe, practical, and—if you prefer—stylish. The following is a list of items that will save you from disaster, outfit you comfortably, and, most important, keep you looking cool.

Helmet. A helmet is an absolute necessity because it protects your head from complete annihilation. It is the only thing that will not disintegrate into a million pieces after a wicked crash on a descent you shouldn't have been on in the first place. A helmet with a solid exterior shell will also protect your head from sharp or protruding objects. Of course, with a hard-shelled helmet, you can paste several stickers from your favorite bicycle manufacturers all over the outer shell, giving companies even more free advertising for *your* dollar.

Shorts. Padded cycle shorts provide cushioning between your body and the bicycle seat. Cycle shorts also wick moisture away from your body and prevent chafing. Form-fitting shorts are made from synthetic material and have smooth seams. If you don't feel comfortable wearing form-fitting shorts, baggy-style padded shorts with pockets are available.

Gloves. You may find well-padded cycling gloves invaluable when traveling over rocky trails and gravelly roads for hours on end. When you fall off your bike and land on your palms, gloves are your best friend. Long-fingered gloves may also be useful, as branches, trees, assorted hard objects, and, occasionally, small animals will reach out and whack your knuckles. Insulated gloves are essential for winter riding.

Sunglasses. Not only do sunglasses give you an imposing presence and make you look cool (both are extremely important), they also protect your eyes from harmful ultraviolet rays, invisible branches, creepy bugs, and dirt.

Shoes. Mountain bike shoes are constructed with stiff soles that help transfer more power from the pedal stroke to the drive train. The soles also provide a solid platform to stand on, thereby decreasing fatigue in your feet. You can use virtually any good light outdoor hiking footwear, but specific mountain bike shoes (especially those with inset cleats) are best. They are light, breathe well, and are constructed to work with your pedal strokes instead of your natural walking cadence.

Other clothing. To prepare for Virginia's weather, it's best to dress in layers that can be added or removed as weather conditions change. In cold weather, wear a wicking layer made of a modern synthetic fiber next to your skin. The next layer should be a wool or synthetic insulating fabric that helps keep you warm but is also breathable. A fleece jacket or vest works well as an insulating layer. The outer layer should be a jacket and pants that are waterproof, windproof, and breathable. Your ears will also welcome a fleece headband when it's cold out. Avoid wearing cotton of any type. It dries slowly and does not wick moisture away from your skin, thus chilling you directly as moisture evaporates.

First-Aid Kit

- Band-Aids
- mole skin
- various sterile gauze and dressings
- white surgical tape
- an Ace bandage
- an antihistamine
- aspirin
- Betadine solution
- a first-aid book
- Tums

- tweezers
- scissors
- antibacterial wipes
- triple-antibiotic ointment
- plastic gloves
- sterile cotton tip applicators
- syrup of ipecac (to induce vomiting)
- thermometer
- wire splint

Oh, Those Chilly Virginia Days

If the weather chooses not to cooperate on the day you've set aside for a bike ride, it's helpful to be prepared.

Tights or leg warmers. These are best in temperatures below fifty-five degrees. Knees are sensitive and can develop all kinds of problems if they get cold. Common problems include tendinitis, bursitis, and arthritis.

Plenty of layers on your upper body. When the air has a nip in it, layers of clothing will keep the chill away from your chest and help prevent the development of bronchitis. If the air is cool, a polypropylene long-sleeved shirt is best to wear against the skin beneath other layers of clothing. Polypropylene, like wool, wicks away moisture from your skin to keep your body dry. Try to avoid wearing cotton or baggy clothing when the temperature falls. Cotton, as mentioned before, holds moisture like a sponge, and baggy clothing catches cold air and swirls it around your body. Good cold-weather clothing should fit snugly against your body, but not be restrictive.

Wool socks. Don't pack too many layers under those shoes, though. You may stand the chance of restricting circulation, and your feet will get real cold fast.

Thinsulate or Gortex gloves. There is nothing worse than frozen feet—unless your hands are frozen. A good pair of Thinsulate or Gortex gloves should keep your hands toasty and warm.

Hat or helmet on cold days? Sometimes, when the weather gets really cold and you still want to hit the trails, it's tough to stay warm. We all know that 130 percent of the body's heat escapes through the head (overactive brains, I imagine). So it's important to keep the cranium warm. Ventilated helmets are designed to keep heads cool in the summer heat, but they do little to keep heads warm during rides in sub-zero temperatures. Cyclists should consider wearing a hat on extremely cold days. Polypropylene skullcaps are great head and ear warmers that snugly fit over your head beneath the helmet. Another option is a helmet cover that covers those ventilating gaps and helps keep the body heat in. It will not, however, keep your ears warm. Some cyclists opt for a simple knit cycling cap sans the helmet, but these have never been shown to be very good cranium protectors.

All of this clothing can be found at your local bike store, where the staff will be happy to help fit you into the seasons of the year.

To Have or Not to Have—Other Very Useful Items

Though mountain biking is relatively new to the cycling scene, there is no shortage of items for you and your bike to make riding better, safer, and easier. We have rummaged through the unending lists and separated the gadgets from the good stuff, coming up with what we believe are items certain to make mountain bike riding easier and more enjoyable.

Tires. Buying a good pair of knobby tires is the quickest way to enhance the off-road handling capabilities of a bike. There are many types of mountain bike tires on the market. Some are made exclusively for very rugged off-road terrain. These big-knobbed, soft rubber tires virtually stick to the ground with magnetic-like traction, but they tend to deteriorate quickly on pavement. There are other tires made exclusively for the road. These are called "slicks" and have no tread at all. For the average cyclist, though, a good tire somewhere in the middle of these two extremes should do the trick. Realize, however, that you get what you pay for. Do not skimp and buy cheap tires. As your primary point of contact with the trail, tires may be the most important piece of equipment on your bike. With inexpensive rubber, the tire's beads may unravel, or chunks of tread may actually rip off the tire. If you're lucky, all you'll suffer is a long walk back to the car. If you're unlucky, your tire could blow out in the middle of a rowdy downhill, causing a wicked crash.

Clipless pedals. Clipless pedals, like ski bindings, attach your shoe directly to the pedal. They allow you to exert pressure on the pedals during down- and upstrokes. They also help you to maneuver the bike in the air or while climbing various obstacles. Toe clips may be less expensive than clipless pedals, but they are also heavier and harder to use. Clipless pedals and toe clips take a little getting used to, but they're definitely worth the trouble.

Bar ends. These clamp-on additions to your original straight handlebar will provide more leverage, an excellent grip for climbing, and a more natural position for your hands. Be aware, however, of the bar end's propensity for hooking trees on fast descents, sending you, the cyclist, airborne. Opinions are divided on the general usefulness of bar ends these days, and, over the last few years, bar ends have fallen out of favor with manufacturers and riders alike.

Backpacks. These bags are ideal for carrying keys, extra food and water, guidebooks, foul-weather clothing, tools, spare tubes, and a cellular phone, in case you need to call for help.

Suspension forks. For off-roaders who want nothing to impede their speed on the trails, investing in a suspension fork or front and rear suspension is a good idea. As with tires, there are plenty of brands to choose from, and they all do the same thing—absorb the brutal beatings of a rough trail. The cost of these forks, however, is sometimes more brutal than the trail itself.

Bike computers. These are fun gadgets to own and are much less expensive than in years past. They offer such information as trip distance, time of day, altitude, average and maximum speed, heart rate, and even global satellite positioning. Bike computers will come in handy when you're following these maps or just want to know how far you've ridden in the wrong direction.

Hydration packs. These are quickly becoming essential items for cyclists pedaling for more than a few hours, especially in hot, dry conditions. The most popular brand is the Camelback. Most packs can carry as much as one hundred ounces of water. The packs strap on your back, with a handy hose running over your shoulder, so you can drink water while still holding the handlebars with both hands. The packs are a great way to carry a lot of extra liquid on hot rides in the middle of nowhere, plus keys, a camera, extra food, guidebooks, tools, spare tubes, and a cellular phone.

Types of Off-Road Terrain

Before roughing it off-road, we may first have to ride the pavement to get to our destination. Don't be dismayed. Some of the country's best rides are on the road. Once we get past these smooth-surfaced pathways, though, adventures in dirt await us.

Rails-to-trails. Abandoned rail lines are converted into usable public resources for exercising, commuting, or just enjoying nature. Old rails and ties are torn up, and a trail, paved or unpaved, is laid along the existing corridor. This process completes the cycle: Ancient Indian trading routes became railroad corridors and then hiking and cycling trails.

Unpaved roads. These are typically found in rural areas and are most often public roads. Be careful when exploring, though, not to ride on someone's unpaved private drive.

Forest roads. These dirt and gravel roads are used primarily as access to forestland and are kept in good condition. They are almost always open to public use.

Singletrack. Singletrack can be the most fun on a mountain bike. These trails, with only one track to follow, are often narrow, challenging pathways through the woods. Remember to make sure these trails are open before zipping into the woods. (At the time of this printing, all trails and roads in this guidebook were open to mountain bikes.)

Open land. Unless there is a marked trail through a field or open space, you should not plan to ride there. Once one person cuts his or her wheels through a field or meadow, many more are sure to follow, causing irreparable damage to the landscape.

Techniques to Sharpen Your Skills

Many of us see ourselves as pure athletes—blessed with power, strength, and endless endurance. However, it may be those with finesse, balance, agility, and grace that get around most quickly on a mountain bike. Although power, strength, and endurance do have their places in mountain biking, these elements don't necessarily form the framework for a champion mountain biker.

The bike should become an extension of your body. Slight shifts in your hips or knees can have remarkable results. Experienced bike handlers seem to flash down technical descents, dashing over obstacles in a smooth and graceful effort as if pirou-etting in *Swan Lake*. Here are some tips and techniques to help you connect with your bike and float gracefully over the dirt.

Braking. Using your brakes requires using your head, especially when descend-ing. This doesn't mean using your head as a stopping block, but rather using it to think intelligently. Use your best judgment in terms of how much or how little to squeeze those brake levers.

The more weight a tire is carrying, the more braking power it has. When you're going downhill, your front wheel carries more weight than the rear. Braking with the front brake will help keep you in control without going into a skid. Be careful, though, not to overdo it with the front brake and accidentally toss yourself over the handlebars. And don't neglect your rear brake! When descending, shift your weight back over the rear wheel, thus increasing your rear braking power as well. This posi-tion will balance the power of both brakes and give you maximum control.

Good riders learn just how much of their weight to shift over each wheel and how to apply just enough braking power to each brake so as not to "endo" over the handlebars or skid down a trail.

Going Uphill—Climbing Those Treacherous Hills

Shift into a low gear (push the thumb shifter away from you). Before shifting, be sure to ease up on your pedaling to decrease pressure on the chain. Find the gear best for you that matches the terrain and steepness of each climb.

Stay seated. Standing out of the saddle is often helpful when climbing steep hills with a road bike, but you may find that on dirt, standing may cause your rear tire to lose its grip and spin out. Climbing requires traction. Stay seated as long as you can, and keep the rear tire digging into the ground. Ascending skyward may prove to be much easier in the saddle.

Lean forward. On very steep hills, the front end may feel unweighted and sud-denly pop up. Slide forward on the saddle and lean over the handlebars. This posi-tion will add more weight to the front wheel and should keep you grounded.

Keep pedaling. On rocky climbs, be sure to keep the pressure on, and don't let up on those pedals! The slower you go through rough trail sections, the harder you will work.

Going Downhill—The Real Reason We Get Up in the Morning

Shift into the big chain ring. Shifting into the big ring before a bumpy descent will help keep the chain from bouncing off. And should you crash or disengage your leg from the pedal, the chain will cover the teeth of the big ring so they don't bite into your leg.

Relax. Stay loose on the bike, and don't lock your elbows or clench your grip. Your elbows need to bend with the bumps and absorb the shock, while your hands should have a firm but controlled grip on the handlebars to keep things steady. Steer with your body, allowing your shoulders to guide you through each turn and around each obstacle.

Don't oversteer or lose control. Mountain biking is much like downhill skiing, since you must shift your weight from side to side down narrow, bumpy descents. Your bike will have the tendency to track in the direction you look and follow the slight shifts and leans of your body. You should not think so much about steering, but rather think about the direction you wish to go.

Rise above the saddle. When racing down bumpy, technical descents, you should not sit on the saddle. Instead, stand on the pedals, allowing your legs and knees to absorb the rocky trail.

Drop your saddle. For steep, technical descents, you may want to drop your saddle 3 or 4 inches. This change lowers your center of gravity, giving you much more room to bounce around.

Keep your pedals parallel to the ground. The front pedal should be slightly higher so that it doesn't catch on small rocks or logs.

Stay focused. Many descents require your utmost concentration and focus just to reach the bottom. You must notice every groove, every root, every rock, every hole, every bump. You, the bike, and the trail should all become one as you seek singletrack nirvana on your way down the mountain. But if your thoughts wander, then so may your bike, and you may instead become one with the trees!

Watch Out!

Back-Road Obstacles

Logs. When you want to hop a log, throw your body back, yank up on the handlebars, and pedal forward in one swift motion. This movement clears the front end of the bike. Then quickly scoot forward and pedal the rear wheel up and over. Keep the forward momentum until you've cleared the log. By all means, don't hit the brakes, or you may do some interesting acrobatic maneuvers!

Rocks. Worse than highway potholes! Stay relaxed, let your elbows and knees absorb the shock, and always continue applying power to your pedals. Staying seated will keep the rear wheel weighted to prevent slipping, and a light front end will help you respond quickly to each new obstacle. The slower you go, the more time your tires will have to get caught between the grooves.

Water. Before crossing a stream or puddle, be sure to first check the depth and bottom surface. There may be an unseen hole or large rock hidden under the water that could wash you up if you're not careful. After you're sure all is safe, hit the water at a good speed, pedal steadily, and allow the bike to steer you through. Once you're across, tap the breaks to squeegee the water off the rims.

Leaves. Be careful of wet leaves. These may look pretty, but a trail covered with leaves may cause your wheels to slip out from under you. Leaves are not nearly as unpredictable and dangerous as ice, but they do warrant your attention on a rainy day.

Mud. If you must ride through mud, hit it head on and keep pedaling. You want to part the ooze with your front wheel and get across before it swallows you up. Above all, don't leave the trail to go around the mud. This just widens the path even more and leads to increased trail erosion.

Urban Obstacles

Curbs are fun to jump, but as with logs, be careful.

Curbside drains are typically not a problem for bikes. Just be careful not to get a wheel caught in the grate.

Dogs make great pets, but they seem to have it in for bicyclists. If you think you can't outrun a dog that's chasing you, stop and walk your bike out of its territory. A loud yell to "Get!" or "Go home!" often works, as does a sharp squirt from your water bottle right between the eyes.

Cars are tremendously convenient when we're in them, but dodging irate motorists in big automobiles becomes a real hazard when you're riding a bike. As a cyclist, you must realize that most drivers aren't expecting you to be there and often wish you weren't. Stay alert and ride carefully, clearly signaling all of your intentions.

Potholes, like grates and back-road canyons, should be avoided. Just because you're on an all-terrain bicycle doesn't mean you're indestructible. Potholes regularly damage rims, pop tires, and sometimes lift unsuspecting cyclists into a spectacular swan dive over the handlebars.

Last-Minute Check

Before a ride, it's a good idea to give your bike a once-over to make sure everything is in working order. Begin by checking the air pressure in your tires to make sure they are properly inflated. Mountain bikes require about forty-five to fifty-five pounds of air pressure per square inch. If your tires are underinflated, there is greater likelihood that the tubes may get pinched on a bump or rock, causing the tires to flat.

Looking over your bike to make sure everything is secure and in its place is the next step. Go through the following checklist before each ride.

- **Pinch the tires to feel for proper inflation.** They should give just a little on the sides, but feel very hard on the treads. If you have a pressure gauge, use it.
- **Check your brakes.** Squeeze the rear brake and roll your bike forward. The rear tire should skid. Next, squeeze the front brake and roll your bike forward. The rear wheel should lift into the air. If this doesn't happen, then your brakes are

too loose. Make sure the brake levers don't touch the handlebars when squeezed with full force.

- **Check all quick releases on your bike.** Make sure they are all securely tightened.
- **Lube up.** If your chain squeaks, apply some lubricant.
- **Check your nuts and bolts.** Check the handlebars, saddle, cranks, and pedals to make sure that each is tight and securely fastened to your bike.
- **Check your wheels.** Spin each wheel to see that it spins through the frame and between the brake pads freely.
- **Have you got everything?** Make sure you have your spare tube, tire irons, patch kit, frame pump, tools, food, water, and guidebook.

Need more info on mountain biking? Consider reading *Basic Essentials Mountain Biking*. You'll discover such things as choosing and maintaining a mountain bike; useful bike-handling techniques; preparing for long rides; overcoming obstacles such as rocks, logs, and water; and even preparing for competition.

Repair and Maintenance

Fixing a Flat

TOOLS YOU WILL NEED

- Two tire irons
- Pump (either a floor pump or a frame pump)
- No screwdrivers!!! (which can puncture the tube)

REMOVING THE WHEEL

The front wheel is easy. Simply disconnect the brake shoes, open the quick-release mechanism or undo the bolts with the proper sized wrench, then remove the wheel from the bike.

The rear wheel is a little trickier. Before you loosen the wheel from the frame, shift the chain into the smallest gear on the freewheel (the cluster of gears in the back). Once you've done this, removing and installing the wheel is much easier.

REMOVING THE TIRE

Step one: Insert a tire iron under the bead of the tire and pry the tire over the lip of the rim. Be careful not to pinch the tube.

Step two: Hold the first tire iron in place. With the second tire iron, repeat step one, 3 or 4 inches down the rim. Alternate tire irons, pulling the bead of the tire over the rim, section by section, until one side of the tire bead is completely off the rim.

Step three: Remove the rest of the tire and tube from the rim. This can be done by hand. It's easiest to remove the valve stem last. Once the tire is off the rim, pull the tube out of the tire.

CLEAN AND SAFETY CHECK

Step four: Using a rag, wipe the inside of the tire to clean out any dirt, sand, glass, or thorns. These may puncture the tube. The inside of a tire should feel smooth. Any pricks or bumps could mean that you have found the culprit responsible for your flat tire.

Step five: Wipe the rim clean, then check the rim strip, making sure it covers the spoke nipples properly on the inside of the rim. If a spoke is poking through the rim strip, it could puncture the tube.

Step six: At this point, you can do one of two things: replace the punctured tube with a new one or patch the hole. It's easiest to just replace the tube with a new tube when you're out on the trails. Roll up the old tube and take it home to repair later that night in front of the TV. Directions on patching a tube are usually included with the patch kit.

INSTALLING THE TIRE AND TUBE

(This can be done entirely by hand.)

Step seven: Inflate the new or repaired tube with enough air to give it shape, then tuck it back into the tire.

Step eight: To put the tire and tube back on the rim, begin by putting the valve in the valve hole. The valve must be straight. Then use your hands to push one of the beaded edges of the tire onto the rim all the way around, so that one side of your tire is on the rim.

Step nine: Let most of the air out of the tube to allow room for the rest of the tire.

Step ten: Beginning opposite the valve, use your thumbs to push the other side of the tire onto the rim. Be careful not to pinch the tube between the tire and the rim. The last few inches may be difficult, and you may need the tire iron to pry the tire onto the rim. If so, be careful not to puncture the tube.

BEFORE INFLATING COMPLETELY

Step eleven: Check to make sure the tire is seated properly and that the tube is not caught between the tire and the rim. Do this by adding about five to ten pounds of air. Watch closely that the tube does not bulge out of the tire.

Step twelve: Once you're sure the tire and tube are properly seated, put the wheel back on the bike before you fill the tire with air. It's easier squeezing the wheel through the brake shoes if the tire is still flat.

Step thirteen: Now fill the tire with the proper amount of air and check constantly to make sure the tube doesn't bulge from the rim. If the tube does appear to bulge out, release all the air as quickly as possible, or you could be in for a big bang. Place the wheel back in the dropout and tighten the quick-release lever Reconnect the brake shoes.

When installing the rear wheel, place the chain back onto the smallest cog (farthest gear on the right) and pull the derailleur out of the way. Your wheel should slide right on.

Lubrication Prevents Deterioration

Lubrication is crucial to maintaining your bike. Dry spots will be eliminated. Creaks, squeaks, grinding, and binding will be gone. The chain will run quietly, and the gears will shift smoothly. The brakes will grip quicker, and your bike may last longer with fewer repairs. Need I say more? Well, yes. Without knowing where to put the lubrication, what good is it?

THINGS YOU WILL NEED

- One can of bicycle lubricant, found at any bike store
- A clean rag (to wipe excess lubricant away)

WHAT GETS LUBRICATED

- Front derailleur
- Rear derailleur
- Shift levers
- Front brake
- Rear brake
- Both brake levers
- Chain

WHERE TO LUBRICATE

To make it easy, simply spray a little lubricant on all the pivot points of your bike. If you're using a squeeze bottle, use just a drop or two. Put a few drops on each point wherever metal moves against metal—for instance, at the center of the brake calipers. Then let the lube sink in.

Once you have applied the lubricant to the derailleurs, shift the gears a few times, working the derailleurs back and forth. This allows the lubricant to work itself into the tiny cracks and spaces it must occupy to do its job. Work the brakes a few times as well.

LUBING THE CHAIN

Lubricating the chain should be done after the chain has been wiped clean of most road grime. Do this by spinning the pedals counterclockwise while gripping the chain with a clean rag. As you add the lubricant, be sure to get some between each link. Spray the chain with an aerosol spray while pedaling backwards (counterclockwise) until the chain is fully lubricated. Let the lubricant soak in for a few seconds before wiping the excess away. Chains will collect dirt much faster if they're loaded with too much lubricant.

Appendix

Bicycle Clubs and Organizations

Charlottesville Albemarle Bicycling Association
Advocating bicycle safety education and bicycle lanes on city streets
www.cycling.org/lists/chaba/

Virginia Bicycling Federation
A state-wide bicycling advocacy organization composed of bicycling clubs
P.O. Box 5621
Arlington, VA 22205

Recreational
Blue Ridge Bicycle Club
A recreational and road-racing club based in Roanoke
Box 13383
Roanoke, VA 24033
www.blueridgebicycleclub.com

Charlottesville Bike Club
Charlottesville's bike touring club
2570 Kendalwood Lane
Charlottesville, VA 22901
www.mindspring.com/~sgdowell/cbc.htm

Eastern Shore of Virginia Bicycle Club
5248 Willow Oaks Road
P.O. Box 882
Eastville, VA 23347
cbes@esva.nets

Eastern Virginia Mountain Bike Association
Concerned with trail access issues in the Tidewater region
P.O. Box 7553
Hampton, VA 23666
www.evma.org

Fredericksburg Cyclists Bicycle Touring Club
Encourages cycling for recreation, sport, fitness, and transportation in and around Fredericksburg
P.O. Box 7844
Fredericksburg, VA 22404
(540) 373–1451
www.bikefred.com

Mid-Atlantic Off Road Enthusiasts
An off-road cycling group based in the D.C. area
14846 Basingstoke Loop
Centerville, VA 22020
scudaman@erols.com
www.more-mtb.org

Milepost Zero Bicycle Club
Road bike club based in Waynesboro
P.O. Box 1693
Waynesboro, VA 22980–2118

Mountain Bike Club of Virginia Tech
An off-road collegiate club at Virginia Tech in Blacksburg
filebox.vt.edu/org/mtnbike

Nelson Bicycle Alliance
Bicycle advocacy organization
9994 Rockfish Valley
Afton, VA 22920
(540) 456–6746

New River Valley Bike Club/Rock 'n' Road Riders
Based in southwestern Virginia (Blacksburg, Christiansburg, Radford, Pulaski)
P.O. Box 488
Blacksburg, VA 24063
www.montgomery-floyd.lib.va.us/compages/nrvbc

Potomac Pedalers Touring Club
A large recreational club in the D.C. area with approximately 5,000 members
6878 Fleetwood Road, Suite D
McLean, VA 22101
(202) 363–TOUR
www.bikepptc.org

Peninsula Bicycling Association
P.O. Box 12115
Newport News, VA 23612
(757) 875–1594

Rappahannock Bicycle Club
P.O. Box 682
Bowling Green, VA 22427
(804) 633–6500

Richmond Area Bicycling Association
For recreational cyclists of all abilities in the Richmond area
Betsy Blevins c/o RABA
409-H North Hamilton Street
Richmond, VA 23221
(804) 266–BIKE
www.erols.com/debraj/raba

Shenandoah Valley Bicycle Club
For recreational cyclists of all abilities; also an advocacy organization
P.O. Box 1014
Harrisonburg, VA 22801
www.math.jmu.edu/~vanwyk/svbc

University of Virginia Mountain Bike Club
A recreational and racing club at the University of Virginia in Charlottesville
www.virginia.edu/~bikeclub

Wheel Power Christian Cyclists
A road and off-road recreational club based in Lynchburg
P.O. Box 4791
Lynchburg, VA 24502
(804) 525–9552
wheelpwr1@aol.com

Williamsburg Area Bicyclists
Road cycling club based in Williamsburg
P.O. Box 2222
Williamsburg, VA 23187

Winchester Wheelmen
Road and off-road club based in Winchester
P.O. Box 1695
Winchester, VA 22604

Racing
Arlington Masters Velo Club/GS Foster
Norm Woodley
2000 North Calvert Street, Apartment 4
Arlington, VA 22201
(703) 528–7194

Beltway Bicycle Club/Golds-Saturn-Dominoes

A road-racing club based in Alexandria with approximately thirty members
Skip Foley
sfoley@erols.com

Blue Ridge Bicycle Club/Team Josta

A recreational and road-racing club based in Roanoke
Box 13383
Roanoke, VA 24033
www.blueridgebicycleclub.com

Chronos Racing/Plow & Hearth

A road-racing club based in Charlottesville
Matthew Butterman
2514 Fontaine Avenue, Apartment A
Charlottesville, VA 22903
(804) 979–7145

CyCor/Richbrau Cycling Team

A road and off-road team focusing on races in the East
Tom Doyle
3202 Hunts Bridge Court
Midlothian, VA 23112
www.cycor.org

East Coasters Bicycle Race Team

A small grassroots road and off-road racing team based in Blacksburg that focuses on events in Virginia, West Virginia, North Carolina, and Maryland.
Mike Matzuk
1001 North Main Street
Blacksburg, VA 24060
(540) 774–7933
www.g3.net/rowdydawg

Hilton Cycling Club/Conte's Bike and Fitness

P.O. Box 1056
Newport News, VA 23612
(757) 595–1333

James River Velo Sport/HDK-Sentara

A road-racing club based in Newport News/Hampton
P.O. Box 12072
Newport News, VA 23612
reality.sgi.com/billh/jrvs

Monticello Velo Club/Powerbar

A road-racing club headquartered in Charlottesville
Ruth Stornetta
19 Elliewood Avenue
Charlottesville, VA 22903
rs3j@virginia.edu
www.bluewheel.com/html/mvc.htm

Old Dominion University Cycling Club

The collegiate racing club at Old Dominion University
111 Constant Hall
Old Dominion University
Norfolk, VA 23529
(757) 683–3585

PDO Velo

The majority of the club members are USCF Category 4 and 5 riders, with many racing masters as well (thus, pretty darn old)
Randy Meadows
category4@home.com

Potomac Velo Club/A-1 Cycling

A road and off-road racing club based
in Dumfries
Ben Williams
15611 Rhame Drive
Dumfries, VA 22026
(703) 670–2665
www.nv.cc.va.us/~nvportg/pvc2.htm

Prince William Elite Racing

Brian Hackett
12312 Mulberry Court
Lake Ridge, VA 22192
(703) 497–1671

Regulators Elite Cycling Team

A road-racing club based in Clifton
Marcel Bengston
12441 Popes Head Road
Clifton, VA 20124
(703) 803–2815

Reston Bicycle Club

A road and off-road racing club based
in Reston
Mark Kukulich
P.O. Box 3389
Reston, VA 20195
(703) 848–5370

Squadra Coppi/Java Shack

A road-racing club based in Arlington;
also known as Unione Sportiva Coppi
Pete Laszcz
(703) 524–5834
pjlaszcz@ix.netcom.com
www.squadracoppi.com

TBA Race Team

A road-racing club based in Norfolk
P.O. Box 12254
Norfolk, VA 23541

Team Anarchy

A road-racing club based in Warrenton
Steve Chalke
748 Cherry Tree Lane
Warrenton, VA 20186
(540) 349–8612

Team Bean Cycling

John Huth
125 King William Drive
Williamsburg, VA 23188
(757) 565–0203

Team Gold

Adam Coon
1175 Herndon Parkway
Suite 500
Herndon, VA 20170
(703) 435–2001

Team Hampton Roads

A USCF racing team based in Hampton, with more than thirty members,
mostly masters. Members race primarily local crits and promote many
events, including a Thursday night crit
series, Winning Edge crits, and the
Lawyer Ashe Dash for Cash.
Dave Venable
17 North Greenfield Avenue
Hampton, VA 23555
(757) 838–7127

Team Richmond/White House Apple Juice

A road-racing club based in Richmond
Thomas J. Sweeney
P.O. Box 11495
Richmond, VA 23230

Team Ultimate Edge
Emily Wilson
1720 Elmsere Avenue
Richmond, VA 23227
(804) 355–7994

Tidewater Bicycle Association
P.O. Box 12254
Norfolk, VA 23541
(804) 490–1831
www.vabch.com/tbapage/INDEX.
HTM

University of Richmond Cycling
Eneas Freyre
310 North Shields Avenue, Apartment 2
Richmond, VA 23220
(804) 353–1164

University of Virginia Cycling Team
The collegiate road-racing club at the
University of Virginia in Charlottesville
cycling@virginia.edu.
www.student.virginia.edu/~cycling

University of Virginia Mountain Bike Club
A recreational and racing club at the
University of Virginia in Charlottesville
www.student.virginia.edu/~bikeclub

Valley Bicycles
Craig Cooper
1236 West Main Street
Salem, VA 24153
(540) 389–2453

Virginia Beach Velo/Fitness Works Racing
A road-racing club based in Virginia
Beach
Bill Collins
1993 Southaven Drive
Virginia Beach, VA 23464
Billbikes2@aol.com

Virginia Tech Cycling Team
The road collegiate cycling team at Virginia Tech in Blacksburg
125 G War Memorial Hall
Blacksburg, VA 24060
(540) 231–7005
www.vt.edu:10021/org/cycling

Whole Wheel Velo Club
A road-racing club based in Arlington
Duwayne Frank
6124 Edsall Road, #103
Alexandria, VA 22304
www.monumental.com/wwvc/WWV
CPAGE.HTM

William and Mary Cycling Team
Ryan McKinney
CSU 4391 P.O. Box 8793
Williamsburg, VA 23186
(757) 221–4533

National
American Trails
The only national, nonprofit organization working on behalf of all trail interests. Members want to create and protect America's network of interconnected trailways.
P.O. Box 200787, Denver, CO 80220
(303) 321–6606
www.outdoorlink.com/amtrails

International Mountain Bicycling Association
Works to keep public lands accessible to bikers and provides information on trail design and maintenance
P.O. Box 7578, Boulder, CO 80306
(303) 545–9011
www.greatoutdoors.com/imba

League of American Wheelmen
190 West Ostend Street #120
Baltimore, MD 21230-3731
(410) 539–3399

National Off-Road Bicycling Association
National governing body of U.S. mountain bike racing
One Olympic Plaza
Colorado Springs, CO 80909
(719) 578–4717
www.usacycling.org/mtb

Outdoor Recreation Coalition of America
Oversees and examines issues for outdoor recreation; based in Boulder, Colorado
(303) 444–3353
www.orca.org, info@orca.org

Rails-to-Trails Conservancy
Organized to promote conversion of abandoned rail corridors to trails for public use
1400 16th Street NW, Suite 300
Washington, D.C. 20036-2222
www.railtrails.org

United States Cycling Federation
Governing body for amateur cycling
Colorado Springs, CO
(719) 578–4581
www.usacycling.org

Ski Resorts

...for Mountain Biking?

Ski resorts offer a great alternative to local trail riding. During the spring, summer, and fall, many resorts open their trails for mountain biking and, just like during ski season, sell lift tickets to take you and your bike to the top of the mountain. Lodging is also available for weekend mountain bike junkies, and rates are often discounted from the normal ski-season prices. Some resorts even rent bikes and lead guided mountain bike tours. Call ahead to find out just what each resort offers in the way of mountain bike riding, and pick the one that best suits your fancy.

The following is a list of many of the ski resorts in the Mid-Atlantic area that say *yes!* to mountain biking when the weather turns too warm for skiing.

Blue Knob
Claysburg, PA
(814) 239–5111

Bryce
Basye, VA
(703) 856–2121

Canaan Valley
Davis, WV
(304) 866–4121

Hidden Valley
Somerset, PA
(814) 443–6454

The Homestead
Hot Springs, VA
(703) 839–5500

Massanutten
Harrisonburg, VA
(703) 289–9441

Seven Springs
Somerset, PA
(800) 452–2223

Ski Liberty
Carroll Valley, PA
(717) 642–8282

Ski Roundtop
Lewisberry, PA
(717) 432–9631

Snowshoe
Marlinton, WV
(304) 572–1000

Timberline
Davis, WV
(800) 843–1751

Whitetail
Mercersburg, PA
(717) 328–9400

Wintergreen
Waynesboro, VA
(804) 325–2200

Wisp
McHenry, MD
(301) 387–4911

Bicycle Touring Companies

There are literally dozens of off-road bicycle tour companies offering an incredible variety of guided tours for mountain bikers. On these pay-as-you-pedal fat-tire vacations, you will have a chance to go places around the globe that only an expert can take you, and your experiences will be so much different than those had on a tour bus.

From hut to hut in the Colorado Rockies or inn to inn through Vermont's Green Mountains, there is a tour company for you. Whether you want hard-core singletrack during the day and camping at night or scenic trails followed by a bottle of wine at night and a mint on each pillow, someone out there offers what you're looking for. The tours are well organized and fully supported with expert guides, bike mechanics, and "sag wagons" that carry gear, food, and tired bodies. Prices range from $100 to $500 for a weekend to more than $2,000 for two-week-long trips to far-off lands such as New Zealand or Ireland. Each of these companies will gladly send you free literature to whet your appetite, with breathtaking photography and titillating stories of each tour.

Selected Touring Companies

Backroads
Berkeley, CA
(800) BIKE–TRIP

Bicycle Adventures
Olympia, WA
(800) 443–6060

Blackwater Bikes
Davis, WV
(304) 259–5286

Elk River Touring Center
Slatyfork, WV
(304) 572–3771

Roads Less Traveled
Longmont, CO
(303) 678–8750

Timberline Bicycle Tours
Denver, CO
(303) 759–3804

Trails Unlimited, Inc.
Nashville, IN
(812) 988–6232

Vermont Bicycling Touring
Bristol, VT
(800) 245–3868

About the Author

Scott Adams has written several mountain biking guidebooks, including *Mountain Biking the Washington, D.C./Baltimore Area* (now in its fourth edition) and *Mountain Bike Madness in Central Pennsylvania.* He is a regular contributor to *MetroSports Magazine* and has competed in more twenty-four-hour races than he cares to remember. A native Virginian, he lives with his wife and growing family in Charlottesville, Virginia. Few things reward him more than a long hike to the top of a mountain or an early-morning bike ride with no particular place to go.